THE MODELING OF
DESIGN IDEAS

THE MODELING OF DESIGN IDEAS

Graphics and Visualization
Techniques for Engineers

Walter Rodriguez, PE, PhD
Georgia Institute of Technology

McGraw-Hill, Inc.
New York St. Louis San Francisco Auckland Bogotá
Caracas Lisbon London Madrid Mexico Milan
Montreal New Delhi Paris San Juan Singapore
Sydney Tokyo Toronto

The Modeling of Design Ideas: Graphics and Visualization Techniques for Engineers

2 3 4 5 6 7 8 9 0 SEM SEM 9 0 9 8 7 6 5 4 3 2

ISBN 0-07-053394-6

This book was originally developed by the author on DOS and UNIX-based workstations using WordPerfect, AutoCAD, CADKEY, ICEM, I-DEAS, and VERSACAD software. The McGraw-Hill editors were B.J. Clark and John M. Morriss; the cover photograph is courtesy of Yagi Studio II/Superstock Inc.; the editors at Business Media Resources were Stacey Sawyer and Pete Alcorn, and the production was supervised by Raleigh Wilson, Lisa Labrecque, and Pamela Mansfield Colbert. Semline, Inc., was printer and binder.

Library of Congress Cataloging–in–Publication Data

Rodríguez, Walter, (date)
The modeling of design ideas: graphics and visualization techniques
for engineers/Walter Rodríguez.
    p.   cm.
    Includes biographical references and index.
    ISBN 0-07-053394-6
1. Computer Graphics 2. Computer-aided design. I. Title.
T385.R5797 1992
620'.0042'0285—dc20   91-44037

To my family and friends

Thanks for teaching me the value of thoughtfulness and the power of thinking in terms of positive visual images.

Quotes

Surgeons think *visually* to perform an operation; chemists to construct molecular models; mathematicians to consider abstract space-time relationships; engineers to design circuits, structures, and mechanisms; businessmen to organize and schedule work; architects to coordinate function with beauty; carpenters and mechanics to translate plans into things.

—Robert H. McKim

The words or the language, as they are written or spoken, do not seem to play any role in my mechanism of thought. The psychical entities which seem to play any role in my mechanism of thought are certain signs and more or less clear *images* which can be 'voluntarily' reproduced and combined.

—Albert Einstein

Table of Contents

Preface

The Modeling of Design Ideas covers the principles and modeling techniques used by engineers and architects to design and develop devices and structures. The book integrates engineering design and visualization techniques and provides a generic (non–software-specific) conceptual background for using computer-aided design and tools for geometric modeling. It is intended as an introductory course in design, graphics, and visualization.

OBJECTIVES

This book will help to enhance the reader's ability to think and communicate in terms of two- and three-dimensional visual images. The reader will learn the methods and standards used in engineering design work. The main objectives are to:

- Master the techniques used in modeling design ideas
- Use effective design communication techniques
- Use the design process to devise new products by experiencing the process and by working on real, open-ended projects
- Discern the design information that will be required by those who will be manufacturing devices, constructing buildings, or supervising production processes
- Employ graphic standards to document design ideas and to avoid potential legal problems
- Use state-of-the-art computer graphics tools to conceive, model, analyze, simulate, evaluate, and select the best design alternatives
- Develop higher cognitive visual thinking functions like observation, visual perception, imagination, creativity, and spatial visualization

BACKGROUND

This book is based on the premise that visualization is the single most important ability required to become an excellent designer and an effective communicator. The reason for this assumption is that no matter what tools are used to model a design (manual or computer), engineers still have to think in terms of three-dimensional visual images in order to conceive, model, analyze, and manufacture a product.

The Modeling of Design Ideas has been designed based on the axioms enumerated below.

Axiom 1: Maintain the essential aspects of visual thinking and design communication, such as design methodology, projection theory, freehand sketching, spatial geometry, and graphics standards.

Axiom 2: Incorporate the state-of-the-art computer graphics visualization techniques, such as computer-aided design (CAD), geometric modeling, and rendering.

Axiom 3: Minimize the need to learn low-level computer programming languages; that is, master high-level visual-oriented languages rather than alphanumeric-based languages.

Axiom 4: Maximize design and visualization problem-solving opportunities by assigning open-ended design projects that would allow the students to be creative and think in terms of visual images.

The Modeling of Design Ideas was born out of several years of unrelenting efforts to integrate design and computer graphics techniques into a single course. In fact, this is the author's fourth textbook integrating modern with valuable traditional approaches. The previous books were entitled *Interactive Engineering Graphics* (1988), *Computer-Aided Engineering Design Graphics* (1989), and *Visualization* (1990). These books were published as preliminary editions and beta-tested by McGraw-Hill Book Company in the U.S, Germany, Japan, and Spain. All the concepts introduced here have been tested by thousands of engineering, architecture, computer, science, arts, management, and technology students who registered for the Introduction to Visual Communication and Engineering Design (EGR 1170) course given at Georgia Institute of Technology between 1985 and 1991.

The basic educational strategy is to integrate traditional visual thinking and design principles with new geometric-modeling techniques. This ensures that the new tidal wave of technological advancements does not erode centuries of design-communication developments by pioneers like Gudea (use of plans), Vitruvius (geometric construction), Gutenberg (printing), Alberti (views), da Vinci (creative design/sketching), Monge (descriptive geometry), and Sutherland (computer graphics).

The Modeling of Design Ideas responds to the new trends in concurrent engineering design, visual communication, and computer graphics visualization techniques. The book combines design processes, 3-D to 2-D and 2-D to 3-D visualizations, spatial geometry, and solids modeling. At the beginning, the book covers design principles and visual annotation techniques like orthographic projection, contour drawing from photographs, and pictorial sketching from real or computer-generated models. Then, it covers design feasibility studies, design shape-analysis, computer graphics tools, and geometric modeling. In this context, the student learns the generic structure of CAD modeling system menus and commands as well as geometric-construction techniques.

The Modeling of Design Ideas presents state-of-the-art techniques to conceptualize, visualize, and communicate design ideas and inventions. It supports three phases—ideation, simulation, and implementation—that are intended to be covered along parallel paths. In Chapters 1 through 5, the students study and practice design-annotation techniques in a lecture recitation setting. In Chapters 6 through 10, the students learn CAD and geometric-modeling techniques in a computer graphics laboratory setting .

The book includes basic terminology in an extensive glossary. It also includes a bibliography at the end of each chapter. The book was designed to be device- and software-independent and as generic in nature as possible. The intent is to provide the fundamentals necessary to understand the CAD modeling programs currently available on the market.

SAMPLE COURSE OUTLINE

Description

Visualization and modeling techniques for product design and development. Design methodology, graphics standards, projection theory, freehand sketching, spatial geometry, CAD, and geometric modeling. Solving open-ended design and visualization problems.

Prerequisites

Coordinate geometry and elementary computer literacy.

Topics

1. Design and Visualization Processes: Principles and Definitions (Chapter 1)

2. 2-D Design Annotation: Orthographic Multiview Projection (Chapter 2)

3. The Design Workstation and Geometric Entities in 3-D (Chapters 6 and 7)

4. 3-D Design Annotation: Axonometric and Oblique Projection (Chapter 3)

5. 3-D Design Annotation: Perspective Projection (Chapter 3)

6. Geometric Modeling: Wireframe, Surface, and Solid Models (Chapter 8)

7. Design Feasibility Study: Case Studies (Chapter 4)

8. Design Shape-Analysis: Spatial Geometry (Chapter 5)

9. Design Documentation: Section Views and Details (Chapter 9)

10. Design Documentation: Dimensioning and Fasteners (Chapter 9)

11. Design Documentation: Geometric Tolerancing Standards (Chapter 9)

12. Design Presentation: Graphing, Rendering, and Prototypes (Chapter 10)

ACKNOWLEDGMENTS

This book is dedicated to my family and friends in acknowledgement of their love, patience, and support. I am indebted to the Georgia Tech students who have helped me in writing this book. Special thanks to A. Opdenbosch, S. McWhorter, W. Patterson, A. Ferrier, S. Otero, W. McCullum, J. Hibbard, C. Merizalde, E. Lynch, D. Dean, W. Petit and B. Murray for their contributions. I am also grateful to Drs. H. Rushmeir (Georgia Institute of Technology), L. Hodges (Georgia Institute of Technology), D. McAllister (NCSU), K. Weiler (Ardent), J. Miller (University of Kansas), and P. Wilson (RPI) for their contributions to the video display, stereoscopic computer graphics, solid modeling, and feature-based modeling sections of this book, respectively. L. Barr, R. Barr, and D. Juricic from University of Texas at Austin, and W. Ross and M. Gabel from Purdue University provided several figures and useful examples. Extended thanks to Ms. S. Gehred and her students at Marquette University for allowing the reproduction of their ASEE '89 Student Design Competition report. I am indebted to past and present colleagues for their inspiration, especially to R. Arheim (Harvard), R. McKim (Stanford), J. Earle (Texas A & M), R. Barr and D. Juricic (University of Texas at Austin), V. Anand (Clemson), G. Bertoline and M. Sadowski (Purdue University), D. Bowers (Arizona), and M. Pleck (University of Illinois at Urbana). Extended thanks to several anonymous reviewers utilized by McGraw-Hill. This book might have never been written without the energetic leadership of B. J. Clark, Executive Editor of Engineering. Pete Alcorn and Stacey Sawyer provided the critical review needed to develop this textbook. Several software developers provided the latest software and gave me permission to reproduce some of the material utilized in this book. Special thanks to the people at AUTODESK, CADKEY, CDC, HP, IBM, SGI, and SUN.

REFERENCES AND SUGGESTED READINGS

Arheim, R. *Visual Thinking*. Berkeley, Calif.: University of California Press, 1969.

Barr, R., and D. Juricic. *Proceedings of the NSF Symposium on Modernization of the Engineering Design Graphics Curriculum*, Austin, Texas, 1990.

Grinter, L. *Report on Evaluation of Engineering Education*. Washington, D.C.: ASEE, 1955.

Hadamard, J. *The Psychology of Invention in Mathematics*. Princeton, N.J.: Princeton University Press, 1945.

Hirsch, E. D. *The Dictionary of Cultural Literacy*. Boston: Houghton Mifflin, 1988.

McKim, R. H. *Experiences in Visual Thinking*. Monterey, Calif.: Brooks/Cole, 1980.

Suh, N. P. *The Principles of Design*. New York: Oxford, 1990.

CHAPTER 1 | Design and Visualization

This chapter covers design as a process and introduces several visualization techniques for conveying and realizing product ideas. The examples show how visual thinking and design-modeling strategies—in conjunction with practical design principles—can be applied to the design, manufacturing, and construction of devices and systems.

1.1 DESIGN AS PROCESS: THE REALIZATION OF IDEAS

What is design? How are engineers involved with design, and what exactly do they do when they design something? Basically, engineers and designers apply scientific and practical knowledge to analyze problems and develop efficient ways of using **resources**, such as people, money, materials, and machines, to solve problems. The byproduct of this activity may be a device, a system, or a process—for example, a mechanical pencil, a laptop computer, a bridge, a software system, a building layout, or a chemical process.

The art of engineering is to take a bright idea and with adequate resources (and proper regard for the environment) design and produce something the public wants at a price that it can afford. Of course, the original idea rarely springs forth complete, polished, and ready to go. Realizing the idea—turning it into a manufacturable product—requires **development**; that is, it requires trying this configuration, these circuits, that arrangement, or some other form, shape, or size until a satisfactory solution is found (Walker, 1989). Such experimentation can be done mentally, on paper, with the use of scale models or computer-generated models, or even—as the Wright Brothers did—by building full-size structures. However, only rarely is the result of the first development efforts completely satisfactory; perhaps the product will be too difficult to build or is too big, too noisy, or too costly to maintain. So, once again the idea goes into the cycle of developing, testing, redeveloping, constructing, and retesting (Walker, 1989). The methodical approach to this cycle is called the **design process**.

All through history, engineers, architects, scientists, and designers have attempted to approach problems in a methodical fashion. The design process is basically a methodological avenue to reach the best solution to a design problem. First, the designer defines the requirements and the constraints of the problem; then, the designer creates alternative design solutions and models and evaluates a number of those solutions; finally, the designer selects the solution that most likely will result in the desired finished product. In short, the design process is basically the combination of imagination and conceptualization (ideation); modeling and analysis (simulation); and building and testing (implementation). These components may be grouped and expressed in the following equation:

$$\text{Design Process} = \text{Ideation} + \text{Simulation} + \text{Implementation}$$

Engineers.encounter extremely intricate problems. However, no matter how complicated a problem may be, engineers follow an approach similar to the design-process procedure shown in Figure 1.1. The design process is **inter-active** and **iterative** in nature, as indicated by the arrows in the figure. This means that a person must provide input to the process and also respond to it (*interact* with it), and that the process does not follow a predetermined sequence of steps—indeed, it can become repetitive (*iterative*). It is difficult to know when one phase finishes and the other begins; that is, process phases can overlap with one another, as illustrated by the shaded areas in Figure 1.1. The figure also shows that the design process is **concurrent** (simultaneous); that is, engineers may design both the product and the procedure by which it is to be built (manufactured or implemented) at the same time. The stages of each phase of the design process—ideation, simulation, and implementation—are discussed briefly below. The function of each is discussed in greater detail in appropriate sections throughout the book.

1.1.1 Phase 1: Ideation—The Conceptualization Phase

Figure 1.1 No matter how compli-cated the design problem, engineers can use the design process below..

Many successful engineering designers and entrepreneurs possess great powers of imagination and creativity, which are essential to ideation—the first phase of

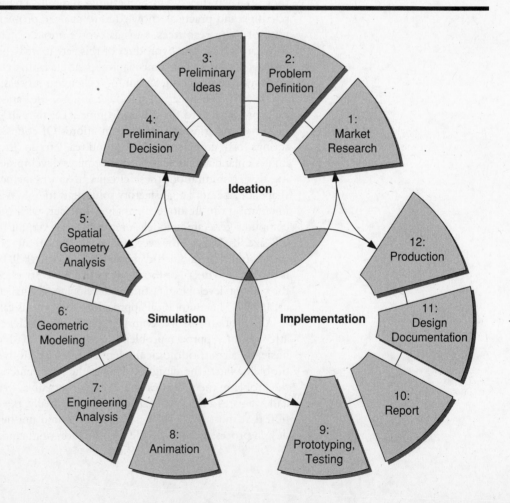

the design process. **Ideation** is the ability to identify a problem and imagine ways to solve it. The "idea person," or designer, is the first person to conceive of a product that will be later developed and manufactured. This person may not necessarily be an engineer; he or she may be an industrial product designer, an architect, or an inventor. However, an engineer would always be employed to develop the design idea into a manufacturable (hence, engineered) device or a constructable system.

Ideation is the conceptualization phase of the design process (Figure 1.1). We may start the ideation phase by doing *market research* (1). Put simply, we need to find out what people want or need. This research is done by surveying the market to determine consumer trends and demands. We may also observe existing devices, systems, or processes to determine deficiencies or possible improvements. Of course, the ideation process may also begin with an opportunity to assist a client with a specific problem or by organizing a group brainstorming session to identify a need or want.

Once we identify the need or want, we need to define the problem. The *problem definition* (2) stage consists of writing a clear statement of the specific design problem. The statement is rewritten as many times as necessary—in a concise and comprehensive way—so that it does not favor a preconceived solution. Concurrently, we need to determine the **functional requirements** (**FRs**) of the problem (Suh, 1990), as illustrated in Example 1.1.

Example 1.1

There is a need for a better mousetrap that uses no poisons, glue, or springs. The FRs may be stated as:
FR1: Provide an enclosure to trap a mouse.
FR2: Minimize the pain caused to the mouse.

In addition, one must state the limitations or constraints of the problem—for instance, in Example 1.1, one must indicate that the trap needs to be disposable and inexpensive. The designer defines these design guidelines based on the client's needs.

The third ideation stage consists of generating *preliminary ideas* (3). The designer or design team brainstorms alternative solutions to the problem without ruling out "illogical" solutions. The **brainstorming** session is simply a meeting during which willing people identify or propose alternative solutions to a given problem or think of possible problems to solve. The objective is to generate a large number of ideas or market needs; therefore, all proposed ideas are accepted. Criticism or ridicule is not permitted. After the brainstorming group is formed, a leader is selected to encourage comments and responses to the questions posed. For example, the leader could pose questions like these: "What are the main needs of society (community, school, home, dormitory)?" "How do we propose to fill these needs?" Someone in the group is usually in charge of writing down (or sketching) the responses (or proposed solutions.) All responses are first written (or sketched) on a board or overhead projector visible to every group member. The design team must then record their ideas on paper or disk, since some of their ideas may need to be refined later.

In addition, some designers perform a **patent search**, which consists of looking up similar products that may have been registered in the government's patent office. Many college libraries and public libraries have computer-based patent information available on CD-ROM (Compact Disk/Read-Only Memory). Other designers may also read certain magazines or visit retail shops to find ways in which other people have attempted to solve similar problems. Figure 1.2 shows a patent for a design solution to the mousetrap problem presented in Example 1.1.

The final stage of the ideation phase is to make a *preliminary decision* (4) of the best design solutions. To make a logical design decision, we need to determine the relevant factors, such as weight, cost, durability, esthetics, and ethics, and assess their relative importance in attaining the specified design (the functional) requirements of the problem. Selecting the best idea(s) to be modeled and evaluated, or analyzed, and then choosing the best design in an objective way are two of the most challenging tasks that a designer faces. A table called a **decision matrix** is used to compare the various design alternatives, as discussed in greater detail in Chapter 4. In this table, a numerical value is assigned to each specific design factor according to the importance of the factor. The design with the greatest cumulative value is the "winner."

1.1.2 Phase 2: Simulation—The Maturation Phase

The intermediate phase of the design-process equation, **simulation** (Figure 1.1), involves modeling and analyzing the object. Computer-generated models are constructed based on the original ideation sketches. The model is analyzed to see how well it behaves under stress, temperature, wind, and other physical factors. Engineers may create computer animations to simulate the product's performance.

Simulation represents the design maturation phase. One often begins this phase by performing *spatial geometry analysis* (5), which consists in part of determining the product's shape and size—that is, the configuration and the proportions of the product. In some cases, the designer may need to perform certain spatial geometry operations such as finding true size, true shape, area, auxiliary views, intersections, and development (unfolding of the surface). And they need to determine any other visual information required to build a model or models of the product.

Before the product is modeled in the computer system, the part's coordinates and strategic points need to be determined. This is the beginning of the *geometric modeling* (6) stage. One may construct geometric models such as **wireframes** (showing only the edges of the object) or **solid models** (showing the surface of the object). These geometric models are constructed using computer-aided design (CAD) and geometric modeling systems, which we will cover in more detail later. Some systems use simple geometric shapes called **primitives** and **boolean algebra** (math operations like subtraction and addition) to create the models. Other computer graphics software systems may also be used to model the product—such as **feature-based modelers**, which use manufacturing/construction terminology, and **virtual-reality modelers**, which create an electronic "reality" within which the user can manipulate the object's model.

Geometric modeling is followed by the *engineering analysis* (7) stage, which consists of determining mass properties, generating stress (due to physical forces and deformations), and creating fluid-flow (using air or water) and/or thermal (heat) simulations that allow the engineer to inspect visually the effects of those factors on the device or structure being studied. If the computer system is

Figure 1.2 Patented solution to the mousetrap problem. (U.S. Patent Office, Nov. 17, 1987. Pat. No. 4,706,407)

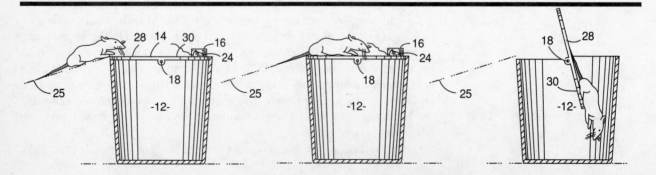

powerful, designers may perform visual simulation or *animation* (8) to determine part clearance, interference, collision detection, and so on. They then evaluate and improve the product based on the simulation results—always seeking to optimize the product's shape, use of materials, and so forth.

1.1.3 Phase 3: Implementation—The Construction Phase

The "final" phase of the design process, **implementation**, refers to building, manufacturing, testing, and documenting the product (Figure 1.1). *Prototyping and testing* (9) are the first stage. This stage consists of building a real model, or *prototype*, of the product; the prototype is then tested under real loads, heat, flow, and stresses and is evaluated for its market appeal and "feel." Figure 1.3 shows a prototype for a design solution to the mousetrap problem presented in Example 1.1.

Next, a design, or technical, *report* (10) is usually prepared. This is done by organizing product presentation materials. Graphs, charts, and other visual information are usually included to support the design solution. Multimedia (audiovisual) presentations using transparencies, slides, sound, and/or animation sequences may also be conducted.

The design must also be documented. This *design documentation* (11) stage consists of extracting detailed drawings (including dimensions and geometric tolerances) from the geometric models previously created. This phase also includes the development of material specifications to support the drawings. Designers may also write patent-pending requests and other documents needed for legal or record-keeping purposes.

The "final" stage is *production* (12). Production involves realization, manufacturing, construction, and/or processing of the product. It consists, in part,

Figure 1.3 Prototype of a solution to the mousetrap problem. (Courtesy of Trap-Ease, Inc.)

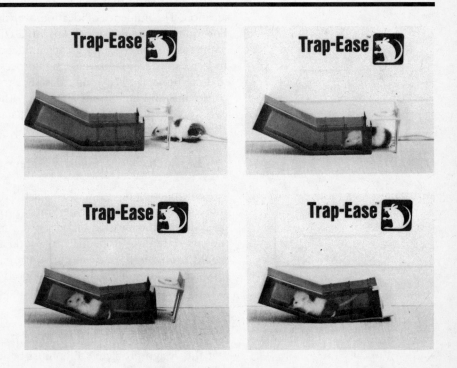

of planning and scheduling—that is, determining the time and the resources needed to manufacture and distribute the product. Marketing (Figure 1.4) and distribution to the consumer, although normally a management activity, should also be regarded as part of the design process. This process never ends: Feedback and continuous improvement of the product are required to remain competitive in today's world economy. Sometimes production is canceled, and the design process begins all over again by redefining the problem—or by going to any other design phase, as necessary.

To minimize production problems and to reduce the number of iterations, or cycles in the design process, it is necessary to apply several design principles.

1.2 DESIGN PRINCIPLES

Design is the central activity of engineers. Design, like any other engineering or scientific endeavor, is based on certain principles. However, the design ideation process has been subjective to a significant extent: it has greatly depended on the designer's creativity, past experiences, and know-how (familiarity with the problem addressed.)

A good designer should be skillful in both analytical thinking and visual thinking. These mental processes are required for the integration of his or her creativity, knowledge, and experiences into a desired design solution. Creativity alone is not enough: it is necessary to use reasoning powers to define and satisfy the functional requirements (FRs) of a particular design problem. Just as laws of nature, like gravitation, exist, so do acceptable principles of good design practice and decision making. Sound design principles help us to conceptualize and choose the best design solution to a problem. In this section, we discuss some fundamental design principles.

It is axiomatic that the most important phase of the design process is ideation. The influence of ideation over the entire design process is profound. For example, the first meeting with a client to define a project's functional requirements, or FRs, may greatly influence other design decisions that follow. In fact, early decisions in the design process affect final design solutions in ways that are difficult for a young designer to imagine. Early selection of design constraints and limitations affects all other stages and can have the greatest effect on the final outcome. This principle can be referred to as the *Ideation Principle* and can be stated as follows:

Early Decisions Greatly Affect the Final Design Outcome

Remembering this principle helps the novice designer recall the importance and consequences of his or her initial problem-definition statement as developed during the ideation phase. For example, if Example 1.1 had stated that the mousetrap was to be made of wood and springs, the mousetrap solution would probably have been conventional (one that harms the mouse and produces an unsanitary mess as opposed to the mousetrap shown in Figure 1.4). In other words, the definition statement would have unnecessarily limited the number of possible solutions.

Two additional design principles have been described by Suh (1990): (1) the *Independence Axiom* and (2) the *Information Axiom*. The first axiom states that the design problem's FRs must be independently satisfied. The second axiom states that designers should minimize the information content. Example 1.2—adapted from Suh's book—illustrates these two principles.

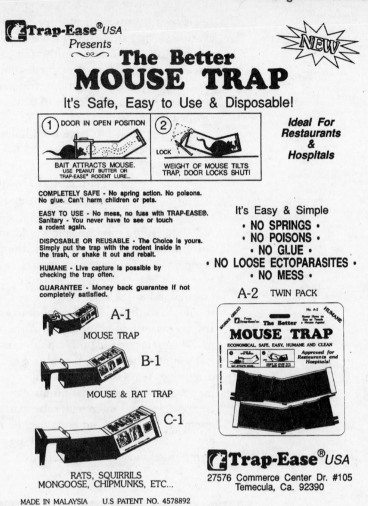

Figure 1.4 Marketing the Better Mousetrap. (Courtesy of Trap-Ease)

Example 1.2

People use refrigerators to keep their food cold and to retard food spoilage. They open their refrigerator door many times during the day. In doing so, the cold air escapes and warm air is let in, forcing the refrigerator's compressor to work harder. Consequently, precious energy is wasted. In this case, the FRs may be defined as follows:

FR1: Facilitate access to the food in the refrigerator.
FR2: Minimize energy loss by providing an insulated enclosure.

As one solution, we may propose the commercial vertical hung-door design commonly found on kitchen refrigerators. However, does such a door satisfy both FRs? Certainly not. When the vertical hung door is opened to satisfy FR1 (access to food), it results in a violation of FR2 (energy loss.) A better design solution consists of a horizontally hinged and vertically opening door, the kind of door used in chest-type freezers. When this vertical door is opened to take out what is inside, the cold air does not escape because it is heavier than the warmer air in the room outside. Therefore, the vertical door will satisfy both FRs. In addition, the vertical door solution has very little **information content**, that is, relevant knowledge needed to produce it. After all, these doors are easy to manufacture.

Of course, this vertical door solution may not be the best solution (for example, it may be inconvenient for some people to retrieve food from such a refrigerator). In addition, although the FRs have been satisfied to a certain extent, when the door is opened some energy is still lost by convection (by removing the food from the refrigerator). However, if we specify a design constraint like "energy loss is to be less than 15 calories," then FR2 would be satisfied to a greater extent.

Note that both FRs have been independently satisfied. We may paraphrase the independence principle as:

**Functional Design Requirements
Must Be Independently Satisfied**

A designer using this principle would attempt to keep each design requirement autonomous from the others in the problem definition. If necessary, the designer would also separate aspects, or parts, that are joined, in order to maintain their independence. However, if it is possible to integrate the design features and at the same time satisfy the independence principle, the designer should do so. It is also a good idea to keep the number of design requirements and constraints to a minimum. An unwieldy number of FRs and limitations would complicate the problem unnecessarily.

Designers should also provide for efficient assemblage, construction, or manufacturing. Ways to accomplish this are suggested by Stoll (1986), who recommends reducing the total number of parts; using modular design, standard components, and interchangeable parts; avoiding separate fasteners; reducing assembly directions; and reducing the material-handling activities required to produce the part. In addition, Stoll suggests designing parts to be multifunctional, multiuseful, and easy to fabricate.

1.3 IMPORTANCE OF VISUALIZATION

The previous sections discussed the design process and several design principles. As stated, design is a concurrent process involving conceptualization (ideation), modeling (simulation), and manufacturing (implementation). This process requires a person with a great capacity to ideate and to form mental images of unique designs. It also requires a person capable of clearly conveying a design's visual information to others. For an engineer to be able to conceive imaginative solutions—and to understand the ideas presented by other members of the design team—he or she needs to possess outstanding visual thinking and design modeling abilities. Luckily, we all possess a certain visual ability that can be greatly enhanced through practice. The next section covers this ability—*visualization*.

1.4 VISUALIZATION PROCESSES: CONVEYING DESIGN IDEAS

Visualization—the creative ability to form mental images—plays a far more important role in our lives than most of us realize. This ability belongs not only to artists, writers, and poets; in fact, engineers, designers, inventors, and scientists continually use their powers of visual thinking to create or modify devices and systems. This unique human ability allows us to think in terms of one, two, three, and four dimensions (lines, planes, pictorials, and animations, respectively.)

In the context of the engineering design process, visualization refers to the visual thinking and design modeling processes that involve perception, imagination, and communication. The visualization process may be expressed as

$$\text{Visualization = Perception + Imagination + Communication}$$

More simply stated, we see (perceive), imagine, and draw (model). (See Figure 1.5; the shaded areas in the Venn diagram—or Euler's circles—indicate the overlapping characteristics of the visualization process.)

Visualization involves wonderful visual thinking and modeling mechanisms that are not yet fully understood. However, it is fairly obvious that visual thinking uses three kinds of visual imagery: (1) the kind we actually see, (2) the kind we imagine (visualize) in our mind's eye, as when we dream, and (3) the kind we draw or model (to help others visualize our ideas). Although visual thinking can occur primarily as one kind—that is, only in the context of actually seeing, only in imagining, or only in modeling, for example—expert visual thinkers use *all* kinds of imagery. They find that seeing, imagining, and drawing (modeling) are interactive and iterative (McKim, 1980); that is, the order of importance of the visualization equation's components vary depending on one's point of view. Am I the designer conveying information to others? Then in descending order of importance, the order is communication, perception, imagination. Am I the client to whom a designer is trying to convey an idea? Then the order is perception, imagination, and communication. If I am drawing or modeling an object based on something I am looking at, then the order is perception, imagination, and communication. If I am conceiving the idea, the order is imagination, perception, and communication to self.

In artistic activity, perceiving and visual thinking are indivisibly intertwined. For example, a person who paints, writes, composes, or dances "thinks" with his or her senses (Arnheim, 1969). Your ability to visualize creative design ideas will depend on how good you are at perceiving the world around you. Developing your visual thinking and design modeling abilities involves developing both visual perception (observation) and analytical (geometry) skills. When you perceive, or "see," an object (that is, its lines, edges, shadows, movement, and so on), you are able to imagine it, and perhaps you can even draw, or model it if you have the necessary knowledge and skills.

Figure 1.5 The overlapping characteristics of the visualization process. Based on a diagram by R.H. McKim.

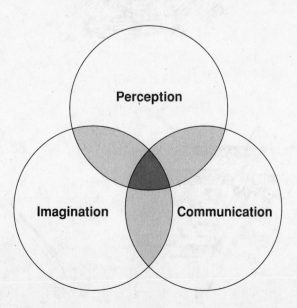

1.5 VISUALIZATION TECHNIQUES: HISTORICAL PERSPECTIVE

The drawing or model you develop to solve a design problem could be a sketch on a piece of paper, a geometric model on a computer display, or a scaled, functional prototype of the real object (**iconic model**). If you design a new device, you have to imagine, model, and communicate it so that others can see, or visualize, the idea. The item's shape and size would be conveyed by detailed drawings, geometric models, animations, iconic models, or a combination of these visualization techniques.

The use of visualization and visualization techniques in design is not new. For example, Leonardo da Vinci (1452–1519) visualized most of his ideas by sketching **pictorials** (drawings showing three faces of the object). Four examples of da Vinci's sketches are shown in Figure 1.6. He developed his talent by observing and studying (perceiving) nature. Leonardo's sketches include brilliant studies of the human body and of natural objects. He used visual annotations to enhance his memory and prepare to create his famous paintings the *Mona Lisa* and *The Last Supper*. He was also a great "design engineer." In *The Codex Atlanticus* he sketched maps, refrigeration systems, printing devices, military artifacts, and aeronautical machines. Because of the technological limitations of the period in physics and engineering, none of these inventions became a reality during da Vinci's lifetime. However, his idea sketches anticipated modern inventions like the refrigerator, the airplane, and military tanks. The quickest way to visualize and remember design ideas is by sketching freehand on a piece of paper. Quick annotations allow us to record our short-term visual memories for later referral and elaboration.

Figure 1.6 Four sketches from Leonardo da Vinci's pictorials. (Courtesy of Biblioteca Ambrosiana-Milan)

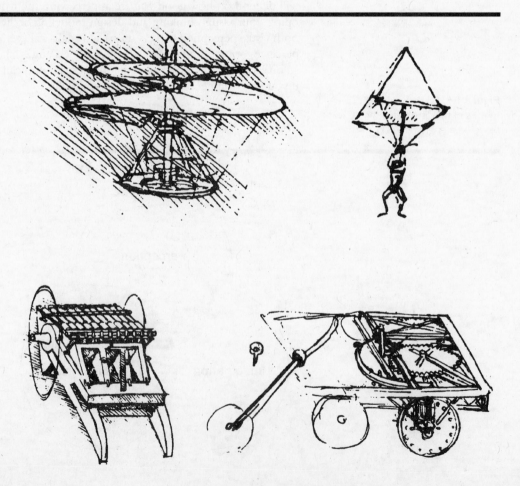

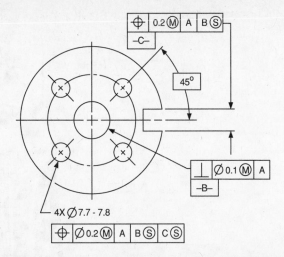

Figure 1.7 Working Drawing
(Courtesy of ANSI)

Visualization was also one of Albert Einstein's most useful tools. The famous scientist said, "Imagination is more important than knowledge, for knowledge is limited, whereas imagination embraces the entire world, stimulating progress or giving birth to evolution" (Earle, 1990). In fact, visual thinking was one of Einstein's favorite tools. When asked about what kind of internal world he made use of, Einstein responded: "The words or the language, as they are written or spoken, do not seem to play any role in my mechanism of thought. The psychical entities which serve as elements in thought are certain signs and more or less clear images which can be voluntarily reproduced and combined" (Hadamard, 1945).

In the same way that Albert Einstein was able to conceptualize his mathematical ideas, we can conceptualize our design ideas, develop new engineering devices, and visualize (simulate) the behavior of materials and processes.

For thousands of years, engineers have used visual communication techniques; particularly, drawings to document and manufacture or build their products. In fact, engineers still use drawings like the one shown in Figure 1.7. This drawing, called also a **working drawing**, illustrates a circular shape that corresponds to the right-side view of a cylindrically shaped part. The numbers and symbols pointing to the part designate its dimensions (size) and tolerances (acceptable margins of error). Manufacturers rely on such design information to determine the size and shape of the product they are going to make. Drawings are also used to illustrate how a part's components should be put together (assembly drawings) and to show the floor, elevations (architectural plans), and structural details (structural plans) of a building.

The first known working drawing is the plan (top view) of a fortress (Figure 1.8) that was recorded on a stone tablet by the Chaldean engineer Gudea (c. 4000 B.C.). Engineers have pointed out "how similar this plan is to those made by architects today, although 'drawn' thousands of years before paper was invented" (Giesecke et al., 1990).

Figure 1.9 charts the historical landmarks of working drawings. As early as 2600–1200 B.C., the Egyptians were using drawings made on papyrus (paper made from a reed-like plant) to design their projects. They used drawings to trace and record land boundaries (Steidel and Henderson, 1983). They also used drawings to show, for example, the stages in an excavation operation and the side views of a shrine or sanctuary (Dobrovolny and O'Bryant, 1984).

Roman architect and engineer Vitruvius (30 B.C.), in *De Architectura*, explains various drawing and construction procedures. His treatise could be considered the first engineering drawing book.

Figure 1.8 Gudea's plan of a fortress—the first known working drawing. (Courtesy ASCE)

Piero della Francesca (1500 A.D.), during the Renaissance period in Italy, first used drawings showing various views of an object. The use of these interrelated views in a working drawing was a cornerstone in the attempts to visually represent an idea for a project (Juricic and Barr, 1987).

Gaspard Monge (1746–1818), a French mathematician, is regarded as the founder of descriptive geometry. **Descriptive geometry** involves the construction of precise drawings. Such drawings provide two-dimensional (2-D) descriptions of and information about three-dimensional (3-D) objects. Monge developed geometric techniques mainly to solve problems in the design of fortifications. He was the first to substitute simple geometric techniques for previously complex mathematical methods. Using simple drawing instruments like

Figure 1.9 Historical Landmarks (Based on a diagram developed by Dr. D. Juricic)

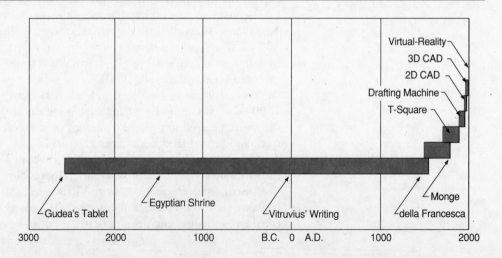

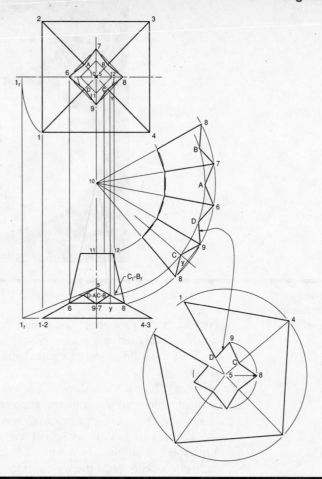

Figure 1.10 Descriptive Geometry (Intersection/Development of a Metal Hood) Such drawings provide 2-D descriptions of 3-D objects. (Courtesy of McGraw-Hill/Source: M. Betterley)

triangles, compasses, and dividers—and Monge's descriptive geometry principles—we are able to determine true shapes and angles of oblique surfaces and to draw the unfolded shape (the development) of physical objects (Figure 1.10). Descriptive geometry, drafting (drawing with instruments such as T-squares and triangles), and design methodology concepts were introduced in the U.S. engineering curriculum during the 20th century under various course titles, for example, descriptive geometry, engineering drawing, engineering graphics, engineering design graphics, visual communication, and design communication.

In the last few decades, computer graphics tools such as CADD (computer-aided design and drafting), solid modeling, stereoscopic computer graphics (illusion of real 3-D), and animation have been introduced as a replacement for drafting instruments. Ivan Sutherland is considered to be the father of computer graphics. In 1961, while a doctoral student at the Massachusetts Institute of Technology, Sutherland developed a computer drawing program called *Sketchpad*. "The name was derived from the proclivity of engineers to rough out an idea on a scrap of paper, then gradually refine it by making innumerable revisions" (McCormick, 1987). This computer program allowed simple geometric construction of lines and arcs on the monitor's screen. Sutherland was able to generate lines by using a series of push-buttons, a light pen, and a cross on the screen. By moving the light pen from one position to another, a line would follow much like a rubberband, with one end tacked to the center of the cross and the other end attached to the light pen. He "sketched" circular arcs by indicating the center of the arc with a push-button, then moving the pen to another position to define the length of the radius. Sutherland's work marks the progress of computer graphics visualization from the laboratory into industry.

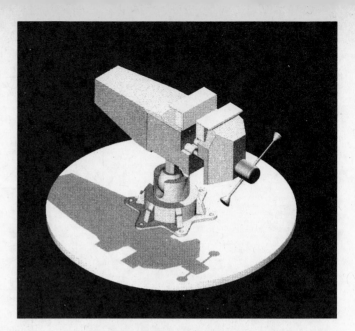

Figure 1.11 Solid Model of a part created using a computer graphics system (Courtesy of CADAM, Inc.)

Nowadays the ability to create geometry using computer graphics visualization tools is regarded as a necessary skill for the engineering designer. Figure 1.11 shows the solid model of a part created using a computer graphics visualization system.

Scientists also use visualization. They regard visualization as a method that "transforms the symbolic into the geometric, enabling researchers to *observe* their simulations and computations. Visualization offers a method for seeing the unseen. It enriches the process of scientific discovery and fosters profound and unexpected insights. In many fields it is already revolutionizing the way scientists do science (and the way engineers design and manufacture devices.) Visualization is a tool for interpreting image data fed into a computer, and for generating images from complex multi-dimensional data sets. It studies those mechanisms in humans and computers which allow them in concert to perceive, use and communicate visual information" (McCormick et al., 1987).

Indeed, scientists have recently used the term *scientific visualization*. **Scientific visualization** involves developing computer software and hardware tools to facilitate the interpretation of scientific data and to better understand physical and chemical behavior in materials or processes. Visualization is emerging as a "major computer-based field, with a body of problems, a commonality of tools and terminology, boundaries, and cohort of trained personnel. As a tool for applying computers to science, it offers a way to see the unseen" (McCormick et al., 1987). Visualization through computing can increase productivity and the potential for major scientific breakthroughs, as well as bring advanced methods into technologically intensive industries and promote the effectiveness of the scientific and engineering communities.

In design, **engineering visualization** is the overall imaging and visual thinking process involved in conceiving, developing, modeling, simulating, testing, documenting, and marketing a device or a system. It also involves analyzing the device being designed and predicting and seeing the response of the device to actual operating conditions (**visual simulation**). Figure 1.12 shows how computer graphics software can be used in the visualization process to build computer models and simulate the behavior of those models under certain design conditions. The engineer begins by logging into the computer system (1) and constructing one or more solid models (2, 3) as necessary from sketches and/or coordinate-geometric data on the product being designed. In this case, the engineer has created a solid model of a Plexiglass valve housing for an aircraft fuel system. The geometric model of the valve housing is exploded to show how its components fit together (4). After executing certain commands, the software then generates solid sections that help the engineer visualize the interior of the part (5). The program can also generate working drawings and details (6) from the model. To analyze the physical effect of factors such as forces and temperature, the program generates a **finite-element mesh**, that is, a set of wire-like elements connected together in a grid (7). Results of thermal (heat) and stress (force) analyses can be visualized easily by executing the finite-element analysis (FEA) capabilities of the software. For example, here a cross-section (8) image is used to illustrate the stresses generated by the fuel pressure in the valve's inlet. The scale on the right indicates the stress in pounds per square inch (psi). When the visual simulation phase of the design is finished, the engineer may prepare the tapes needed by a numerically controlled (NC) machine-tool cutter for machining the products' parts (9, 10). In this case, NC

Figure 1.12 Computer-aided design and manufacturing process. Computer graphics software aids in the overall visualization process. (Courtesy Control Data Corp. and High Tech.)

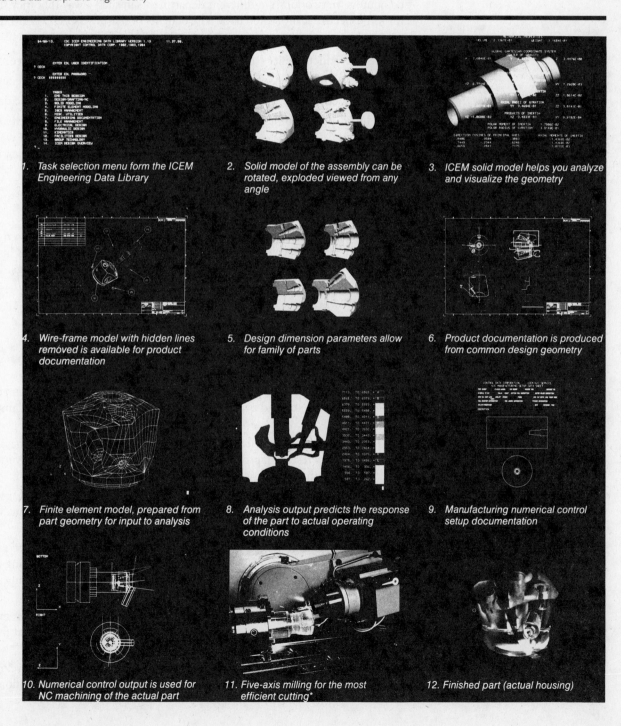

1. *Task selection menu form the ICEM Engineering Data Library*

2. *Solid model of the assembly can be rotated, exploded viewed from any angle*

3. *ICEM solid model helps you analyze and visualize the geometry*

4. *Wire-frame model with hidden lines removed is available for product documentation*

5. *Design dimension parameters allow for family of parts*

6. *Product documentation is produced from common design geometry*

7. *Finite element model, prepared from part geometry for input to analysis*

8. *Analysis output predicts the response of the part to actual operating conditions*

9. *Manufacturing numerical control setup documentation*

10. *Numerical control output is used for NC machining of the actual part*

11. *Five-axis milling for the most efficient cutting*

12. *Finished part (actual housing)*

tapes were used to set up the data for the cutter (11) that machined the valve housing (12) from a real piece of Plexiglass.

As you can imagine, with computer graphics visualization tools we are now able to model and simulate the product being designed before building the first physical prototype. Two of the most useful computer-based visualization tools are **geometric modeling** and **computer-aided design** (CAD)—software programs that use the designer's input to generate an electronic 3-D graphic model on the computer screen. The model created by a geometric modeler or a CAD package represents a **database**. The database is a collection of data—such as the X, Y, and Z coordinates of the products' parts—having organization and structure. If the same database is shared with the manufacturing or building engineers, the process is called **CAD/CAM**, or **computer-aided design** and **computer-aided manufacturing**. Sharing a database involves hooking up computers (networking) in different departments in such a way that they share the same electronically stored data. The benefits of sharing a CAD/CAM database include the following:

- Better product quality (since the manufacturing process is easier to control)
- Greater accuracy (by specifying an acceptable margin of error or tolerance)
- Shorter design time (since designers and manufacturers use the same data)
- Reduced prototyping cost (since a real model is generated directly by a machine)
- Faster analysis (by using the same computer model from an earlier design stage)
- Added manufacturing flexibility (by being able to change the database)
- Reduced inventory (record-keeping of needed parts is easier)

CAD/CAM and the other design and visualization techniques discussed allow engineers to develop new products or improve existing products in less time than ever before and without using traditional paper drawings. The reduced design-cycle time facilitates the evaluation of more design alternatives and, ultimately, assists in obtaining better products.

Chapter Summary

Chapter 1 detailed the following points:

- The realization of a design is a process that can be considered a combination of three interrelated and overlapping phases: ideation, simulation, and implementation.
- Ideation involves the conceptualization of a design. The ideation phase includes market research, problem definition, generation of preliminary ideas, and the preliminary decision on choice of design.
- Simulation involves the maturation of a design. The simulation phase includes geometric modeling, spatial geometry analysis, engineering analysis, and sometimes animation.
- Implementation involves the construction or manufacturing of the product from a mature design. The implementation phase includes prototyping and testing, generating a report, creating design documentation, carrying out production, and marketing the product.
- Two important design principles for the beginning designer to keep in mind are that early decisions greatly affect the final design outcome, and that functional design requirements must be independently met.
- The cognitive process of visualization can be considered a skill to be developed through the combination of perception, imagination, and communication.

- The history of design communication dates back to at least 4000 B.C., to the first known working drawing. The field was given a great push forward by the work of such notable figures as Leonardo da Vinci, who developed the "pictorial" sketching method during the late 15th and early 16th centuries, and Gaspard Monge, who developed techniques of "descriptive geometry" about 300 years after da Vinci's time. Design communication has progressed rapidly during the latter half of this century with the advent of computer-aided design (CAD), geometric modeling, and other visualization techniques.

REFERENCES AND SUGGESTED READINGS

Arnheim, R. *Visual Thinking*. Berkeley, Calif.: University of California Press, 1969.

Dobrovolny, J. S., and D. C. O'Bryant. *Graphics for Engineers: Visualization, Communication and Design*. New York: Wiley, 1984.

Earle, J. H. *Engineering Design Graphics*. Reading, Mass.: Addison-Wesley, 1990.

Giesecke, F. E., et al. *Principles of Engineering Graphics*. New York: Macmillan, 1990.

Hadamard, J. *The Psychology of Invention in the Mathematical Field*. New York: Dover, 1954. Originally published by Princeton University Press, 1945.

Juricic, D., and R. Barr. "Engineering Graphics and Computer Graphics: About Their Past, Present, and Future." *Engineering Design Graphics Journal*, 51(3):13–16, 1987.

McCormick, J., et al. (Eds.). *Computer Graphics*, 21(6), 1987.

McKim, R. S. *Experiences in Visual Thinking*. Monterey, Calif.: Brooks/Cole, 1980.

Rodriguez, W. E. "Design As an ISI Process." *Journal of Theoretical Graphics and Computing*, 3(2):65–71, 1990a.

Rodriguez, W. E. *Visualization*. New York: McGraw-Hill, 1990b.

Steidel, R. F., and J.M. Henderson. *The Graphics Languages of Engineering*. New York: Wiley, 1983.

Stoll, T. W. "Design for Manufacture: An Overview." *Applied Mechanics Review*, 39(9), 1986.

Suh, N. P. *The Principles of Design*. New York: Oxford, 1990.

Walker, E. A. "Engineering Schools Share the Blame for Declining Productivity." *The Bent of Tau Beta Pi*, 80(2), 1989.

EXERCISES

1.1 Try to paint the following picture in your mind: Imagine you are on the coast of a beautiful tropical island. You are walking down the beach and you pick up a sea shell. Imagine a sea shell that still has its natural color and luster because it has not yet been bleached by the sun or worn down by the sand. Imagine that the shell is as hard as a suit of armor. Then, look at the overall shape and perceive the paper-thin walls of the shell. Note the ridges, stripes, lining, texture, and curvature of the outer surface. Rotate the sea shell and make it dance.

You have just experienced the power of creative imagination, or visualization. Your brain is capable of generating such images faster than the most powerful supercomputer—for example, one type of supercomputer would require over 70 billion calculations and two minutes to produce an animated sequence or scene like the one you just imagined!

1.2 Look at a simple object or a device nearby—for instance, a pencil or a book. Pay close attention to the overall shape of the object. Then look very carefully at all the contours and details. Now close your eyes for a minute and imagine the object. You will be able to "see" the object in your mind by simply thinking about the contour and details you pictured earlier. Now, with your eyes closed, imagine the object moving to different positions.

1.3 Write a one-page essay about how you would approach one of the following design problems. Include a short statement of the problem—the way you perceive it—and determine the FRs and constraints of the problem. You are encouraged to use drawings to reinforce your ideas.

a. Rubberband-Propelled Vehicle Project

A child wants a small tabletop vehicle powered by rubber bands for a competition. No high-tech electromechanical or solar propelled gadgets are allowed. The vehicle will be raced on a table that measures 3 meters long. The vehicle will compete against other similar "cars" set on one edge of the table. The children will release the vehicles with the objective of the vehicles reaching the opposite end of the table without falling off. The kids are not permitted to protect their vehicles in the event of a mechanical failure or a fall. The vehicle that ends up closest to the opposite edge is the winner. The following specifications are given:

Width: Overall width shall not exceed 180 mm.

Length: Overall length shall not exceed 350 mm.

Weight: Weight shall not exceed 285 grams.

Material: Any safe and legal material.

Other: The entire vehicle needs to reach the finish line.

(*Equivalents:* 1 mm = .039 in., 1 gram = 0.035 ounce)

Hints:

1. Start fresh! Work through a brainstorming session.

2. Consider air resistance and wheelbase, axle, and wheel-surface friction.

3. Consider lubricating the rubber band; it might reduce breakage.

4. Test drive your vehicle well in advance.

5. Consider protection against damage incurred during a possible failure (such as falling off the edge of the table).

b. Clipboard Design

Students frequently use clipboards to write on while standing, lying in bed, or sitting in the car. There is always the need for direct lighting on the board; however, traditional lamps are not easily adjustable to this task. Occasional light is often obscured by the projected shade of an obstacle. Design a clipboard lighting device that is portable and lightweight. It should provide bright and even illumination. Cost should be under $15.

c. Sailboat Rack Design

Because of lack of space, the local sailing club needs a new boat rack that will store two Force-5 sailboats with masts down above a fleet of Coronado-15s. The Coronados are in drydock on trailers, and they must be loaded with their masts up, 25 feet in the air. The rack should be designed so that a Force-5 can be loaded and unloaded between two C-15s. A small (or handicapped) person should be able to load and unload the boats with a minimum of effort.

d. Overhead Projector Antiglare Shield

Overhead projectors are useful lecturing tools. They are commonly used in classrooms to display figures and diagrams prepared beforehand. This enables the speaker to save time and effort during the class or lecture. However, while the overhead projector is in use, it produces an intense light reflection. This light reflection is so intense that it can irritate the eyes of the person using it. Also, it produces a glare that forces the user to position himself or herself in uncomfortable positions to avoid the glare. A secondary problem is created when the user wants to write on the transparencies while lecturing. The overhead projector stage glass is very hot, causing discomfort to the lecturer. Design an overhead projector antiglare device that will solve these problems. The device should be easy to attach and detach, and materials should not cost more that $10. The device should allow the user to be in a comfortable position.

1.4 Research and draw Leonardo da Vinci's inventions:

a. Anemometer	k. Pile driver
b. Flying machine	l. Military tank
c. Cone-headed mitre valve	m. Odometer
d. Double-hulled ship	n. Paddlewheel ship
e. Drill press	o. Parachute
f. Gear study	p. Scaling ladder
g. Machine for placing columns	q. Rotating bridge
h. Helicopter	r. Triple-tier machine gun
i. Hygrometer	s. Variable speed device
j. Inclinometer	t. Wire-testing device

1.5 Write a one-page essay that describes the design process.

1.6 Write a one-page essay that explains how visualization is used in the design process.

1.7 Describe some of the benefits of using CAD/CAM.

1.8 Research the history of the design and visualization fields, and write a one-page report on the topic.

1.9 Draw an image and/or write a short statement that describes or defines each of the key terms, listed below, used in this chapter:

Boolean algebra	Implementation
Brainstorming	Interactive
Computer-aided design (CAD)	Information content
Computer-aided manufacturing (CAM)	Iterative
Concurrent	Patent search
Database	Pictorials
Decision matrix	Primitives
Descriptive geometry	Resources
Design process	Scientific visualization
Development	Simulation
Engineering visualization	Solid models
Feature-based modelers	Virtual-reality modelers
Functional requirements (FRs)	Visual annotation
Finite-element mesh	Visualization
Geometric modeling	Visual simulation
Iconic model	Wireframes
Ideation	Working drawing

CHAPTER 2 2-D Design Annotation

Design annotation techniques—such as sketching and projecting a visual image on a plane—allow us to record and describe the shape of our product design ideas quickly and effectively. Although the real world is three-dimensional (3-D), engineers, architects, and designers commonly sketch or display two-dimensional (2-D) views, or faces, of the device or structure being described.

2.1 PROJECTION OF VISUAL IMAGES

One of the most popular 2-D design annotation techniques is called *view projection*, or simply **projection**. By projection, one produces an image by mapping a face of an object onto a plane, as shown in Figure 2.1. Projection provides a convenient way to draw the object's geometry (its shape) on a sheet of paper or to display it on a computer screen. It involves establishing the relationship between a series of visual variables including one's point of view, the plane on which one is projecting the image, and the object to be portrayed, among others.

As a design engineer, your ability to communicate to other members of the design or manufacturing/construction team will be enhanced by knowing the various projection rules, standards, and practices (Rodriguez, 1988, 1990). You will use projection standards almost every day in discussions with other members of the design team. These standards have been established by the **American National Standards Institute (ANSI)**, the **International Standards Organization (ISO)**, and other similar organizations around the world. In this day of international competition and broad markets, design engineers should be familiar with at least the ISO and the ANSI standards, which are the most widely accepted in practice. Engineers, designers, and technicians should be able to prepare or interpret sketches, mechanical production drawings, and construction plans according to either ANSI or ISO conventions. They should also be familiar with the principles of projection theory.

2.1.1 Projection Theory: 3-D to 2-D Visualization

Projection theory comprises a set of rules and principles devised to analyze, draw, and display spatial geometry on two-dimensional surfaces (for example, a sheet of paper or a computer screen). The aim of projection theory is to describe the shape and geometry of objects. Gaspard Monge—described in Chapter 1 as the founder of descriptive geometry—wrote a book about projection theory principles entitled *Descriptive Geometry* (1795). Monge used drawing instruments, such as compasses and rulers, to solve complex mathematical problems involved in the design of military fortifications. The problems dealt with calculations of true (actual) length, angles, and the shape of oblique or irregular objects. His methods also extended to the determination of the points of intersection between, say, two objects in contact. Monge solved three-dimensional problems that originally required extensive and tedious mathematical calculations by devising a method for projecting the objects onto a two-dimensional plane. He developed this method while still a student in France (it was said that his teacher used to reprimand him for not following traditional approaches). The descriptive geometry method became so useful that during Napoleon's reign, Monge served as his technical adviser. Monge's techniques were kept as a French military secret for almost two decades; however, descriptive geometry has been used in engineering design and geometric space analysis for the last 200 years. Chapter 5 shows how the principles of descriptive geometry (or *spatial geometry*, as it is called today) are used to solve some modern visualization problems.

2.2 PARALLEL PROJECTION

Projections can be classified as either (1) parallel projections or (2) perspective projections. When we use **parallel projection** to represent an object, we assume that the observer has many "eyes" adjacent to one another (or more precisely, lines of sight parallel to one another, as shown in Figure 2.1).

Parallel projection simplifies the problem of representation by portraying an object as a geometric abstraction of human visual reality. It allows us to visualize an object in greater depth and communicate it to members of a design team in a clear and concise way. In parallel projection, the observer is assumed to be at an infinite distance from the object (as opposed to a finite distance, as in perspective projection). Since observer and object are so far apart, the visual rays are parallel to each other. These rays, or **lines of sight**, are used to project the object onto a standard projection plane, or 2-D display (Figure 2.1).

In contrast, when we use perspective projection we assume that the observer has binocular vision, creating an illusion that the object's faces vanish toward certain points—as is the case in actual visual perception. Perspective projections are much more difficult to draw than parallel projections; this topic is discussed in Chapter 3.

Figure 2.1 Projection—the mapping of an object's face onto a plane.

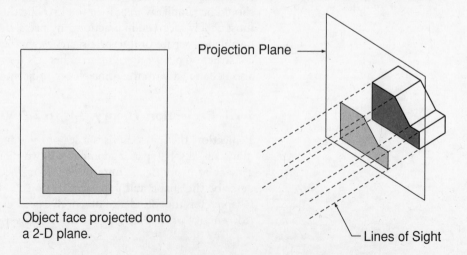

Projection Plane

Object face projected onto a 2-D plane.

Lines of Sight

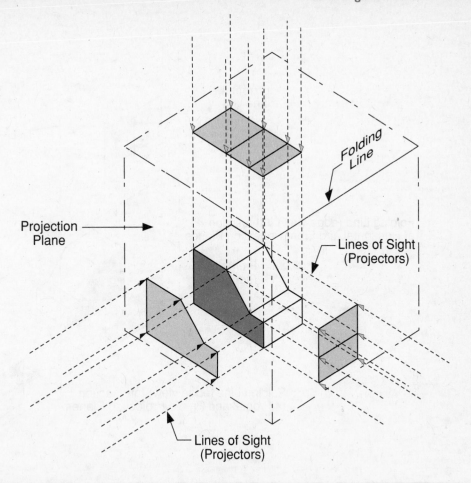

Projection → Plane

Folding Line

Lines of Sight (Projectors)

Lines of Sight (Projectors)

Figure 2.2 Orthographic projection. The faces of the imaginary transparent box portray the projection planes between the object and the observer.

2.2.1 Orthographic Projection

Parallel projections are subclassified by the angle formed between projection planes and the observer's line of sight. One type of parallel projection is **orthographic projection**. This term derives from the Greek word *orthogonios*, which means "composed of right angles." Orthographic projection uses parallel lines of sight at right angles (90 degrees) to an imaginary plane to represent 3-D objects, as shown in Figure 2.2. This standard method allows the designer to describe a specific device, in every detail, on a 2-D plane.

Orthographic projection uses 2-D planes. As the name implies, **projection planes** are imaginary two-dimensional surfaces on which one draws and/or displays an object's views. Figure 2.2 depicts a solid object enclosed by an imaginary transparent, or "glass," box. The illustrated faces of the box portray the projection planes between the object and the observer. The projection planes are used to project orthographic views.

Figure 2.3 shows three main standard planes of projection:

1. Horizontal plane
2. Frontal plane
3. Profile plane

The projection planes are separated by imaginary reference lines, or folding lines. The **folding line** is the line of intersection between two projection planes. If the imaginary transparent box is unfolded (Figure 2.3), each folding line becomes an *edge view* of the projection plane.

Orthographic views are constructed by projecting orthogonal lines of sight onto the projection planes. As mentioned earlier, lines of sight (also known as

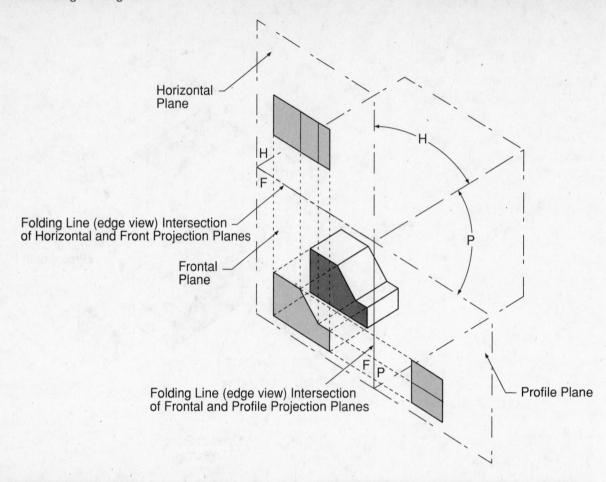

Horizontal
Plane

Folding Line (edge view) Intersection
of Horizontal and Front Projection Planes

Frontal
Plane

H

F

H

P

F P

Profile Plane

Folding Line (edge view) Intersection
of Frontal and Profile Projection Planes

Figure 2.3 Simulation of the unfolding of the profile and horizontal projection planes of the box in Figure 2.2.

projectors, or *visual rays*) are straight lines from the eye of the observer to points located on the object. In orthographic projection, all lines of sight are parallel to one another, and the eye of the observer is assumed to be an infinite distance away from the object. When generating orthographic views, one assumes that the eye of the observer changes position with each projected point, so as to keep each line of sight parallel to the others. The object's orthographic views are always projected onto a projection plane perpendicular to the lines of sight. According to the ANSI standards, the projection plane is located between the observer and the object.

2.2.2 Multiview Projection

The ANSI method of displaying orthographic projection views of an object is illustrated in Figure 2.4. These views, or **multiviews**, as they are usually called, are obtained by an imaginary unfolding of the projection planes of the transparent box, similar to the unfolding illustrated in Figure 2.3. In fact, **multiview projection** refers to the relative arrangement of the orthographic projection views on the computer screen or the sheet of paper as the result of the unfolding. Figure 2.4 shows a total of six views projected in their respective projection planes. The six principal views are top, front, right side, left side, bottom, and rear. Ordinarily, it is not necessary to draw all six views. For simple objects, three standard views—namely, top, front, and right side—will suffice to describe completely the object's shape. Note that these three views describe the height (H), length (L), and depth (D) dimensions of the object. Figures 2.5 and 2.6 show sequences illustrating the projection of top, front, and right-side multiviews for two given objects.

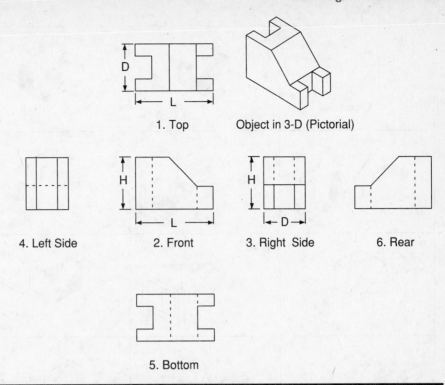

Figure 2.4 Orthographic multiviews, according to ANSI standards.

2.2.3 Linetype Conventions

Figures 2.4, 2.5, and 2.6 contain several types of lines that have been projected onto the projection plane. These **linetypes**, or types of lines, have been standardized to enable proper identification of an object's features. Figure 2.7 defines the standard linetype conventions, and Figure 2.8 shows some linetype uses.

The dashed lines represent lines that are not visible from a specific multiview and are therefore called **hidden lines**. Hidden lines are drawn to clarify details and indicate important features of the object. Omission of hidden lines from multiviews might cause important aspects of a device to be overlooked. Nevertheless, sometimes they must be omitted—for example, when they occur behind a visible line or when they will confuse, rather than simplify, the drawing. Hidden lines that intersect other lines should be drawn so that their end dashes are in contact with the intersecting lines, with one exception: when the dash makes a continuation with another linetype. ANSI recommends that features located behind transparent material also be drawn with hidden lines.

Solid, thick lines delineating the object's edges are called **visible lines**. Visible lines are usually drawn heavier than hidden lines so that they stand out. Note that two line widths are recommended for visible and hidden lines: thick (.032 inches [.7 mm]) and thin (.016 inches [.35 mm]), respectively. In other words, line thickness should contrast at a recommended ratio of approximately 2:1 between visible and hidden lines. In fact, adequate contrast between the visible lines and all other lines makes a drawing more legible. The legibility of a drawing is called its **line quality**.

Center lines should always be drawn at the centers of circles and arcs to aid in the view's interpretation. These alternating long and short dashes are used in all orthographic views to identify the circular features of the objects and to locate the centers of the circles. Center lines are partially omitted only when they coincide with hidden or visible lines. However, whenever possible, you should draw their **extends**—the portions of the center lines that protrude beyond the edge of the circle. Center lines are also used as an axis of symmetry—for example, to represent the other half of a partially drawn view, to indicate the path of a part in motion, and to clarify partial sections of symmetrical parts.

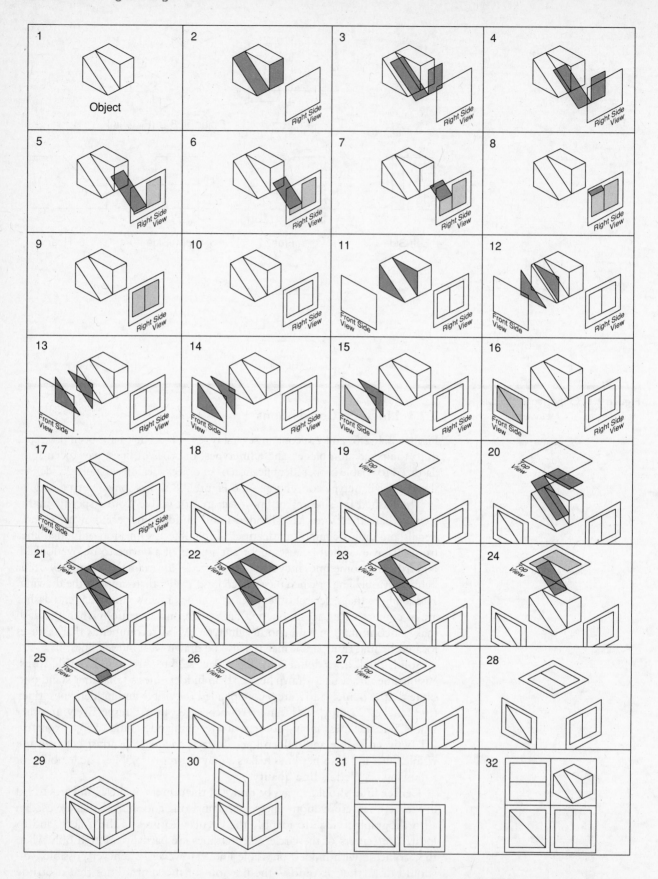

Figure 2.5 Sequence showing the projection of three multiviews (top, front, and right side) for the given object..

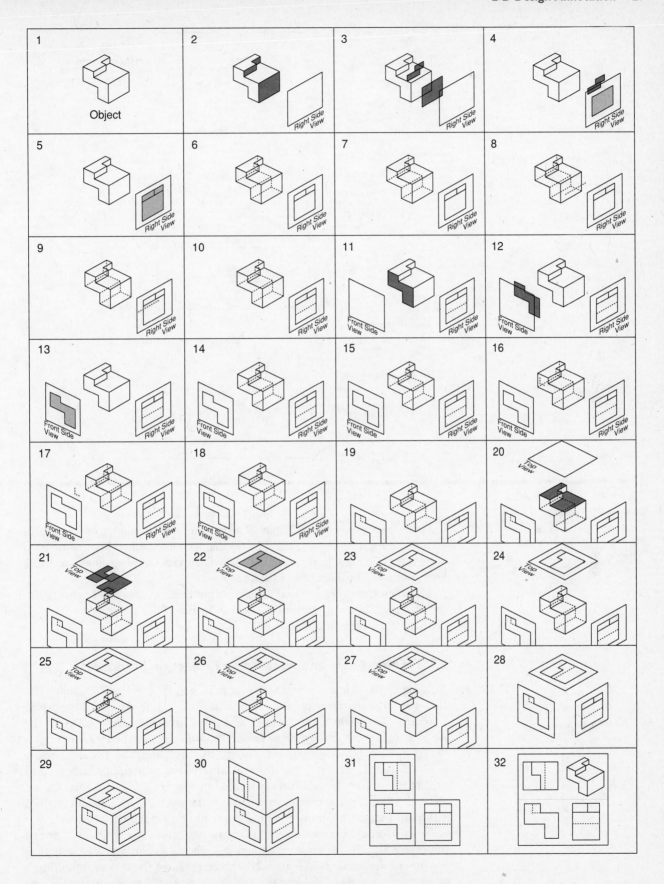

Figure 2.6 Sequence showing hidden line projection on multiviews.

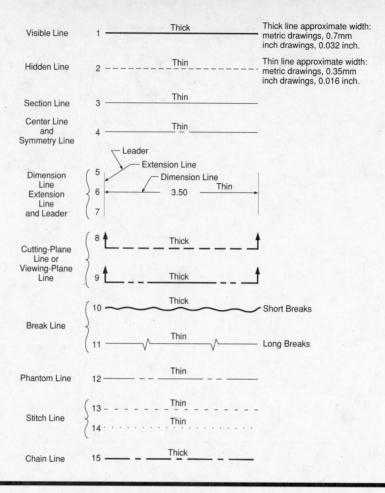

Figure 2.7 Standard linetype conventions. (Courtesy of ASME)

Other linetypes (Figures 2.7 and 2.8) used for design annotation and documentation are section lines, chain lines, phantom lines, stitch lines, dimension lines, extension lines, leaders, cutting-plane lines, viewing-plane lines, and break lines; these will be discussed in Chapter 9.

Construction lines are used to assist in guiding the drawing. In contrast to the linetypes shown in Figures 2.7 and 2.8, these lines are erased or deleted once the drawing is finished.

2.2.4 Third-Angle and First-Angle Projection Standards

As mentioned earlier, there are two types of graphic standards systems. The ISO system is the most popular system in Europe and Asia, and the ANSI system is used in the United States and some other western countries. The ANSI system uses the *third-angle projection standard*, and the ISO system uses the *first-angle projection standard*. The words "first" and "third" designate the assumed spatial location of the object relative to the projection planes used to project the object. If the object is located in the first quadrant, then we are using the first-angle projection standard; if the object is located in the third quadrant, then we are using the third-angle projection standard (Figure 2.9).

In **third-angle projection**, the plane of projection is positioned between the object and the observer, as shown in Figure 2.9. Imagine a hinged glass box inscribing an object (Figure 2.10), each wall of the box representing a projection plane. By unfolding this imaginary box in the form illustrated, we obtain the standard six third-angle orthographic views arrangement. In the arrangement of views in third-angle projection, the front view is the most significant view (Spence, 1988) and constitutes the core of the system—since the top view folds up and the bottom view folds down, forming the front view. The right-side view and the left-side view fold off each edge of the front view, and the rear view normally folds off the left-side view.

ANSI uses the standard graphic symbol (for the third-angle projection) portrayed in Figure 2.11. Whenever possible you should include this symbol in your multiview drawings, as shown in Figure 2.12. This figure illustrates the standard third-angle view arrangement for the object shown in Figure 2.11.

In **first-angle projection**, the object is located between the observer and the plane of projection (Figures 2.13 and 2.14).

Since the visibility of lines is obtained from the observer's point of view, the orthographic views of the object are the same for both the third-angle and first-angle projection standard systems. However, the arrangement or relative positioning of the orthographic views may be different. Figure 2.15 illustrates an example of the first-angle projection standard. Figure 2.16 illustrates a first-angle working drawing of a bicycle stand made out of finished concrete.

Figure 2.8 Use of standard line-types. (Courtesy of ASME)

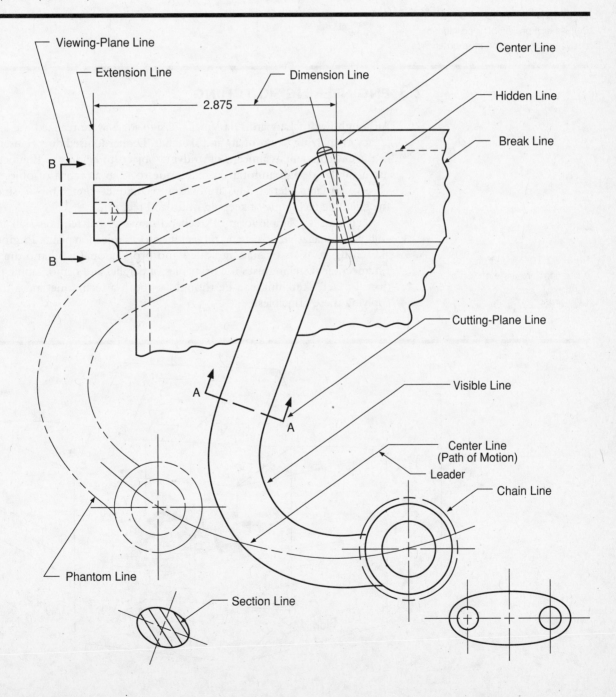

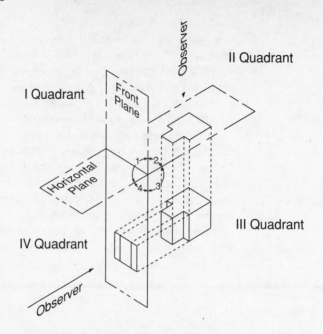

Figure 2.9 In third-angle projection, the plane of projection is positioned between the object and the observer.

2.3 ENGINEERING SKETCHING

Although few of Leonardo da Vinci's design ideas were realized, he left us a legacy of amazing works of art and sketches. Leonardo used direct observation of the environment as a means of studying objects to be drawn. Engineers can use a similar design annotation technique to keep a record of objects they observe for later referral. This annotation technique—sketching—is similar to the scientific technique of keeping notes and records.

Sketching is a simple form of freehand drawing that requires skill and the ability to visualize an object and project it onto a projection plane. **Engineering sketching** consists of making scaled and proportional freehand drawings. Engineering sketching uses the principles of parallel and orthographic projection. In fact, sketching can be thought as both a technique and a tool for applying these principles.

Figure 2.10 Hinged glass box illustrating third-angle projection standard. (Courtesy of McGraw-Hill, Source: H.E. Grant, *Engineering Drawing*)

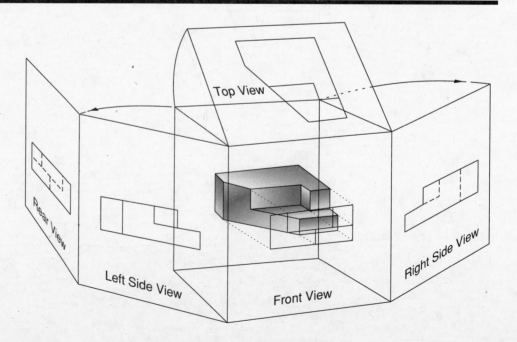

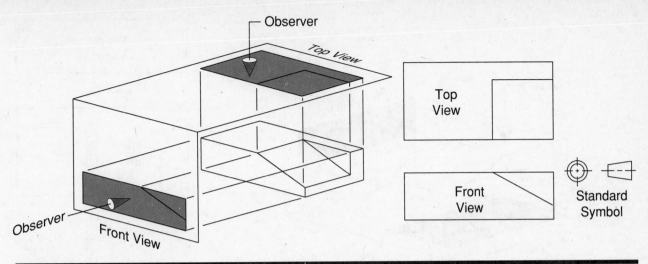

Figure 2.11 Third-angle projection and third-angle standard symbol. (Courtesy of ASME)

The eye and the brain are the most important elements of sketching. For example, while observing a certain object, we visualize the object by constructing an organized mental image based on our experience and the stimuli reaching our eyes. In constructing this visual image, we should seize on the unique physical characteristics of the object. In other words, we need to study its main features, form, proportions, orientation, material, color, symmetry, contrast, repetition, and so on. Then, we sketch the general outline of the object, imagining that the pencil is actually touching the object as we sketch it on the drawing pad or computer screen. Some engineering designers have the good habit of carrying a sketch pad (or laptop computer) wherever they go, to take "visual notes" of what they observe and think. Like Leonardo, they "get" ideas by observing the environment and by interacting with people.

Sketching is particularly useful in the early brainstorming and formulation stages of the design process and in the generation of alternative solutions to a particular design problem. During this ideation phase, designers use sketching to stimulate their imagination as well as to communicate visually. A sketch usually serves to define an initial idea and at the same time suggest additional alternatives and improvements. Sketching helps in organizing our thoughts,

Figure 2.12 Standard third-angle multiviews and third-angle symbol. (Courtesy of ASME)

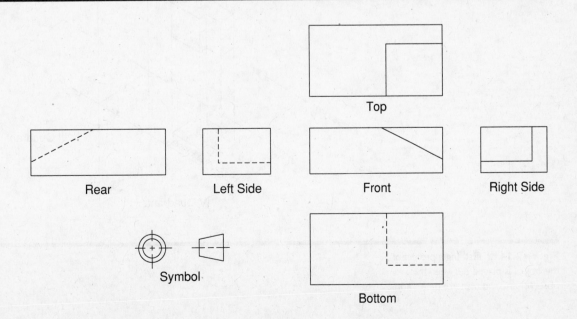

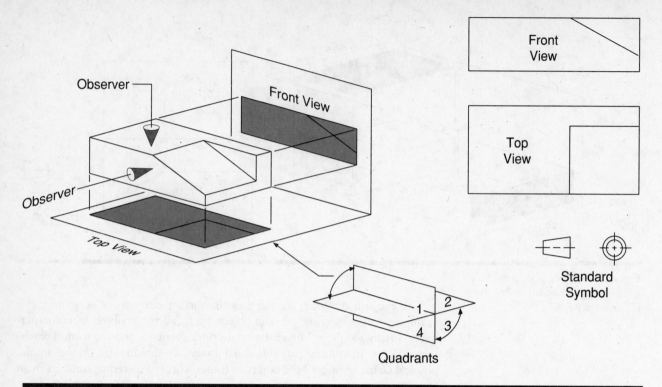

Figure 2.13 First-angle projection
and first-angle standard symbol.
Notice that the concentric circles are
to the right of the quadrilateral of the
first-angle symbol. (Courtesy of
ASME)

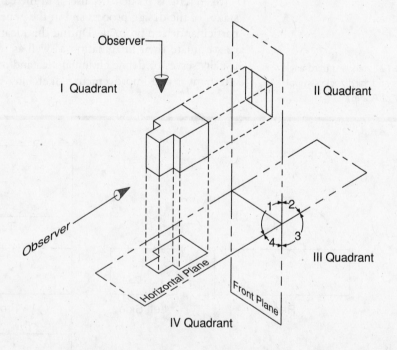

Figure 2.14 In first-angle projection,
the object is placed between the
observer and the plane of projection.

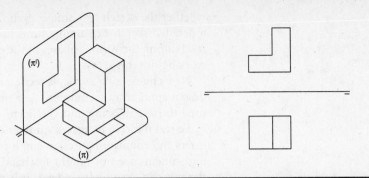

Figure 2.15 Example of the first-angle projection standard. (Courtesy of M. Rodrigues, Brazil)

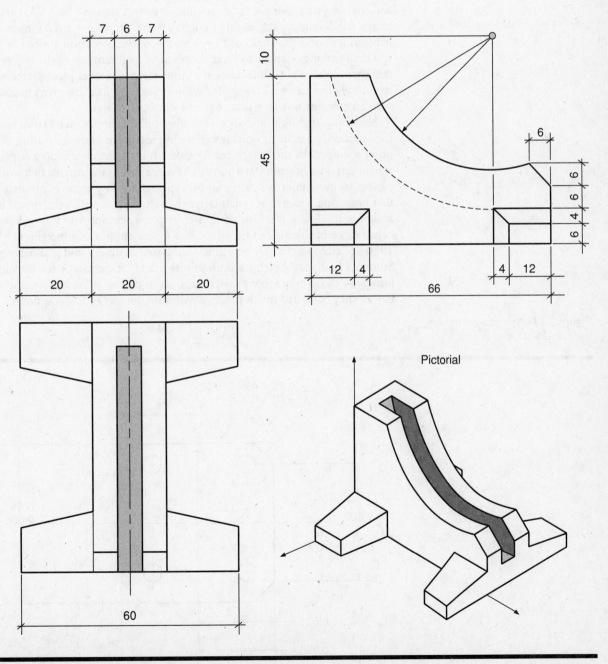

Pictorial

Figure 2.16 Bicycle stand illustrating first-angle projection drawings; dimensions are given in centimeters. (Courtesy of P. Mayrhofer and Beton-Katzenberger)

whether the sketch be a simple graph summarizing points of a presentation or a detailed sketch explaining a mechanism (Beakley, 1975). Sketching is also used during the various phases of the design process and while revising the final working drawings.

New engineering curricula recognize the importance of sketching and other design annotation techniques. As a matter of fact, early engineering programs used to have drawing and visualization courses, but they were abandoned to make room for an increased number of technical courses. However, manufacturers and engineering design employers have often complained that engineering students are not taught freehand drawing. They have always recognized the value of sketching. Indeed, it is difficult to imagine an engineer without freehand sketching talent.

Engineering and manufacturing companies are recognizing more than ever the importance of being able to produce proficient freehand, instrumental, and/or computer-aided sketches to quickly convey design ideas. CAD and geometric-modeling packages allows engineering sketching (with an input device like a mouse or a trackball) of the geometry of the object on a monitor screen and then making changes to meet the physical requirements of the object being designed. Figure 2.17 illustrates the front view of a steel plate sketched by a structural engineer on a computer system. Sketches like this provide designers with an efficient way to visualize the object in question.

Sketching orthographic views and three-dimensional pictorial drawings is the engineer's means of quickly generating ideas and communicating them to other members of the design team. A sketch on a computer, on a napkin in a restaurant, on a blueprint at a construction site, or on the surface of a workshop table is far more effective than a verbal explanation. Engineers in industry know that preparing a sketch is much faster than drawing it with mechanical instruments or modeling it with a computer graphics system. And by working freehand, more problems can be solved in a given amount of time (French et al., 1986). Sketching can also be a time-saving tool in design and graphics courses. Students find that sketching is an effective and efficient tool for learning the principles of orthographic projection, since it can be done by beginners even before they have had much practice with instruments or the computer.

Figure 2.17 Preliminary computer-aided sketch of a steel plate.

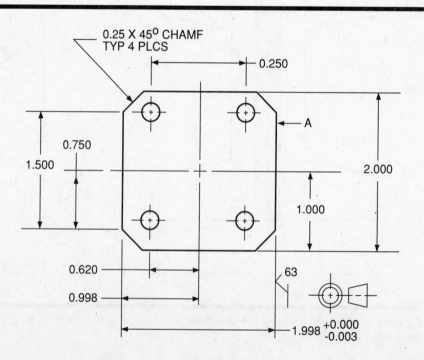

A good sketch is not the same thing as a carelessly made drawing. Sketching does not give us a license to become sloppy or incomplete (Edel, 1967). Sketches should reflect high quality, and completeness of thought.

2.3.1 Sketching Tools: Triangles, Paper, and Scales

Sketch quality can be improved by using straight edges, triangles, and other tools. Manual drafting tools can be used to prepare the final form of a sketch. But you do not need to have a complete set of instruments or a computer to prepare a neat sketch. If you have the ability, pencil and paper will suffice. However, a set of 30-, 60-, and 45-degree triangles will help you gain confidence and sketching skill.

What are the tools required to start a sketch? Normally, the tools needed are a drawing or input device (for example, pencil, stylus, mouse), and a display surface (sheet of paper, tablet, monitor). Most beginners prefer to use a sketch pad. Such pads are commercially available in several rulings, including 4, 5, 6, or 8 squares to the inch and 5 squares to the centimeter. Pads with overlaid orthographic grids are also available. However, an engineer should be capable of sketching a proportional drawing on any type of paper—including a napkin at lunch time! Preliminary sketches are later drafted on a standard sheet of paper.

The following is a list of the ANSI standard paper-size designations. All dimensions are given in inches (1 in. = 25.4 mm):

TYPE	WIDTH	LENGTH
A	8.5	11.0
B	11.0	17.0
C	17.0	22.0
D	22.0	34.0
E	34.0	44.0
F	28.0	40.0

The international (ISO) paper sizes are listed below (all dimensions are given in millimeters):

TYPE	WIDTH	LENGTH	NEAREST U.S. TYPE
A0	841	1189	E
A1	594	841	D
A2	420	594	C
A3	297	420	B
A4	210	297	A

What if you have to draw or sketch an object, a device, or a system larger than the standard sheets of paper listed above? You can reduce, or "scale-down," the drawing. **Scaling** is the process of drawing an object to a specified size. The object may be drawn to the same size, or *full scale* (1:1); it may also be reduced in size, making it appear smaller, by using a different scale. For example, a part may be reduced by half (50 percent) at a ratio of reduction equal to 1:2, or *half scale*. A very small device, like a microchip, may be enlarged, making it appear larger than the actual size.

The designer who is using a computer graphics system does not have to be concerned about scaling until the drawing is ready to be plotted (output sent to a plotter). CAD can output drawings on almost any scale. Nevertheless, all designers should be familiar with the different types of scales and learn how to use them.

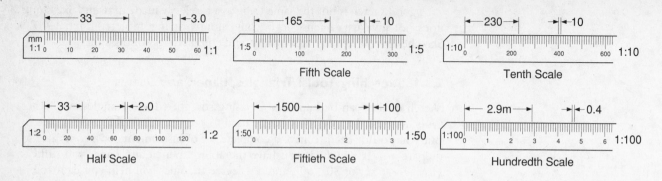

Figure 2.18 Metric scale. (Courtesy of McGraw-Hill)

The **metric scale** is used in the international system of measurements. The *Système International d'Unités*, or SI, is the accepted metric system. According to the metric scale, 1:1 (full size) means 1 mm calibration represents 1 mm actual size; 1:2 (half size) means each 1 mm calibration represents 2 mm actual size. Other ratios are 1:5, 1:25, 1:33, 1:75, and so on. Each of these metric scales can be used for other ratios. For example, the 1:1 scale could be used as 1:10, 1:100, and other multiples of 10, as shown in Figure 2.18.

The **engineer's scale** is graduated in decimals of an inch (English System). One inch is divided in 10, 20, 30, 40, 50, and 60 parts. Figure 2.19 shows the relative effect of using the 10 or 30 scale to measure 21 or 210 feet. Each scale could be used for other ratios, for example: 1"=10', or 1"=0.1".

In the **architect's scale**, the major divisions represent feet, and the sub-divisions represent inches (English System). The main ratios are 16 Full Size (each division is $\frac{1}{16}$ inch); 3"=1'0"; 1½"=1'0"; 1"=1'0"; ¾"=1'0"; ½"=1'0"; ⅜"=1'0"; ¼"=1'0"; ³⁄₃₂"=1'0"; ⅛"=1'0"; ³⁄₁₆"=1'0". Figure 2.20 shows the architect's scale.

Figure 2.19 Engineer's scale. (Courtesy of McGraw-Hill)

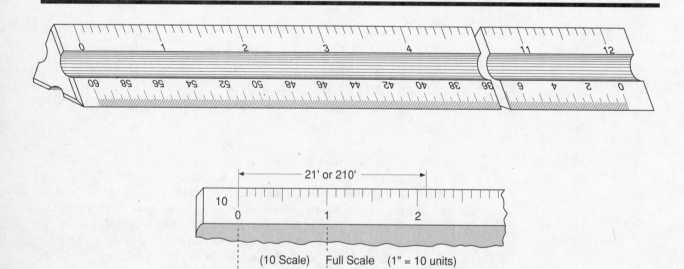

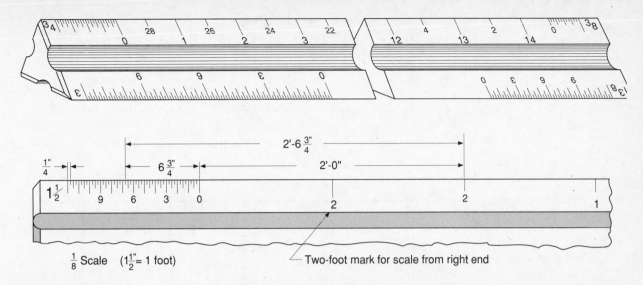

Figure 2.20 Architect's scale. (Courtesy of McGraw-Hill)

2.3.2 Sketching Procedure for Multiview Projection

The best way to learn how to use scales, triangles, and other engineering sketching tools is to practice, practice, and practice again. Careful observation of the object is also required. Refining visual perception skills is fundamental in sketching. Not only do we need to be able to express the construction, form, and size of the design, but we must also describe the highlights, textures, characteristics, and spatial geometry of the 3-D object we are trying to represent.

Let's study the procedure for sketching orthographic multiviews of a certain object. First, we need to observe the object's overall shape. We also need to ask what the features are that need to be emphasized. Then we decide on the best position and point of view to represent the object and analyze the proportions and determine the object's outer boundary limits. Based on the object's dimensions and the sketching surface available, we determine the scale to use. We measure the height, width, and depth of all the object's features. We need

Figure 2.21 Solid model of the bracket to be sketched.

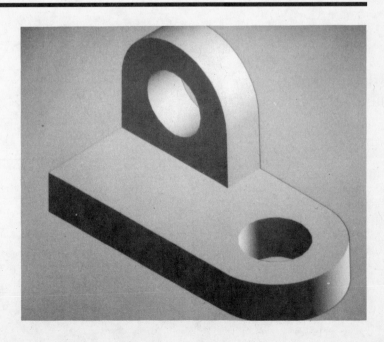

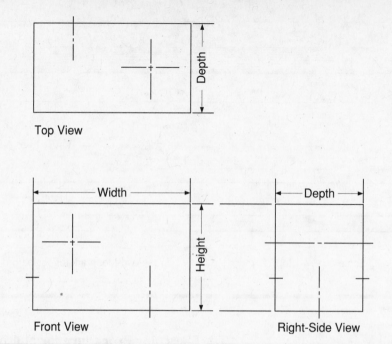

Figure 2.22 Block the overall outside boundaries of the bracket.

to picture ourselves as looking at a large glass window onto which the edges of the object are projected. Then, we imagine that visual rays—parallel to one another—are hitting the surface of the window (the projection plane) at right angles. Finally, we sketch the image of the object projected onto the window's surface. Example 2.1 presents the procedure in more detail.

Example 2.1

Sketch the three standard orthographic views of the bracket shown in Figure 2.21. Try to do this problem manually, without the assistance of a grid paper or computer. Use a medium grade pencil (B, HB, F) and a standard sheet of paper (A or A4 size). Use the same pencil throughout the sketching process, but sharpen it accordingly to obtain *heavy* visible lines, *medium* hidden lines, *thin* center lines, and *light* construction lines (refer to Figure 2.7).

Figure 2.23 Draw mitre line to transpose dimensions.

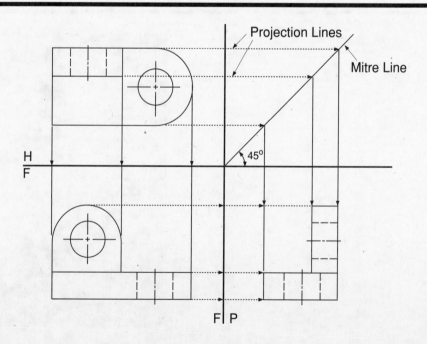

1. Visually estimate the overall measurements and proportions from Figure 2.21.

2. Block the object (sketch its overall outside boundaries) on the horizontal and frontal faces of an unfolded transparent box, as shown in Figure 2.22. Note that parallel lines in the 3-D image remain parallel to one another in the orthographic views. Object surfaces parallel to the projection plane appear in true shape in the multiview sketch.

3. Indicate the centers of circles and label the views.

4. Draw a *mitre* line (that is, a 45-degree line to extend the right-side view dimensions), as illustrated in Figure 2.23.

5. To transpose the depth dimensions, draw projectors to the right, until they hit the mitre line, and then downward, locating the important features of the right-side view.

6. Draw light construction lines to aid in sketching circles. For example, sketch a centered square around the location of the circles. Outline the prominent features of the part: curves, changes in direction, and so on. Note that oblique or inclined surfaces (those not parallel to the projection planes) are not in true shape. Note also that the elliptical shapes of the object's hole appear as circles in the orthographic projections.

7. Finish the drawing by heavily darkening the visible lines. Lightly darken the hidden lines. Erase all construction lines (Figure 2.24).

2.4 COMPUTER-AIDED SKETCHING

As stated earlier, making a freehand sketch requires only pencil and paper. However, **computer-aided sketching** requires several computer graphics visualization tools (see Chapter 6) and knowledge of the particular CAD or geometric modeling system being used. CAD software packages can be used to produce high-quality sketches and conceptual drawings. As with freehand sketching, the goal is to produce rapidly a drawing to communicate and stimulate ideas. Although a computer sketch may take slightly longer to construct

Figure 2.24 Finished multiview sketch of the bracket.

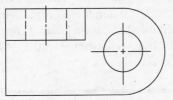

Top View

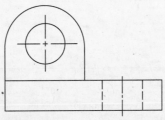

Front View

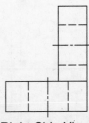

Right-Side View

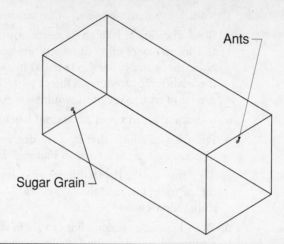

Figure 2.25 Box showing the location of the ants and the grain of sugar.

than a manual sketch, it can be recalled, modified, and reproduced on a printer or a plotter. The adaptation of a computer to quick sketching is limited only by the user's knowledge of the tools provided by the CAD system. Commercial CAD packages provide dozens of commands, menus, options, and functions to produce any type of engineering drawing or sketch you can imagine. However, it does take some time for the beginner to become completely familiar with their capabilities.

2.5 COMPUTER GRAPHICS APPLICATION OF PROJECTION

We have studied how orthographic projection standards and computer graphics visualization techniques can be used to draw or display 3-D spatial geometry on a 2-D surface. In this section, we discuss a "minimum path" application of these techniques. The application is to find the minimum path for an ant to travel to reach a grain of sugar before other ants, located in the same position and traveling at the same velocity, reach the sugar.

Example 2.2

Once upon a time there were three lonely ants—Bit, Aby, and Comp—in a Plexiglass rectangular box. The ant-box measurements are 60 mm high, 60 mm wide, and 150 mm long. From their observation post, the ants look at the opposite end wall and see a grain of sugar stuck in the center, 5 mm above the floor of the box, as illustrated in the 3-D wireframe representation of the box

Figure 2.26 Ant Bit's route.

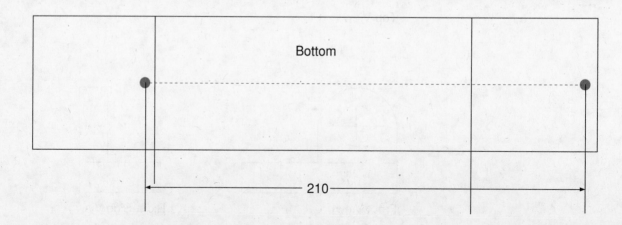

(Figure 2.25). The ants are located very close to one another in the middle of the opposite wall, 5 mm below the ceiling. Each ant will take a different path. Which ant will get the grain of sugar first? Determine the minimum distance traveled. Assume none of the ants will waste time fighting!

Graphical Solution: A three-dimensional box is modeled on a CAD system, as shown in Figure 2.25. Then a two-dimensional representation (a partial development) of the unfolded box is displayed in several ways. The distance traveled by each ant is calculated by using the "Data Verify" features of the CAD system.

1. Ant Bit takes the most obvious route, illustrated in Figure 2.26. Note that two walls of the box have been "unfolded." This ant travels straight down 55 mm, then 150 mm across the bottom, and 5 mm up only to realize that both the other ants are already eating the sugar. Total travel distance is 210 mm.

2. Ant Aby takes the route illustrated in Figure 2.27. Note that the box has been "unfolded" (developed) to mark the path. Aby traveled diagonally down, across the wall, and across the side wall and bottom, a total of 203.59 mm—but Ant Comp was already having a banquet.

3. Ant Comp won by following the path in Figure 2.28. Again, a similar development of the box is generated. But Comp travels up across the ceiling for a total distance of exactly 200 mm. Ant Comp followed an ingenious (engineered) path rather than the apparently straightest route.

As you have seen in this hypothetical problem, projection and 3-D wireframe representation can be very useful. Actually, engineers use similar graphical optimization techniques to solve real-life facility planning problems.

Figure 2.27 Ant Aby's route.

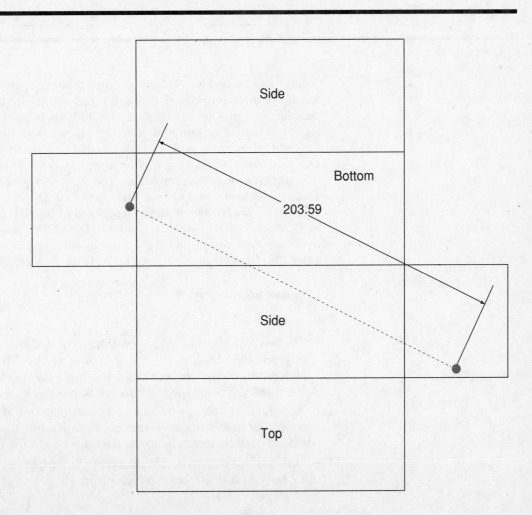

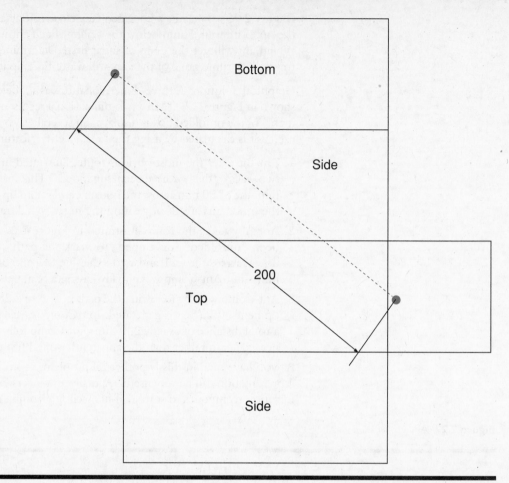

Figure 2.28 The winner is Ant Comp.

Since engineering is a problem-oriented profession, most academic training consists of solving hypothetical as well as real-life technical problems. You will discover, very early in your career, that in addition to gaining technical knowledge, you must also learn how to record problem solutions and design alternatives. Orthographic projection and computer graphics programs will assist you in this process. As an engineering student, you will be required to solve various analytical and design problems. You will apply your knowledge, experience, deductions, and even a little bit of intuition to reach solutions. Background knowledge of mathematical and graphical procedures will be extremely useful in attaining these solutions. In addition, as an engineer, you will use visualization tools and techniques in conjunction with your technical knowledge to assess real-life problems and satisfy society's needs and wants.

Chapter Summary

Chapter 2 detailed the following points:

- The two-dimensional design annotation technique known as projection displays an object by mapping an image onto a plane. The standards for displaying projections have been established by the American National Standards Institute (ANSI) and the International Standards Organization (ISO).

- Projections can be constructed with parallel lines of sight or lines of sight emanating from a single vantage point. In the first case, the projection is called a parallel projection; in the second, a perspective projection.

- Orthographic projections are parallel projections, in which the lines of sight are perpendicular to the projection plane.

- Standard sets of orthographic projections into frontal, horizontal, and profile planes are called multiviews.

- All types of lines in projections—such as visible, hidden, center, and construction lines—are governed by linetype conventions.

- Engineering sketches, drawn freehand or with manual or computer tools, provide a quick and efficient method for communicating new ideas.

- To represent objects too large or small to be drawn on standard sizes of paper, a designer must be able to scale his or her drawings using either a metric scale, an architect's scale, or an engineer's scale.

- Computer-aided sketches may take longer to create than freehand sketches, especially for beginners, but the quality of the finished sketch can be very high, and the sketch can be easily recalled, modified, and reproduced.

REFERENCES AND SUGGESTED READINGS

Beakley, G. C. *Introduction to Engineering Graphics.* New York: Macmillan, 1975.

Edel, D. H. *Introduction to Creative Design.* Englewood Cliffs, N.J.: Prentice-Hall, 1967.

French, T. E., C.J. Vierck, and R. Foster, *Engineering Drawing and Graphic Technology.* New York: McGraw-Hill, 1986.

Rodrigues, M. *Geometria Descriptiva.* Brazil: INCISA, 1988.

Rodriguez, W. E. "Axiom-Based Spatial Analysis and Visualization" *Journal of Theoretical Graphics and Computing,* 1(1): , 1988.

Rodriguez, W. E. *Visualization.* New York: McGraw-Hill, 1990.

Ross, W. A. "An Examination of the Graphical Representation of First and Third Angle Projections," *Proceedings,* ASEE/EDGD Conference, New Harmony, Indiana, Nov. 20-22, 1988.

Spence, W. *Engineering Graphics.* Englewood Cliffs, N.J.: Prentice-Hall, 1988

EXERCISES

2.1 The table below (A through I) contains a series of multiview projection problems. A view is missing in each of the problems. Select the correct third-angle orthographic view from the given multiple choices (1 through 9).

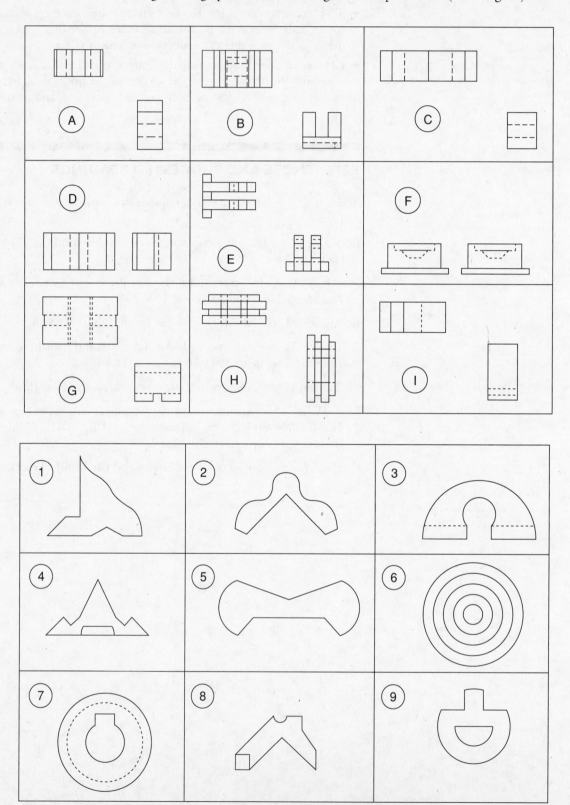

2.2 The table below contains a series of multiview projection problems (J through R). A view is missing in each of the problems. Select the correct third-angle orthogonal view from the given multiple choices (10 through 18).

2.3 Measure the object below, and sketch the front, top, and right-side orthographic views.

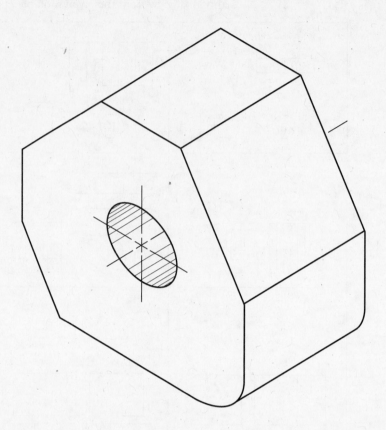

2.4 Measure the object below, and sketch the front, top, and right-side orthographic views in the space provided.

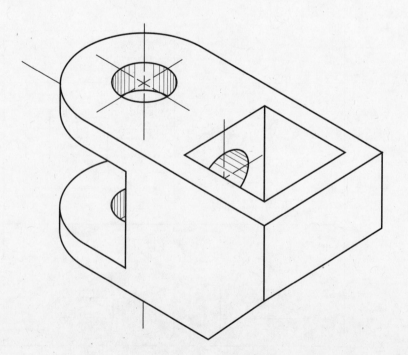

2.5 Measure the object below, and sketch the front, top, and right-side orthographic views.

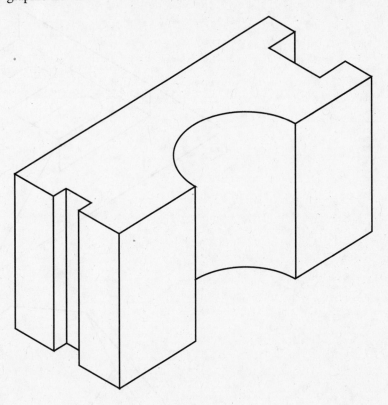

2.6 Measure the object below, and sketch the front, top, and right side orthographic views.

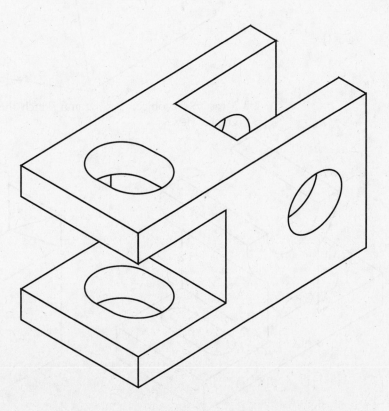

2.7 Measure the objects below, and sketch the front, top, and right-side orthographic views.

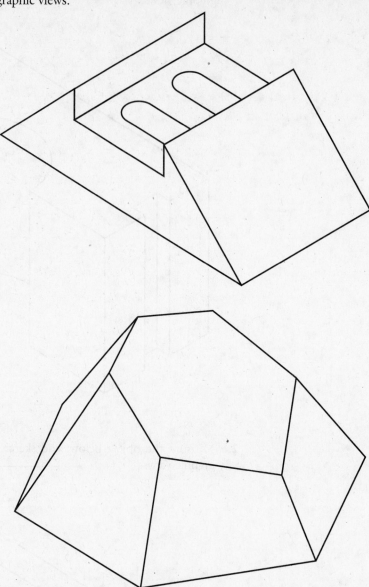

2.8 Measure the objects below, and sketch the front, top, and right-side orthographic views.

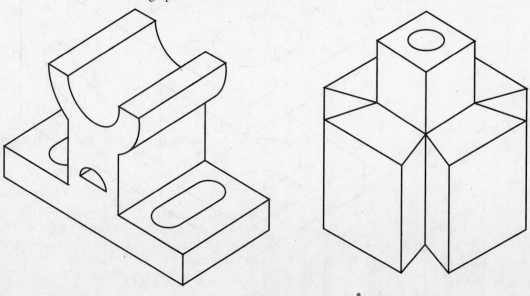

2.9 Measure the objects below, and sketch the front, top, and right-side orthographic views.

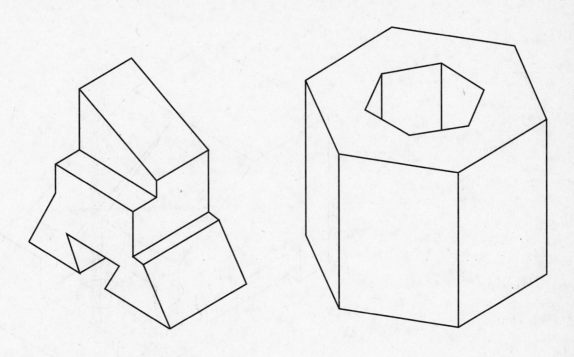

2.10 Measure the objects below, and sketch the front, top, and right-side orthographic views.

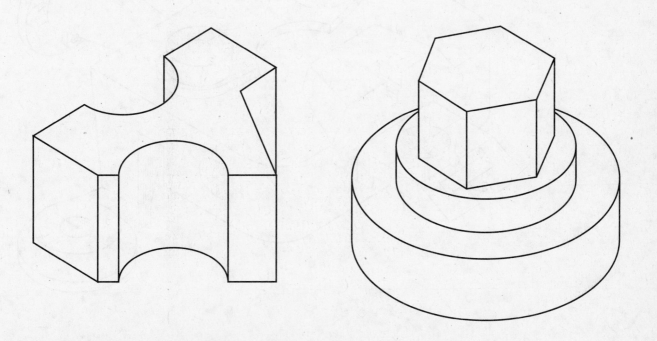

2.11 Measure the objects below, and sketch the front, top, and right-side orthogonal views.

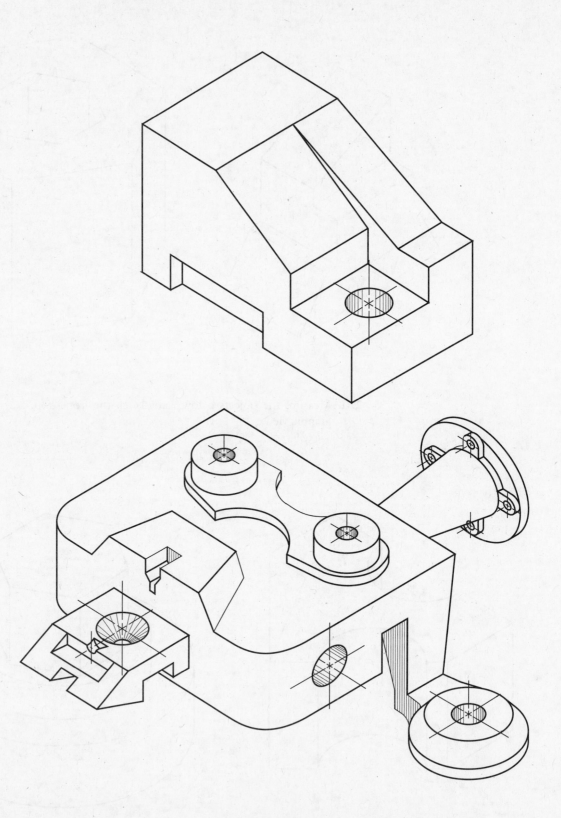

2.12 Carefully study each of the following problems. Sketch the third-angle and first-angle orthographic projection view (see Figure 2.29). Use a metric scale to obtain the proportions and measurements of the given objects. Draw the objects on a scale of 1:1 or 1:2, depending on the space available. If available, use a CAD software package to present your solutions.

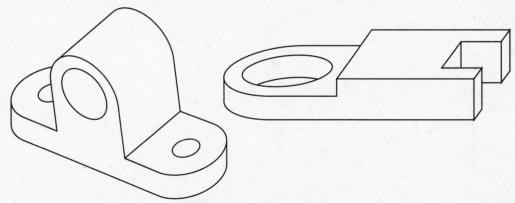

2.13 Carefully study each of the following problems. Sketch the third-angle and first-angle orthographic projection views. Use a metric scale to obtain the proportions and measurements of the given objects. Draw the objects on a scale of 1:1 or 1:2, depending on the space available. If available, use a CAD software package to present your solutions.

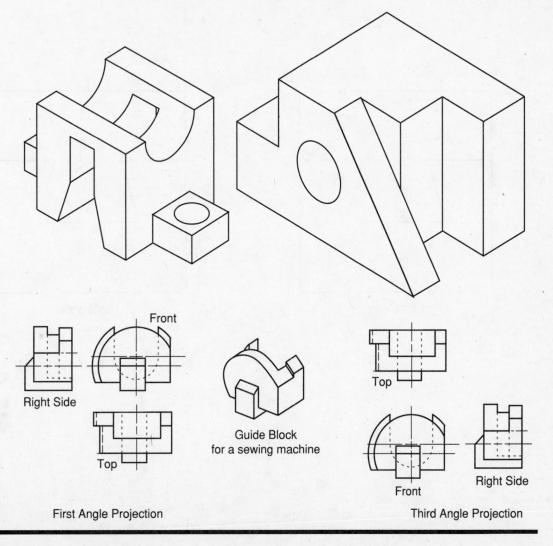

Figure 2.29

2.14 Sketch the top view complete with all hidden lines. These two parts each have sliding, interlocking dovetail joints and can be easily assembled and disassembled.

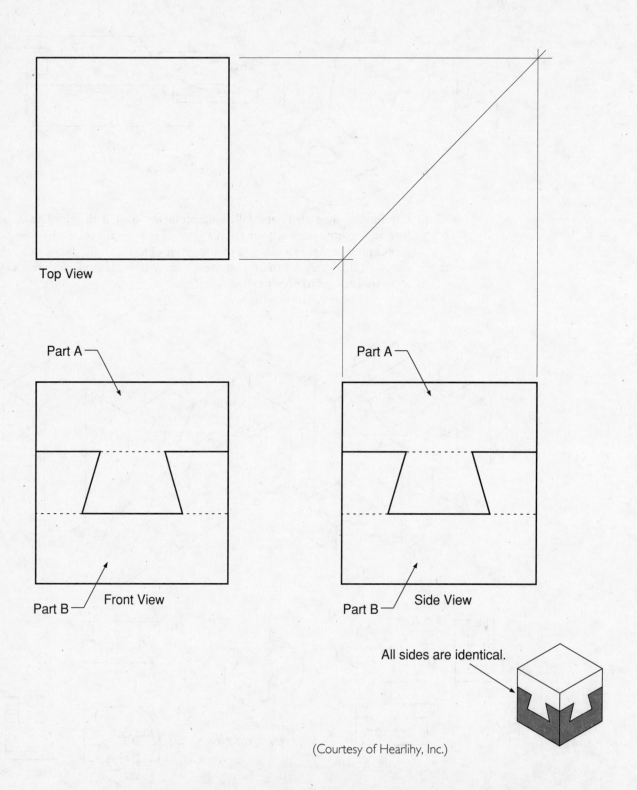

Top View

Part A

Part A

Part B — Front View

Part B — Side View

All sides are identical.

(Courtesy of Hearlihy, Inc.)

2.15 Sketch the missing view for the given problems. Transfer dimensions by using mitre and projection lines.

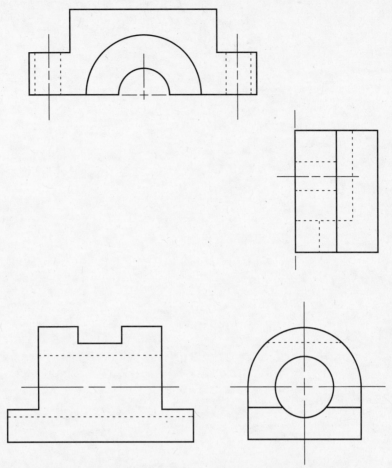

2.16 Draw an image and/or write a short statement that describes or defines each of the key terms, listed below, used in this chapter:

American National Standards Institute (ANSI)

Architect's scale

Center lines

Computer-aided sketching

Construction lines

Edit

Engineering sketching

Engineer's scale

Extend

First-angle projection

Folding line

Hidden line

International Standards Organization (ISO)

Line quality

Line of sight

Linetype

Menubar

Metric scale

Multiview

Multiview projection

Object

Orthographic projection

Parallel projection

Projection

Projection plane

Projection theory

Pull-down menu

Scaling

Third-angle projection

Visible line

3 3-D Design Annotation

Since we live in a three-dimensional (3-D) world, the best method of visualizing and conveying our design ideas is to use the three dimensions or features of width, height, and depth. This chapter covers various 3-D annotation, or visual-representation, techniques used in the design process. The examples given show how these techniques are used for creating geometric models and freehand sketches.

3.1 PICTORIALS: 3-D VISUALIZATION

The depiction of an object may be classified as a pictorial representation if it shows at least three faces of the object in a given view or display. Since the pictorial faces show the width, height, and depth of the object, a pictorial is classified as a 3-D representation. Computer graphics software programs are particularly valuable in creating 3-D geometric models in the early stages of design.

We can identify three types of pictorial representation techniques: perspective, axonometric, and oblique. A perspective is a realistic image that emulates our vision. In perspective representation, the depth features of the object represented converge to one or more points. Conversely, in axonometric representation (being orthographically based), the depth features remain parallel and do not converge. In oblique representation, one face of the object is viewed parallel to the projection plane. These three design annotation, or representation, techniques will be discussed in detail in the next sections. As you will see,

Figure 3.1 Dots representing the mapping of a perspective on a plane.

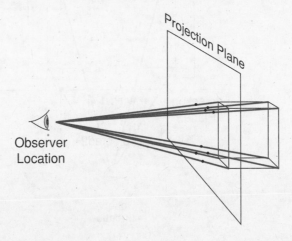

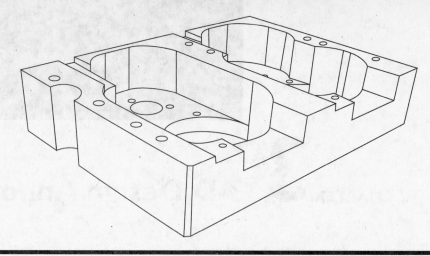

Figure 3.2 Perspective view of a valve block.

since axonometric and oblique pictorials are constructed using parallel projection, they are easier to construct than a perspective pictorial. However, perspectives have one important advantage: they show how an object or designed product would look in real life.

3.2 PERSPECTIVE: A REALISTIC REPRESENTATION TECHNIQUE

Figure 3.3 Although the two original distances are equal, Original 1 appears smaller to the observer than Original 2, because Original 1 is farther from the projection plane.

Perspective is the form of pictorial representation that most nearly resembles an object as seen by our own eyes—that is, as a result of our vision. If we imagine a vertical projection plane between the observer's location and a cube (Figure 3.1), the visual rays from the eye to the cube—if intercepted by the projection plane—will form an image that exactly coincides with the edges of the cube. The intercepting dots, shown in the figure, map the perspective image on the projection plane. In other words, the perspective is generated by the intersection

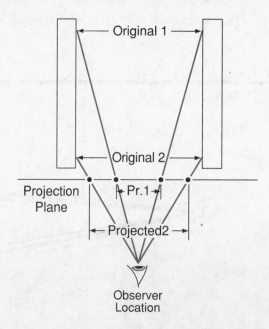

of the observer's visual rays, or lines of sight on the projection plane. Note that the location of the observer's eye (also called the station point or point of sight) is located at a finite (measurable) distance from the projection plane.

Figure 3.2 shows a perspective drawing of a valve block. As you can see, because the point of sight is at a finite distance from the object, perspective projection does not involve any kind of parallel projections. (Recall from Chapter 2 that in parallel projection the observer is considered to be at an infinite location relative to the object.) In short, in perspective projection the lines of sight are not parallel to one another, and not all of them intercept the projection plane at 90-degree angles.

An interesting perspective effect, usually unnoticed by the casual observer, is the size reduction of the projected object's image that results from increasing the distance between the observer's location and the projection plane (Figure 3.3). In perspective projection, parallel lines in space—for example, two parallel edges of an object—will not appear parallel when drawn in perspective projection because they are not parallel to the projection plane. Therefore, the distance between them will appear to decrease as the lines recede from the projection plane. The result is that every set of parallel lines not parallel to the projection plane will seem to vanish to a point. You may see this effect of lines vanishing to a point in a photograph taken with a camera.

Figure 3.4 shows a building photographed by a camera in a certain position. Note that the sets of parallel lines formed by different surface planes (for example, the edges of the roof) that are supposed to be parallel to each other, "vanish" toward a certain imaginary vanishing point to the left. A **vanishing point** (**VP**) is a particular imaginary point at which parallel lines seem to converge.

Figure 3.4 Perspective effect on a photograph of a building. (Courtesy of Georgia Tech)

Figure 3.5 A computer-generated perspective. (Courtesy of Intergraph and ALIAS)

Perspectives are used extensively by artists, architects, and designers to realistically depict sculptures, buildings, and other structures before they are built. Some geometric modeling programs can generate perspectives that simulates a designer "walking around" a model. This capability allows the user to inspect the interior and exterior of the design. A great number of computer-based interactive graphics systems also provide the designer with the ability to rotate the image and view it from a different point of sight (in CAD, this is referred to as the **viewpoint** from which you request to see the model of the object).

Perspective projections have not been traditionally used in engineering practice. However, with the advent of computer graphics, the use of perspectives is becoming more common for modeling buildings and engineering devices. Computer-generated perspectives allow the designer to quickly depict the actual appearance of the device or structure before a prototype or iconic model is developed (see Figure 3.5).

Figure 3.6 One-point perspective. (Courtesy of ASME)

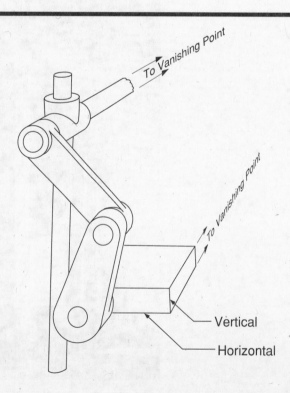

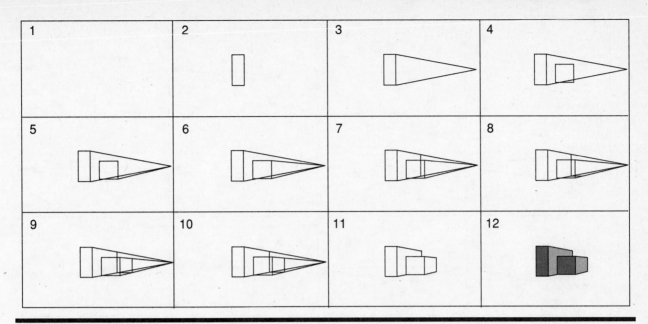

Figure 3.7 Sequence showing the construction of a one-point perspective.

Figure 3.8 Two-point perspective. (Courtesy of ASME)

Perspective projections (also known as **central projections**) are classified based on the number of vanishing points used to generate them: one-point, two-point, and three-point. In a **one-point perspective** (also known as a **parallel perspective**) two of the principal axes of the object are depicted as parallel to the picture plane, and the third as perpendicular. Figure 3.6 illustrates a one-point perspective of a mechanical device in which the vertical and horizontal axes are parallel and the depth axis is perpendicular to the picture plane. Note how the depth features of this device tend to vanish toward a single point.

Figure 3.7 shows the process involved in constructing a one-point perspective of two contiguous boxes on a surface. The process is simple: (1) start with a clear screen or a clear piece of paper; (2) sketch the frontal orthographic view of the first box; (3) define a vanishing point at a convenient distance to the right or left (depending on whether you want to show the left- or right-side view of the object), then draw vanishing lines from each corner to the vanishing

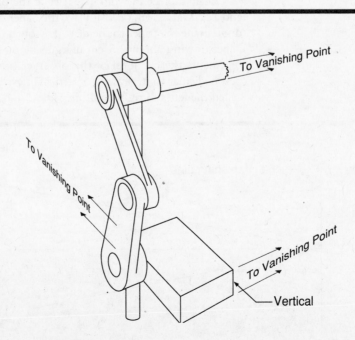

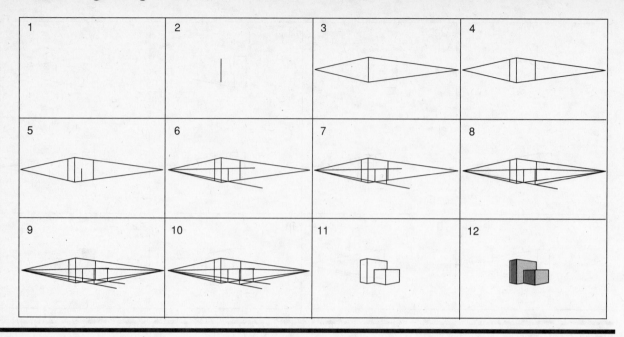

Figure 3.9 Sequence showing the construction of a two-point perspective.

point; (4) position the next frontal face of the box at a convenient distance from the first; (5–10) extend vanishing lines from each of the box's vertices to the previously defined vanishing point; (11) erase the hidden lines; and (12) shade the model if necessary.

When two of the object's axes are inclined to and one axis is parallel to the picture plane, we obtain a **two-point**, or **angular**, **perspective**. Figure 3.8 illustrates a two-point perspective drawing of a mechanical device. Note that the vertical axis is parallel to the plane of projection, whereas the horizontal and depth axes converge toward their respective VPs. Figure 3.9 shows a construction sequence of a two-point perspective. Note that the procedure is similar to the one-point perspective construction process, except that now we define two vanishing points. Example 3.1 details the process for sketching a two-point perspective.

Example 3.1

In this example you will practice drawing a two-point perspective of a 5 cm x 5 cm x 5 cm cube, or closed box, as perceived by the human eye.

Obtain a piece of white paper (like the ones used in photocopy machines) and a pencil (F, HB, or #2). Place the paper on a desk or similar flat surface, but do not tape the paper to the desk. Lay out a horizontal line in the middle of the paper, leaving about 2.5-cm margins along both sides of the paper. This line represents the eye level of the observer (you). At each end of the line, and perpendicular to it, draw two vertical lines. The left and right vertical lines are called the left and right vanishing lines, respectively.

Figure 3.10 Direct perspective construction method.

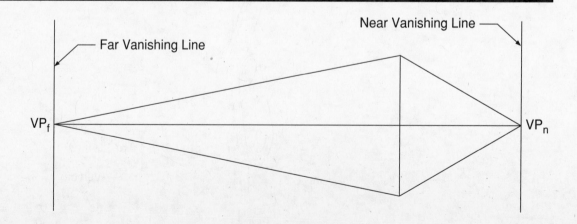

Now sketch the 5-cm front vertical edge of the cube at a horizontal distance of 2.5 cm from the right vanishing line. Draw the edge so that its center is at eye level (2.5 cm above and below the eye level horizontal vanishing line). This vertical line on the right will be called the near vanishing line, and the left vertical line will be referred to as the far vanishing line. (Of course, we would reverse the terminology if the front-edge vertical line were placed near the left vanishing line.)

Label the point where the near vanishing line intersects the horizontal vanishing line VP_n (for Vanishing Point, near), and the point where the far vanishing line intersects the horizontal vanishing line VP_f. Draw lines from VP_n and VP_f to the ends of the vertical edge of the cube (your drawing should now look like Figure 3.10). These lines will correspond to the frontal "horizontal lines" of the outside boundaries of the cube. Of course, since we are drawing a perspective view, the "horizontal lines" are no longer truly horizontal but rather vanish toward each vanishing point.

The next step is to draw the left front vertical edge of the box. Simply draw a line parallel to the initial front vertical edge. Draw a vertical line approximately 5 cm to the left of the front edge of the cube. Now draw the back vertical edge of the box by drawing a vertical line approximately halfway between VP_n and the initial front vertical edge. If you shade the right side of the cube, your final sketch should look like Figure 3.11.

In Example 3.1, the observer was located at the level of the horizon. Figure 3.12 shows another procedure for constructing a view of the box (Powell, 1987). Follow the sequence of numbers in the figure to construct a two-point perspective. By changing the location of the first vertical reference line—that is, left or right—and its relative position above or below the horizon, you obtain different views of the box.

Finally, Figure 3.13 shows a **three-point**, or **oblique**, **perspective** in which all axes of the object incline with respect to the projection plane. ANSI recommends that the point of sight in a three-point perspective should be placed so that the observer's cone of visual rays, which covers the object, is not greater than 30 degrees, as shown in Figure 3.13. In addition, the point of sight should be centralized in the front face and located at a convenient height to expose the horizontal surfaces of the object. Figure 3.14 shows a construction sequence of a three-point perspective.

Figure 3.11 Finished cube by the direct perspective construction method.

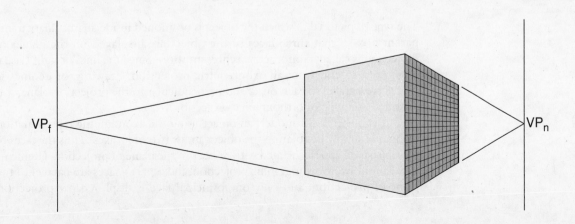

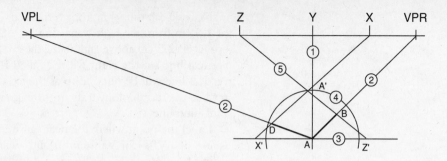

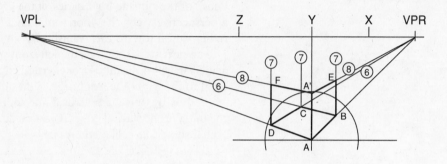

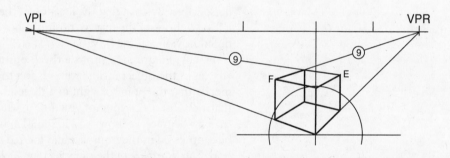

Figure 3.12 Construction sequence for a bird's-eye view of a box using two-point perspective. (Powell, 1987)

3.3 AXONOMETRIC: A PRACTICAL REPRESENTATION TECHNIQUE

The type of pictorial in which the object is positioned inside an imaginary transparent box so that three faces of the object are displayed on the planes of projection is called **axonometric representation**. Since the lines of sight (visual rays) used to construct an axonometric projection, drawing, or geometric model are parallel to each other and perpendicular to the projection plane, it is classified as a type of orthographic projection.

One can sketch (or model) an object using the axonometric representation technique simply by rotating the object about two of its axes. Thus the faces of the object will appear inclined with respect to the plane of projection. (Remember: In multiview orthographic projection, the object's faces are parallel to the plane of projection, and only one principal face is displayed per projection

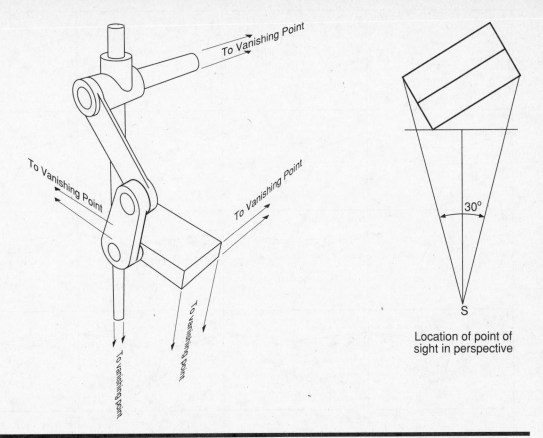

To Vanishing Point

To Vanishing Point

To Vanishing Point

To Vanishing Point

To vanishing point

To vanishing point

30°

S

Location of point of
sight in perspective

Figure 3.13 Left: Three-point perspective. Right: Recommended location of point of sight in perspective. (Courtesy of ASME)

plane. In axonometric projection, you see three faces of the object.) The axes of an axonometric projection can make any angle with each other except 90 degrees. If the axes were to make a 90-degree angle, the result would be a multiview orthographic projection (see Chapter 2) and not an axonometric projection. Example 3.2 will help you understand the axonometric technique.

Example 3.2

Choose a thick book from your library (a dictionary will do). Place the book on a table parallel to the table edge; then sit down and look straight at the front of the book. The front face of the book is parallel to an imaginary projection plane (running along the table edge) located between you and the book. Now stand up and look at the book from the top. Turn the book 45 degrees relative to the projection plane. Then look at the side view. Draw an imaginary diagonal line across the side view of the book. Tilt the book up until the diagonal of the side view is horizontal. Note that you are now able to see three faces of the book; the front view of the book has become an axonometric projection.

You probably noted in Example 3.2 that the faces, views, and axes of the book appeared foreshortened, since the book was inclined with respect to the projection plane. This foreshortening also occurs when we draw the axonometric projection of an object. In fact, the degree of foreshortening depends on the angle of inclination that the object makes with respect to the projection plane. For practical purposes, the scale is foreshortened about 80% on each of the affected axes. Due to the inclination, the rectangular faces of the object will appear as parallelograms.

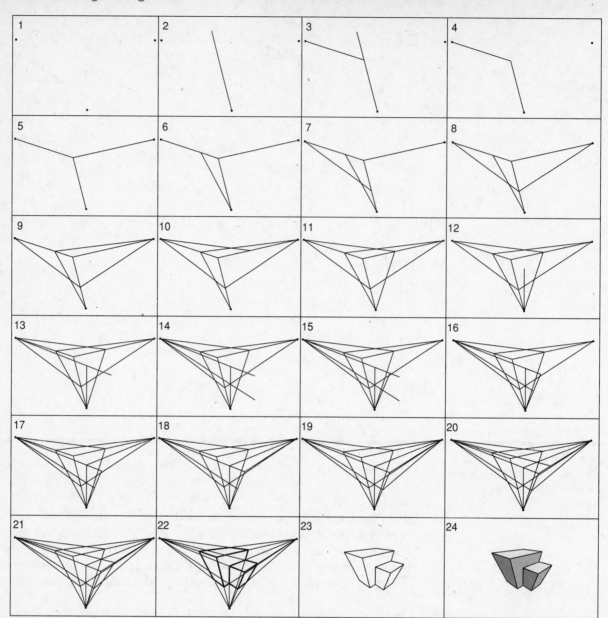

Figure 3.14 Construction sequence for a three-point perspective.

Axonometric drawings resemble axonometric projections; however, in the former, the distances along the axes are measured in true length. This makes construction easy, because there is no need to calculate the degree of foreshortening on the axes. We may think of an axonometric as basically a projection of a tilted part (Grant, 1968). In fact, the axonometric theory is best explained by referring to a cube. Figure 3.15 (a) shows a cube turned 45 degrees on its base. In (b) the side view has been tilted until the diagonal of the cube is horizontal when viewed from the side and appears as a point when viewed from the front. The resulting view is an axonometric projection. The same view could have been obtained by using an 81/100 scale to measure the lengths of the edges vertically and at 30 degrees upward to the left and right.

Instead of producing an axonometric projection, it is more convenient to create an axonometric drawing or model, because the foreshortened measurements are replaced with true length measurements to obtain the cube shown in Figure 3.15 (c). Axonometric drawings are used in practice more than axonometric projections because axonometric drawings are simpler to measure and draw.

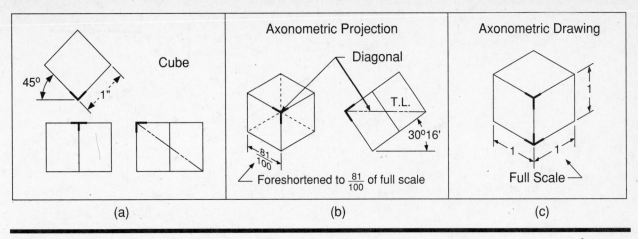

(a) (b) (c)

Figure 3.15 Axonometric Projection and Axonometric Drawing. (Courtesy of McGraw-Hill)

Further, axonometric drawings can be classified according to the degree of inclination between the object's axes and the projection planes as *isometric*, *dimetric*, and *trimetric*. The terms **isometric drawing** and **isometric model** come from the Greek *isometros*, which means "equal measure." Isometric drawings or models (referred to commonly as isometrics) are obtained by positioning the object axes at equal angles with respect to the plane of projection. An isometric is a type of axonometric whereby the edges (that is, axes) and faces of the object are equally projected onto a projection plane; that is, the three principal axes and faces are inclined at equal angles to the projection plane. Axes can be placed in several positions, but they always make equal angles with each other. Figure 3.16 (a) illustrates the positioning of the axes in the orthographic multiviews of a cube. In Figure 3.16 (b) the object has been revolved 45 degrees through the vertical axis. If the cube is then tilted about the horizontal axis we can visualize the position of the axes in the isometric. The resulting construction is an isometric projection in which all edges of the cube are 35.26 degrees from the projection plane (see Figure 3.17). However, instead of foreshortening the edges to about 81.6% of the original size, it is

Figure 3.16 (a) Positioning of axes in orthographic multiviews. (b) Rotating the object around the vertical axis, then tilting it around the horizontal axis, allows us to visualize the position of the axes in an isometric.

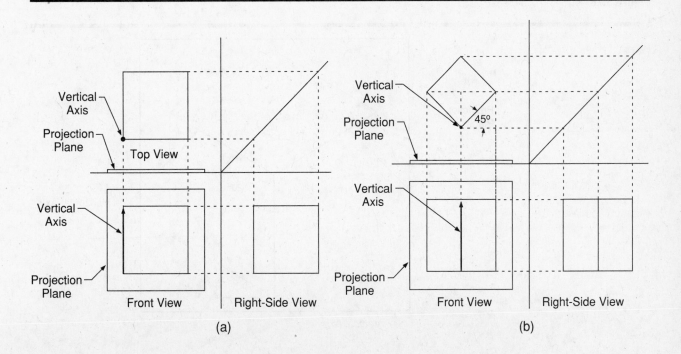

(a) (b)

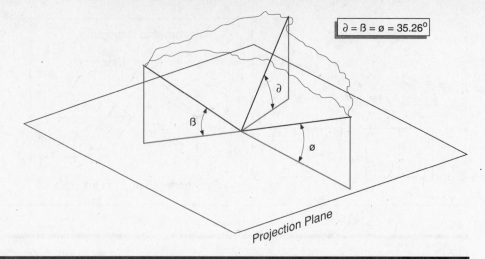

$\partial = \beta = \emptyset = 35.26°$

Projection Plane

Figure 3.17 True isometric —all edges of the cube are 35.26 degrees from the frontal plane.

better to measure the actual true size along each axis. Figure 3.18 shows the resulting isometric drawing of a cube where the object was tilted with respect to the projection plane until angles A, B, and C are each 120 degrees.

As mentioned earlier, since it is awkward to work with foreshortened sides, the preferred procedure is to draw an isometric model with lengths parallel to the axes shown in true size instead of using foreshortened lengths. To do this, simply construct the isometric axes and measure actual width, height, and depth along the axes, rather than measuring the projected image of the lines. Figure 3.19 (a) and (b) compares an isometric projection with an isometric drawing. Example 3.3 shows how to draw an object using the isometric representation technique.

Example 3.3

Based on the multiview projections of an object shown in Figure 3.20, draw the object using the isometric representation technique.

1. Start by drawing an imaginary box that is big enough to enclose the object. With the assistance of a 30–60 degree triangle, construct a vertical line and two 30-degree inclined lines from an arbitrary point in a horizontal reference line, as shown in Figure 3.21 (a).

Figure 3.18 Isometric of a cube.

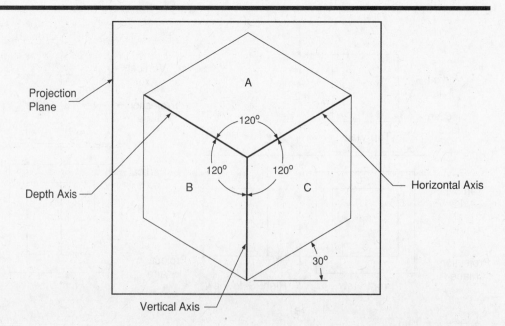

Projection Plane

A

120°

120° 120°

Depth Axis

B

C

Horizontal Axis

30°

Vertical Axis

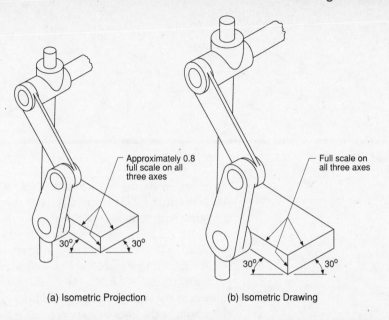

(a) Isometric Projection   (b) Isometric Drawing

Approximately 0.8
full scale on all
three axes

Full scale on
all three axes

30°   30°   30°   30°

Figure 3.19 (a) Isometric projection
and (b) isometric drawing. (Courtesy
of McGraw-Hill)

2. Lay out the overall depth, width, and height of the object. Draw the inclined surfaces or faces of the object as if you were projecting them onto the
   isometric box planes (b).

3. Establish the end points of the groove (c).

4. Reinforce the visible lines of the object and delete unnecessary construction
   and hidden lines (d).

Not all objects are as simple to visualize or sketch as a box. For example,
how can we visualize and sketch oblique surfaces isometrically? Oblique surfaces
are not parallel to the orthographic projection planes (that is, they appear as
foreshortened views in the projection plane). Therefore, the projected lines and
edges that form these surfaces are not in true length. Your ability to visualize
complex objects with oblique surfaces will improve if you carefully analyze the
surfaces of an object (as represented by a given set of multiviews) by locating
certain strategic points on those surfaces and imagining you are removing material from the object—in other words, sculpting the shape.

Figure 3.22 shows how to locate and sketch inclined surfaces and edges on
an isometric pictorial (Grant, 1968). Study the given top and front multiview
projections (a). To locate line AB, lay out orthographically a 30-degree triangle
of convenient size (b). Use your scale to find dimension *e*. Draw the same
triangle on the isometric drawing, using 2 inches and dimension *e* as shown in
Figure 3.22 (c). The 45-degree triangle is easily located in a similar fashion, as

Figure 3.20 Draw an isometric for
the given views.

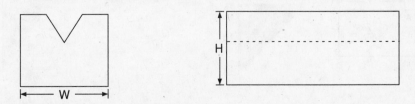

W

H

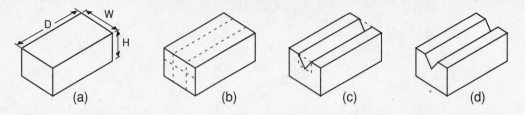

Figure 3.21 Isometric construction procedure.

illustrated in (b) and (d). Figure 3.22 (d) also shows how to determine line AC (note that CD is parallel to AB). Finally, Figure 3.22 (e) illustrates the isometric representation of the given orthographic multiviews.

Figure 3.23 illustrates the process of solving oblique-surface intersection problems in isometric drawing construction. This figure uses the same oblique surface shown in Figure 3.22 (e), with an additional cut. This solution uses parallelism (that is, AE // FG // CD and EF // DG). Note that each of the surfaces of the cut are drawn on the front face and back face of the enclosed box (b); also that the lines of intersection on the top and side surfaces locate points E and G. Finally, lines GF and EF are drawn using parallelism (c). The completed project is shown in (d).

Another type of axonometric representation is **dimetric projection**. Figure 3.24 (a) shows the positioning of the axes in dimetric projection, and (b) a mechanical device in dimetric projection. In dimetric projection, two of the object's axes make equal angles with the plane of projection. The third axis makes a different angle with the frontal plane; therefore, it is foreshortened at a different ratio than are the other two axes. Dimetric projections are rarely used, except occasionally to explode views of devices that have predominant frontal features.

The last type of axonometric projection to be covered here is **trimetric projection**. In trimetric projection, no two axes make equal angles with the projection planes, as shown in Figure 3.25 (a) and (b). Its advantage is the flexibility obtained by being able to position the object in almost any direction. Nevertheless, this type of projection is not very popular.

Note: If you have been wondering how to construct isometrics features with a set of 30/60 and 45/90 triangles, study Figure 3.26. You can manipulate or position the triangles in various ways to obtain the desired angled line. However, for our purposes it suffices to sketch approximate values for angles. Also, you can sketch curves free-hand (Figure 3.26 a & b).

Figure 3.22 Construction of an isometric with oblique surfaces. (Courtesy of McGraw-Hill)

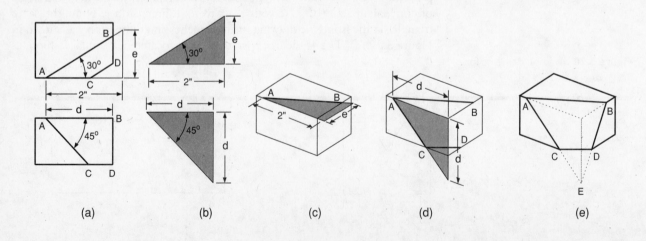

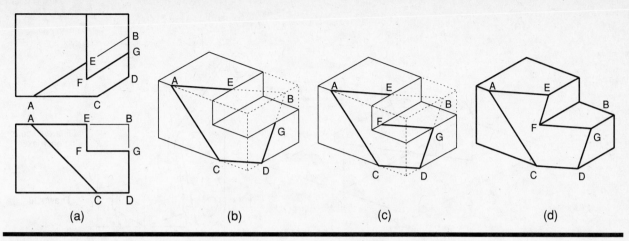

Figure 3.23 Construction of oblique plane intersections in isometric. (Courtesy of McGraw-Hill, Grant, 1968)

3.4 OBLIQUE PICTORIAL: THE SIMPLEST TO SKETCH

An oblique is a pictorial produced by looking at an angle through the projection plane, instead of perpendicularly, or like looking at a frontal view. Hence, it is *not* a type of orthographic projection. Since there is no need to rotate or tilt the object in order to obtain the 3-D effect, an oblique is the simplest pictorial to sketch. The result of projecting from the object with parallel projectors that are oblique to the projection plane is that the object's image appears as a pictorial. As mentioned earlier, oblique pictorials are easy to sketch by hand; however, they are not as popular as isometric pictorials because most computer programs do not support 3-D oblique modeling.

Oblique pictorials are classified as *cavalier, cabinet,* and *general oblique*. The **cavalier oblique** projection is drawn by recessing an axis at any angle between 0 and 90 degrees (usually 45 degrees) with respect to the horizontal, and using true-length measurements, as shown in Figure 3.27 (a) and (b). Lines of sight

Figure 3.24 (a) Positioning of the axes in dimetric projection; (b) dimetric projection of a mechanical device. (Courtesy of ASME)

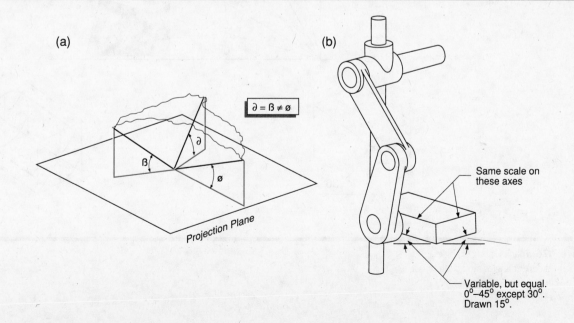

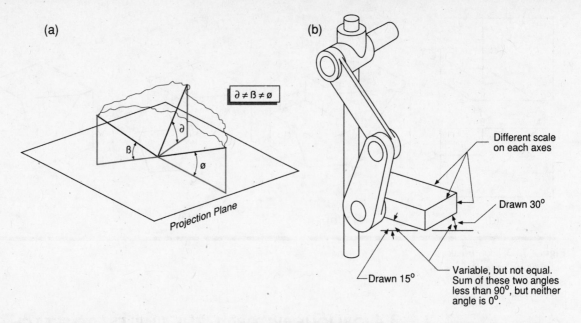

(a)

(b)

$\partial \neq \beta \neq \emptyset$

Projection Plane

Different scale
on each axes

Drawn 30°

Drawn 15°

Variable, but not equal.
Sum of these two angles
less than 90°, but neither
angle is 0°.

Figure 3.25 (a) Positioning of the
axes in trimetric projection;
(b) trimetric projection of a mechanical device. (Courtesy of ASME)

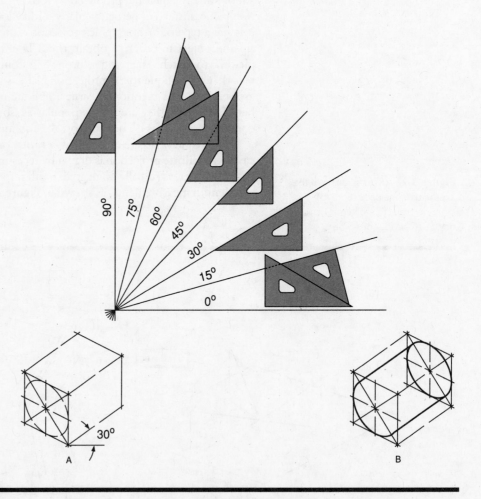

Figure 3.26 Manipulating triangles
to obtain different angles, and sketch
isometric features. (Courtesy of
McGraw-Hill)

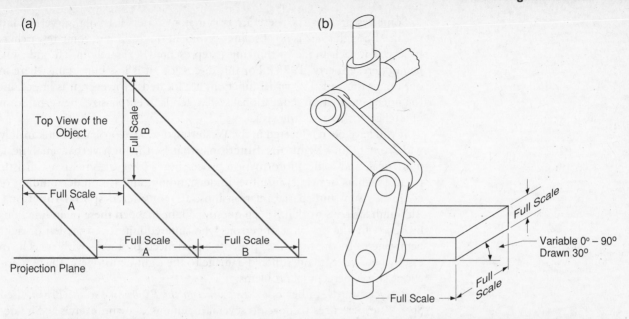

(a)

(b)

Top View of the Object

Full Scale B

Full Scale A

Full Scale A

Full Scale B

Projection Plane

Full Scale

Variable 0° – 90°
Drawn 30°

Full Scale

Full Scale

Figure 3.27 (a) Cavalier oblique projection uses full scale measurements. (b) Cavalier oblique projection of a mechanical part.

in cavalier oblique projections are projected onto the plane of projection at an angle of 45 degrees. In contrast, the **cabinet oblique projection** is generated by visual rays striking the plane of projection at an angle of approximately 63 degrees. The receding axis measurements are half the actual size, as shown in Figure 3.28 (a) and (b). Finally, the **general oblique projection** is constructed by drawing a true-size view, say a frontal view, with lines of sight at any angle other than 45 or 63 degrees from the plane of projection. The receding axis contains the depth features of the object, as illustrated in Figure 3.29. The depth scale will be other than the true-length and half-size ratios.

3.5 VISUAL PERCEPTION AND NATURAL FREE-FORM SKETCHING

The three types of pictorial techniques used in design and visualization that we have just covered depend on human sight, or vision. Designers use this sense to extract visual information to aid understanding of the surrounding environment.

Visual perception is the ability to see and understand the objects or environment we are observing (Wiley, 1988). Our ability to visually perceive objects—to see objects and to extract their meaning—is governed by various visual inputs: reflection, color, texture, depth, and three-dimensional shape. We are able to see features of an object in depth—that is, to judge the distance and thickness of objects—because our eyes are set slightly apart. Each eye sees the object from a different angle, sending a slightly different signal to the brain. The brain puts the images together, providing depth perception, also called **stereoscopic vision**, binocular vision, or "real" 3-D vision.

Our eyes can see only the reflection of light off objects, not the object themselves. They can see only in the presence of light. When light rays enter the eye, the rays are converted to electrical signals. The signals are sent to the brain, which interprets them as visual images. In fact, half of the brain's neurons are associated with the way we see, perceive, or visualize objects.

The human brain is divided in two halves, called **hemispheres**. The hemispheres are connected by the **corpus callosum**, which enables communications, mainly transmission of memory messages, between the hemispheres. Each hemisphere has its own independent functions and characteristics.

Some researchers say there are two major modes of thinking: verbal and visual. Although there is no absolute agreement on this point, some researchers believe that each mode of thinking is represented separately in left and right hemispheres (Sperry, 1973). For this discussion, it is less important where in our brains the verbal or visual functions are located. However, it is important to understand that our educational system tends to emphasize the verbal form of intellect rather than the visual.

If you have been educated in the Western world, you probably think mainly with your brain's **symbolic functions**, that is, through verbal, analytical, numerical, and logical information processing. However, creativity, artistic talent (such as drawing) intuitive understanding, and the understanding of complex visual and spatial relationships, are considered **spatial functions**. Although Sperry's work has been questioned, he mapped these brain functions by observing the behavior of persons who suffered injuries to the left or right hemisphere: In the first case, patients experienced problems with speech. In cases where the patients suffered damage to the right hemisphere, they experienced visual/perceptual problems.

Betty Edwards, in her book *Drawing on the Right Side of the Brain*, used Sperry's experiences to develop several ingenious drawing exercises. She describes in one of her exercises a method whereby a line drawing of an image is turned upside-down, or inverted, and copied just the way a person sees it. Observe the inverted drawing shown in Figure 3.30 for a few seconds. Edwards explains her observational, or visual perception, method as follows:

> Regard the angles and shapes and lines. You can see that the lines all fit together. Where one line ends another starts. The lines lie at certain angles in relation to each other and in relation to the edges of the paper. Curved lines fit into certain spaces, and you can look at the spaces within the lines. . . .
>
> When you start your drawing, begin at the top and copy each line, moving from line to adjacent line, putting it all together just like a jigsaw puzzle. Don't concern yourself with naming the parts; it is not necessary. In fact, if you come to parts that perhaps you *could name* (remember we are not *naming things*), just continue to think to yourself, 'Well, this line curves that way; this line crosses over, making that

Figure 3.28 (a) In cabinet oblique the depth features are reduced by one half. (b) Cabinet oblique projection of a mechanical part. (Courtesy of ASME)

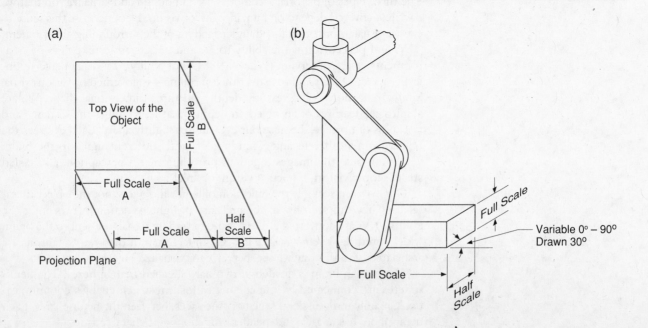

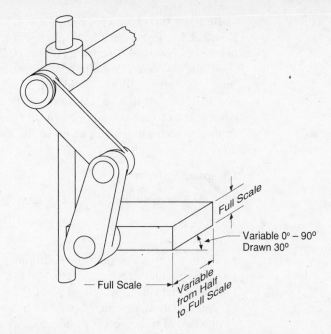

Figure 3.29 General oblique projection. (Courtesy of ASME)

little shape there; this line is at that angle, compared to the edge of the paper,' and so on. Again, try not to think about what the forms are and avoid any attempt to recognize or name the various parts.

Example 3.4 uses modifications of Edwards's inversion method of drawing. The modifications have been made to incorporate ideas regarding "contours" discussed in *The Natural Way to Draw* by Kimon Nicolaides.

Example 3.4

Find a line drawing of an object. Invert it, as in Figure 3.30. Then copy (do not trace) the image the way you see it (upside down). Do not try to identify specific items in the picture, simply observe and copy what you see; that is, observe and copy the line inclinations, curves, angles, and spatial relationships. The first time you do this exercise go very slowly. Imagine that you are actually touching the lines and shapes as you draw the image. Nicolaides explains that "merely to see . . . is not enough. It is necessary to have a fresh, vivid, physical contact with the object you draw through as many of the senses as possible." You should visually identify the edges, or **contours**; that is, the locations where the different planes of the object intersect. Finally, do not worry about the final result; this is not a test. When you are finished, turn the drawing right side up. You might be surprised to see that you can really draw!

Figure 3.30 Upside-down drawing. (Courtesy of Mr. Rodis & Lucas Film.)

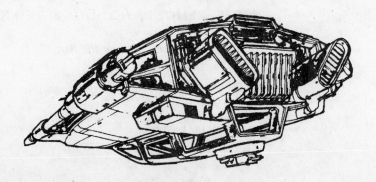

In doing the exercise in Example 3.4, you should have experienced a shift from the left (symbolic) hemisphere's way of thinking to the right (spatial) hemisphere's way of perceiving (Edwards, 1979). If you had drawn the picture right side up, your symbolic hemisphere would probably have perceived the image as "easy to draw," and you would have ended up with your own symbolic version of a spaceship rather than the actual image in the picture. Also, the fact that you are drawing very slowly—and thinking in terms of contours—helps in making a shift to the spatial hemisphere.

Chapter Summary

Chapter 3 detailed the following points:

- To be classified as a pictorial, a representation must show at least three faces of an object.

- The three types of pictorial techniques are perspective representation, in which parallel depth features converge to a vanishing point; axonometric representation, in which all parallel features appear parallel; and oblique representation, in which the object is viewed from an angle even though the one face of the object is parallel to the projection plane.

- Perspective representations are classified as one-point, two-point, and three-point perspectives. Perspectives are the most realistic type of pictorial, but they are also the most difficult to draw.

- Axonometric representations are a type of orthographic representation, since the lines of sight are parallel to each other and perpendicular to the projection plane; axonometrics, however, show three faces of an object on a single projection plane by tilting the object so that none of its axes is parallel to the projection plane.

- Axonometric projections display foreshortened distances along the object's axes, because the axes are not parallel to the projection plane. In axonometric drawings, however, distances along the axes are drawn in true length; axonometric drawings are therefore easier to create than axonometric projections.

- Axonometric drawings are classified as isometric, dimetric, or trimetric, depending on whether none, two, or three of the object's axes are positioned at equal angles to the projection plane.

- Oblique representations—classified as cavalier, cabinet, and general—are the easiest pictorial to sketch because they do not require that the object's axes be tilted. The oblique modeling technique, however, is not supported by most computer programs.

- The skills involved in freehand sketching can be enhanced by exercises that encourage the use of the visual, rather than the verbal, functions of the brain.

REFERENCES AND SUGGESTED READINGS

Edwards, B. *Drawing on the Right Side of the Brain*. Los Angeles: Tarcher, 1979.

Giesecke, F. E., et al. *Principles of Engineering Graphics*. New York: Macmillan, 1990.

Grant, H. E. *Engineering Drawing with Creative Design*. New York: McGraw-Hill, 1968.

Johnson, J., and J. Rodis-Jamero. *The Empire Strikes Back: Sketchbook.* New York: Ballantine, 1980.

Helms, M. *Perspective Drawing: A Step-by-Step Handbook.* Englewood Cliffs, N.J.: Prentice-Hall, 1990.

Lockard, W. K. *Design Drawing Experiences.* Tucson, Az.: Pepper, 1987.

Nicolaides, K. *The Natural Way to Draw.* Boston: Houghton Miffin, 1941.

Powell, D. *Design Rendering Techniques.* Cincinnati, Oh.: Northlight, 1987.

Rodriguez, J., and V. Alvarez. *Geometria Descriptiva—Tomo III Sistema Axonometrico.* Alcoy, Spain: Marfil, 1987.

Sperry, R. W. *The Psychophysiology of Thinking.* New York: Academic Press, 1973.

Wiley, S. W., "Curricular Considerations for Developing the Visual Perception Ability of Technical Illustration Students." Proceedings, Engineering Design Graphics Mid-Year Conference, American Society for Engineering Education, New Harmony, Ind., November 20–22, 1988.

EXERCISES

3.1. Study the multiview sets shown below, and sketch an isometric drawing for each set. Use a 2:1 scale (double the size shown).

a

b

c

d

e

f

g

h

i

j

3.2. Study the multiview projections given below, and sketch an isometric drawing of the object. Use a 1:1 scale (same size shown).

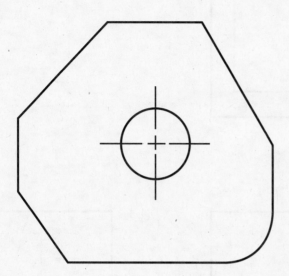

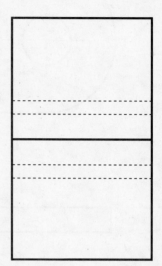

3.3. Study the multiview projections given below, and sketch a cavalier oblique drawing of the object. Use a 1:1 scale.

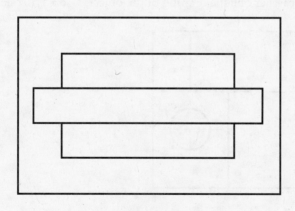

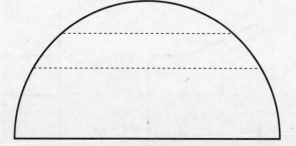

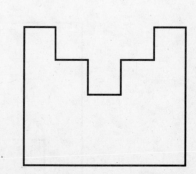

3.4. Study the multiview projections given below, and sketch an isometric drawing and a cavalier oblique drawing of the object. Use a 1:1 scale.

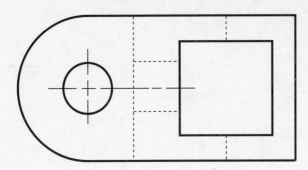

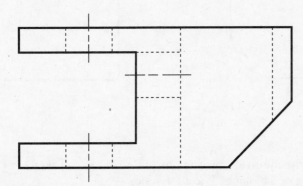

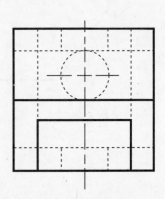

3.5. Study the multiview projections given below, and sketch an isometric drawing and a cavalier oblique drawing of the object. Use a 1:1 scale.

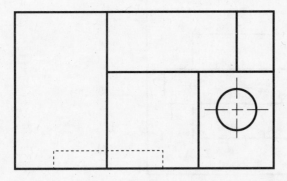

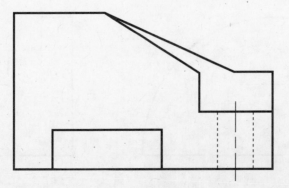

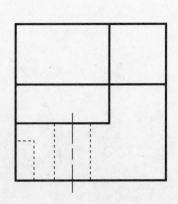

3.6. Study the two multiview projections given below, sketch the missing top view and the corresponding isometric drawing of the object. Use a 1:1 scale.

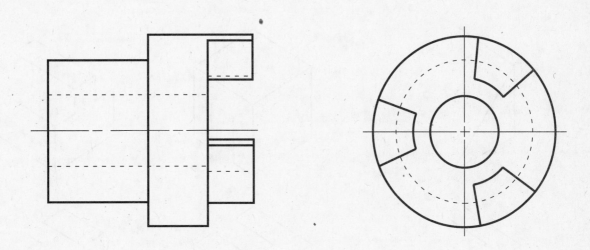

3.7. Study the two multiview projections given below, sketch the missing right-side view and the corresponding isometric drawing of the object. Use a 1:1 scale.

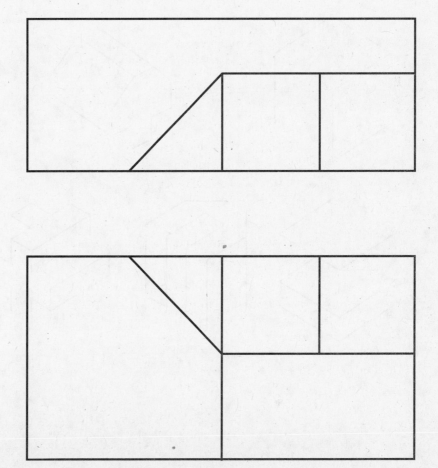

3.8. Sketch the missing lines in the isometric drawings given below.

3.9. Visualize and sketch at least one solid part (as an isometric drawing) that will pass through all three holes of the hollowed block shown below. The circle's diameter, the triangle's altitude and base, and the square's sides all have the same 2.00 dimension (courtesy of Hearlihy).

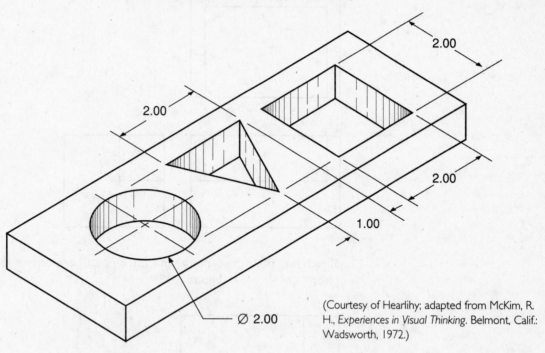

(Courtesy of Hearlihy; adapted from McKim, R. H., *Experiences in Visual Thinking*. Belmont, Calif.: Wadsworth, 1972.)

3.10. Using the modified contour/upside-down technique, sketch the drawings below.

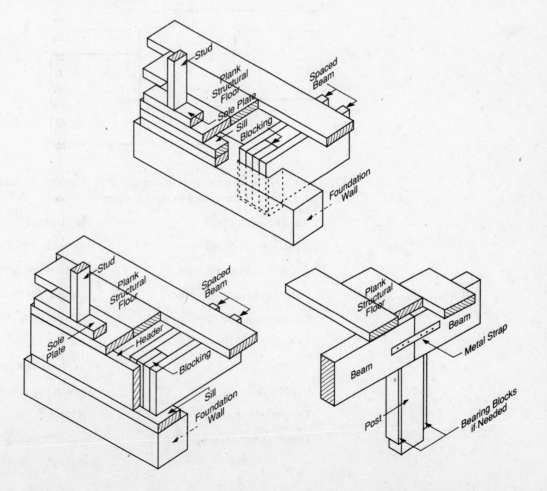

3.11. Sketch one-point, two-point, and three-point perspectives for the multiview projections shown below.

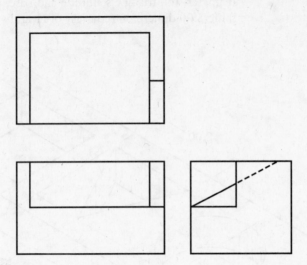

3.12. Sketch one-point, two-point, and three-point perspectives for the multiview projections shown in Figure 3.42.

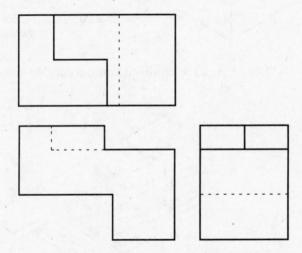

3.13. Draw and/or write a short statement that describes or defines each of the key terms, listed below, used in this chapter:

Angular perspective	Hemisphere
Axonometric drawing	Isometric drawing
Axonometric projection	Isometric projection
Cabinet oblique projection	Oblique perspective
Cavalier oblique projection	Oblique projection
Central projection	One-point perspective
Contour	Parallel perspective
Corpus callosum	Perspective projection
Dimetric projection	Pictorial
General oblique projection	Spatial hemisphere

Stereoscopic vision

Symbolic hemisphere

Three-point perspective

Trimetric projection

Two-point perspective

Vanishing point (VP)

Viewpoint

Visual perception

CHAPTER 4 Design Feasibility

The best way to present the initial stages of the design process uses real-life examples or case studies. The examples presented in this chapter illustrate the use of the design methodology and annotation techniques covered in Chapters 1, 2, and 3. The purpose of this chapter is to show you how to prepare and present an initial report for any given design problem. Most product developers designate this report as the "design feasibility study" because it is where they find out whether a product is viable before they commit further resources to it.

4.1 DESIGN FEASIBILITY STUDY

A **design feasibility** study provides a realistic and convenient format for presenting the initial stages of the design process. It consists of written and oral presentations of the design concept. The feasibility study addresses the following questions: What exactly is the problem? What do we want to achieve? What are the functional design requirements? Are there any practical solutions to the problem? How are we going to achieve those solutions? Which is the best solution, and why? Does the solution satisfy sound design and construction/manufacturing principles? Does it work? How effective and efficient is the solution? Can it be easily manufactured or built? How much will it cost? Will people buy it?

Because engineering design problems are normally open-ended, you may experience some initial frustration when you are learning to prepare design feasibility studies. However, you will derive plenty of satisfaction when you achieve your goal.

The feasibility study has four sections, which are the same as the four stages in the ideation phase of the design process discussed in Chapter 1 (refer to Figure 1.1). The four sections needed in the report are: market research, problem definition, preliminary ideas, and preliminary decision. However, these sections do not necessarily need to be organized in a given order. (Remember: The design process is not sequential; it is iterative, interactive, and in many cases, concurrent.) When preparing the feasibility study, the designer may go back and forth between sections of the report or may even consider all the stages covered by the sections at the same time.

The following sections and examples illustrate the recommended sections of a design feasibility study.

4.1.1 Market Research

The **market research** section of a design feasibility study usually begins with an introduction to the market survey results (that is, consumer needs or wants) as obtained in the ideation phase of the design process (see Chapter 1). While some members of your design team prepare graphs and diagrams showing the survey results, you may report on the existing devices, systems, or processes obtained in the patent search. For example, you may photocopy, sketch, photograph, and/or write a description of the existing devices. You may also write about deficiencies of or possible improvements to existing products.

In addition, the market research section should contain the results of the group's brainstorming session (that is, the identification of needs or wants as perceived by your group). In reporting the brainstorming session, you may write about the market needs explored and their importance. Although the objective is to try to identify an urgent market need, it should be one related to your group's interests and abilities. Following the discussion of needs, the group provides a summary statement indicating the particular need to be defined and the reasons for that decision.

Sometimes, someone like your professor, a supervisor, or a client may assign you a particular design problem. In this case, you do not need to search for a need. However, you must first gather information about the problem. The following information was gathered by students doing market research as the first stage of designing a new aluminum can crusher.* We will present the entire case study in five sections (Examples 4.1 through 4.5) corresponding to the sections of the design feasibility study and the study's presentation.

| **Example 4.1** |

Aluminum-Can Crusher: Market Research

In 1985, 85 billion aluminum cans were sold in the United States. Alcoa, the nation's leading aluminum can recycler, recycles 11.6 billion cans annually. Reynolds Metals Company processes 8.7 billion cans per year. These two corporations are the two largest recycling companies in the country; however, they are joined by several smaller salvage and recycling businesses.

With costs of aluminum rising and the need for metal resources increasing, there has been an enormous jump in demand for this material. In 1984, the price of aluminum was $.30 per pound. In 1989 this figure escalated to $.70 per pound in some areas; the average rate of return for a recycler in Milwaukee was $.60 per pound. Milwaukee had more than ten aluminum reclamation centers, resulting in intense competition.

According to the ten reclamation centers surveyed in Milwaukee in 1989, 96% of the aluminum cans that come to the centers were not crushed. All the center managers except one said that they would prefer the aluminum cans crushed. The tenth center accepted cans in either form and did not express a preference for either. However, an employee at one recycling center noted that the volume of 300 intact aluminum cans equals the volume of 1,000 crushed aluminum cans, indicating that there is definitely an advantage to crushing the cans before transporting and recycling them. It was determined that all but one of the ten recycling centers were interested in selling aluminum-can crushers directly to the public, thus providing a prime marketplace for the product.

There are essentially two ways to crush (that is, decrease the volume of) an aluminum can: (1) manually, with no assistance from any type of device, or (2) by using some sort of tool or apparatus. Crushing the aluminum cans manually

---

*This design project won the 1989 American Society for Engineering Education, Engineering Design Graphics Competition. (Courtesy of S. Gehred and her students J. B. Ferguson, D. M. Jakopin, P. T. McGowan, and W. W. Verkuilenwon at Marquette University.)

(usually by stepping on them or by applying pressure with the hands) exposes a person to possible injury—for example, losing one's balance and falling by twisting an ankle when a can crushes unevenly and flies out from underfoot, or cutting one's hand when crushing cans or handling cans after they are crushed. The majority of the aluminum-can–crushing devices on the market today avoid these problems only partially at best. Figure 4.1 (a) and (b) show two examples of commercially available aluminum-can–crushing devices.

When an aluminum can is crushed manually, its volume is reduced by approximately 70%. Mechanical can crushers reduce the volume of the can by 90%.

As stated previously, the survey of recycling center managers indicated that a large demand exists for an efficient aluminum-can crusher. All the managers had inquired after the availability of such a device. The number of these inquiries increased greatly when the price of aluminum more than doubled, creating greater interest in collecting aluminum.

The managers said that people were now willing to spend more for an aluminum-can crusher than they had been—from $15 to as much as $200. The average amount was in the range of $40 to $60, up from $10 to $20 just three years previously.

The design group tested several aluminum-can crushers. It was determined that the few aluminum-can crushers on the market in 1989 were far from being ideal solutions to the can-crushing problem. They still left people exposed to possible injury, required large amounts of human effort, and were time-consuming to use. The can crushers on the market in 1989 were all basically the same. An arm with a weighted crushing mechanism was attached to an existing wall, and a metal cylinder was attached to the floor. The arm was lifted, a can was placed in the cylinder, and the arm was lowered, crushing the can. The

Figure 4.1(a) Side-way crushing device (Courtesy of PF Consumer Products, Inc.).

Figure 4.1(b) Top-down crushing device (Courtesy of PF Consumer Products, Inc.).

arm was lifted again, the person operating the crusher reached in and pulled out the crushed can, and a new can was placed in position to be crushed. The main complaint about this system concerned safety. While the operator used one hand to remove the crushed can and put a new can in place, he or she had to hold up the device's arm with the other hand. Should the device arm slip, and it often did, it could injure the operator's hand. The recycling center managers said they all had heard many comments about the severity of the bruises that people suffered while crushing cans with such devices. Another safety problem occurred when the operator reached into the cylinder to grab the crushed can: many people cut their hands severely.

As one manager put it, "A friend of mine bought a crusher a few months ago. A couple weeks later he told me he was going to quit using it because he was bruising his hands something awful. When he brought in his carload of cans the next week, he was on crutches because he had severely sprained his ankle stomping on them."

For these reasons, the design group decided to design and build a better aluminum-can crusher by either altering an existing solution or developing an entirely new one. With this information in hand, we are ready to write the aluminum-can crusher problem-definition report.

4.1.2 Problem Definition

The **problem definition** section of the design feasibility report consists of writing a preliminary statement of the specific need identified in the market research section. This statement is rewritten as many times as necessary in order to define the design problem without bias. Obviously, we need to describe and summarize the functional design requirements, goals, limitations, and constraints of the design problem before proposing preliminary solutions to it.

DESIGN #1

HUMAN-ASSISTED GUIDED DEAD WEIGHT

DECISION MATRIX SCORE: 1198 (Refer to Figure 4.10.)

DESCRIPTION: This system utilizes a dead weight guided by four steel rods. Human effort is used
to complete crushing.

INSTRUCTIONS: 1. Lift weight.
2. Place can vertically between top and bottom weights.
3. Press weight down (crushing can).
4. Lift weight and remove crushed can.

PLUSES: Very inexpensive   MINUSES: Extreme human force required
Simple instructions for use   Not very safe
Little maintenance required   Not very efficient
Easily portable

INTERESTING POINTS: Simple design
Symmetrical in construction
Adaptable to hand or foot power
Can crush many cans at once

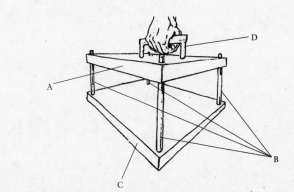

DESIGN #1

A–top weight
B–guide rods
C–bottom weight
D–handle

Figure 4.2 Aluminum-Can Crusher:
Design alternative #1.

DESIGN #2

LEVER WITH AUTOMATIC CAN EJECTOR

DECISION MATRIX SCORE: 1438 (Refer to Figure 4.10.)

DESCRIPTION: This design uses a simple lever action to crush the cans. It is a variation of current
crushers, with a can ejector built in.

INSTRUCTIONS: 1. Place can in cylinder.
2. Push down on lever. (This pulls the ejector out of the chamber and smashes can.)
3. Lift lever. (This pushes the ejector into the chamber, pushing the crushed can out.)

PLUSES: Quick   MINUSES: Very bulky
Efficient   Somewhat expensive
Fairly safe   Will not achieve minimum can volume because
crushing mechanism comes down at angle

INTERESTING POINTS: Several standard parts
Might need to be clamped down
Original adaptation to unoriginal design

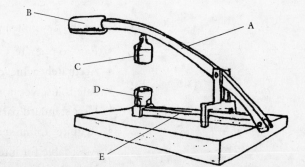

DESIGN #2

A-lever
B-handle
C-crushing mechanisim
D-cylinder
E-can ejector

Figure 4.3 Aluminum-Can Crusher:
Design alternative #2.

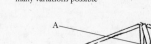

DESIGN #3

GUIDED DEAD WEIGHT

DECISION MATRIX SCORE: 1195 (Refer to Figure 4.10.)

DESCRIPTION: This design is an adaptation of the first one. Instead of using human effort to crush the can, the weight is lifted higher, allowing it to gain enough downward force to completely crush the can. A block and tackle is used to raise the weight.

INSTRUCTIONS: 1. Pull string to raise weight.
2. Place can between weight and bottom plate.
3. Release string, allowing weight to crush can.
4. Pull string to raise weight.
5. Remove crushed can.

PLUSES: Little human force required   MINUSES: Dangerous
                 Minimizes volume well   Heavy
                                                                   Cans must be inserted
INTERESTING POINTS: May be used for other purposes as well   manually
                      many variations possible

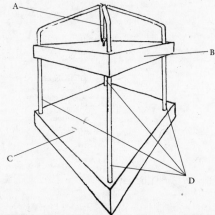

DESIGN #3

A–block and tackle
B–weight
C–bottom plate
D–guide rods

Figure 4.4 Aluminum-Can Crusher:
Design alternative #3.

| Example 4.2 |

The Aluminum-Can Crusher: Problem Definition

Based on the results of the market research section (see Example 4.1), the design team defined the problem in a concise way:

Design a simple device to reduce the volume of empty aluminum cans safely.

Note that the problem has been defined free of bias for or against any particular solution. For example, if the design team had stated "design a trash can compactor made of plastic," this may have prevented the team from exploring other volume-reduction or manufacturing-material options.

The design team determined the two major functional requirements (FRs) for the aluminum-can–crusher design problem as follows:

FR1: Minimize can volume
FR2: Maximize safety of operation

Then the design team listed the desirable features or goals of the device:

• Easy to operate

• Accurately achieves minimum volume

• Safe to use yet not a nuisance

• Uses standard parts

• Requires minimum human force

• Affordable for intended market

• Durable

- Storable
- Adaptable
- Fun to use

Because of some disagreement as to which of the listed features are most important, the group went back to interview recycling center managers (that is, back to the market research stage). It was found that two additional goals were named frequently: speed and ease of installation. For example, eighty percent of the managers said that having to reach all the way into the crusher's cylinder to pull out the crushed can slowed down the entire crushing process tremendously. Installation was a problem because the arm and cylinder of the crusher were designed to be nailed or screwed to a wooden wall and floor, causing significant problems for users who wanted to attach the mechanism to their cement garage or basement floor. This problem was noted by 60% of the managers. Initially, the design team decided to add to the goals the requirement that the mechanism be a stand-alone device; however, they later changed the requirement to "portable."

Finally, the design group listed the constraints or boundaries of the design problem as follows:

- Either safe for young children to use or impossible for them to use
- Less strength required than manual can-crushing methods
- As fast as manual crushing methods
- No force used except human power (no motors, hydraulics, and so on)
- Construction of prototype to be completed in two months

Figure 4.5 Aluminum-Can Crusher: Design alternative #4.

DESIGN #4

SPRING-LOADED VERTICAL PRESS

DECISION MATRIX SCORE: 954 (Refer to Figure 4.10.)

DESCRIPTION: This design utilizes a compression spring and gravity to crush the can. It is basically a slight adaptation of the first design.

INSTRUCTIONS: 1. Pull top plate up until latch catches.
2. Place can on bottom plate.
3. Release latches to release spring, crushing can.
4. Lift top plate until latches catch again.
5. Remove crushed can.

PLUSES: Accurate in achieving minimum volume   MINUSES: Strong spring would be
                                                                       expensive
INTERESTING POINTS: May be used for other purposes   Extreme human force needed
                      Must find a feasible way to operate it   to compress
                                                                       Spring
                                                                       Dangerous
                                                                       Not very durable

DESIGN #4

A–Compression spring
B–Latch support
C–Top plate
D–Bottom plate
E–Latch
F–Guide rods

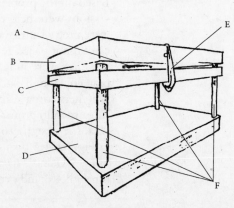

DESIGN #5

HORIZONTAL SPRING PRESS WITH CAN EJECTOR

DECISION MATRIX SCORE: 1219 (Refer to Figure 4.10.)

DESCRIPTION: This is a variation of design #4, only laid on its side. Gravity is not used to crush the can, but gravity does not work against the operator when compressing the spring either.

INSTRUCTIONS: 1. Pull plate back until latch catches.
  2. Lay can on lower platform.
  3. Pull latch, releasing plate.
  4. Pull plate back until latch catches.
  5. Crushed can falls through hole in platform bottom.

PLUSES: Quick   MINUSES: Compression spring is expensive
               Safe if effective latch is developed   Much human force required
               Achieves small volume well   Not very durable

INTERESTING POINTS: A can feeder may be added to this design.

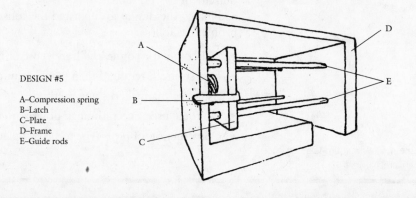

DESIGN #5

A–Compression spring
B–Latch
C–Plate
D–Frame
E–Guide rods

Figure 4.6 Aluminum-Can Crusher:
Design alternative #5.

After identifying the problem, FRs, goals, and constraints, the design team held brainstorming sessions to generate preliminary ideas for solutions.

4.1.3 Preliminary Ideas

The preliminary ideas section of the design feasibility study consists of organizing and refining the alternative solutions recorded in the preliminary ideas stage of the design process. Designers may report preliminary ideas by using common design annotation techniques (for example, perspectives, isometrics, and obliques). Designers may also use computer-based techniques of modeling and specifying the geometry of their ideas. These design modeling techniques will be discussed in Chapters 7, 8, and 9.

The Aluminum-Can Crusher: Preliminary Ideas

Example 4.3

Based on the problem definition section (see Example 4.2), two brainstorming sessions were held to come up with possible solutions to the problem. Some were pretty outrageous, others were quite practical, but every participant was careful not to judge or criticize any of them at this time. At the next meeting, the ideas were judged and poor ideas were eliminated—these included dropping concrete slabs out of third-story windows onto the cans and hiring Weight Watchers to have its members sit on the cans during their weekly meetings. After spending much time debating the positive and negative aspects of each idea, the design group narrowed the list to eight possible solutions, as shown in Figures 4.2 through 4.9. Note that design alternatives have been sketched using 3-D and 2-D annotation techniques—perspective pictorial in Figures 4.2 through 4.8 and orthographic multiview in Figure 4.9.

DESIGN #6

SCREW PRESS

DECISION MATRIX SCORE: 1071 (Refer to Figure 4.10.)

DESCRIPTION: This is another adaptation of the first solution, this one using a screw device to lower the plate.

INSTRUCTIONS: 1. Rasie plate by turning handle.
2. Place can on bottom platform.
3. Lower plate by turning handle.
4. Raise plate again by turning handle.
5. Remove crushed can.

PLUSES:		MINUSES:	
Very safe		Extremely slow	
Little strength needed		Higher than average cost	
Easy instructions		Tedious	
		Not very durable (threads wear quickly)	

INTERESTING POINTS: Able to crush more than one can at once
adaptable to using a power drill to operate

DESIGN #6

A–Screw
B–Screw support
C–Bottom platform
D–Handle
E–Plate
F–Guide rods

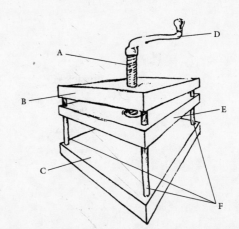

Figure 4.7 Aluminum-Can Crusher:
Design alternative #6.

DESIGN #7

VERTICAL LEVER AND TOGGLE

DECISION MATRIX SCORE: 1506 (Refer to Figure 4.10.)

DESCRIPTION: This is a variation of design #2. It was noted that design #2 crushed the can unevenly because the lever caused the crushing mechanism to come down at an angle. This design corrects that problem by guiding the crusher straight down. This design may be adapted to include a cylinder and a can ejector, as in design #2, although these are not included in the concept drawing.

INSTRUCTIONS: 1. Place can under crushing mechanism.
2. Pul down on handle to crush can.
3. Raise handle.
4. Remove crushed can.

PLUSES:		MINUSES:	
Very fast		Uses some expensive parts	
Quite safe		Might require more than	
Easily cleaned		average maintenance	
Very accurate in reducing volume		Would have to be clamped down	

INTERESTING POINTS: Many different unique features
Fun to watch while in operation

DESIGN #7

A–Toggle support braces
B–Crushing mechanism
C–Crushing platform
D–Handle
E–Lever

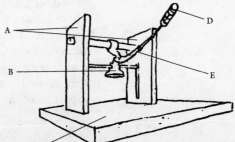
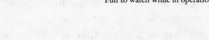

Figure 4.8 Aluminum-Can Crusher:
Design alternative #7.

DESIGN #8

FOOT-POWERED CAN FLATTENER

DECISION MATRIX SCORE: 1580 (Refer to Figure 4.10.)

DESCRIPTION: This design is almost completely different in nearly all aspects from any of the previous seven. It is the only one to crush from beneath, it is the only one that does not crush the can from top to bottom (rather, it smashes the can in the middle and folds the ends over), and it is the only one that is exclusively foot powered.

INSTRUCTIONS: 1. Place cans on ramp.
2. Push down on pedal with foot. This raises the shaft and crushes the can flat.
3. Release pedal.
4. Crushed can falls into container. Next can slides into place to be crushed.

PLUSES: Minimizes volume accurately   MINUSES: Might be expensive
                Very fast   Might get clogged
                Very safe   Bulky, hard to store or transport
                Could be modified easily before final production

INTERESTING POINTS: Works like a soda machine
                      Uses gravity in ejecting crushed cans
                      Crushing mechanism entirely enclosed

DESIGN #8

A–Crushed can container
B–Shaft
C–Ramp
D–Foot pedal
E–Center crusher
F–End smasher

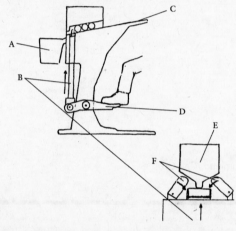

Figure 4.9 Aluminum-Can Crusher:
Design alternative #8.

4.1.4 Preliminary Decision

In the preliminary decision section of the design feasibility study you need to document your unbiased decision about which design solution is the best. Designers sometimes evaluate the proposed solutions in relation to existing devices and patent searches. This patent information may be used as a benchmark against which designers can compare proposed design solutions. In addition to satisfying the functional requirements and goals of the problem, you may include manufacturing considerations such as the number of different parts needed to manufacture the product, the modularity of the design (that is, made out of parts that fit with other parts), the multifunctionality of parts (that is, parts that can perform several functions), the use of standard components, the ease of fabrication and assembly, the ease of handling, compliance with government regulations, and so on.

The design group then selects the best solutions for computer modeling and further analysis by a technician or an engineer. The designers should then revise the parameters and the value factors of each of the design goals and requirements considered. This quantitative information forms the rationale for selecting and presenting the best design solution. The decision matrix (Figure 4.10) is then revised, redrawn, and labeled neatly, because it is the most important component of the design feasibility study.

Example 4.5

The Aluminum-Can Crusher: Preliminary Decision

Based on the preliminary ideas section (see Example 4.3), the design group assigned value factors to each of the design goals or features (Figure 4.10). It was arbitrarily decided to have the factors total two hundred. The design team selected the top three goals or features: (1) safety (that is, safe to use yet not a nuisance), (2) minimum volume (of can after crushing), and (3) minimum human force required (note that the first two goals, safety and minimum volume, are similar to two of the FRs defined in Example 4.2).

Safety was assigned the highest priority because of the danger involved in stomping on cans—the primary reason this project was undertaken—and

Figure 4.10 Decision matrix: Evaluating the design ideas for the aluminum-can crusher.

Decision Matrix

Design Goal/Feature		Value Factor
1.	Safe to use yet not a nuisance	33
2.	Accurately achieves minimum volume	30
3.	Requires minimum human force	30
4.	Affordable for intended market	21
5.	Operates quickly	19
6.	Not complex instructions	14
7.	New features can be adapted during design	14
8.	Uses of standard parts	12
9.	Durable	11
10.	Storable	7
11.	Portable (size, weight, shape)	5
12.	Fun to use	4

		Design #							
		1	2	3	4	5	6	7	8
Goal #	1	5 165	7 231	3 99	2 66	7 231	9 297	7 231	9.5 314
	2	8 240	8 240	9 270	9 270	8 240	9 270	9 270	9 270
	3	3 90	7 210	9 270	4 120	6 180	2 60	7 210	7 210
	4	9 189	7 147	5 105	5 105	4 84	5 105	6 126	7 147
	5	4 76	8 152	3 57	2 38	7 133	0 0	8 152	9 171
	6	10 140	9 126	10 140	8 112	7 98	8 112	10 140	8 112
	7	3 42	8 112	3 42	3 42	5 70	2 28	8 112	9 126
	8	8 96	6 72	8 96	7 84	5 60	5 60	8 96	6 72
	9	7 77	6 66	5 55	4 44	4 44	5 55	7 77	6 66
	10	5 35	4 28	4 28	4 28	4 28	7 49	5 35	5 35
	11	8 40	6 30	1 5	5 25	3 15	7 35	5 25	5 25
	12	2 8	6 24	7 28	5 20	9 36	0 0	8 32	8 32
	Total	1198	1438	1195	954	1219	1071	1506	1580

because safety is a major problem with current crushing devices. Achieving minimum volume was ranked highly because it is the primary reason for crushing cans in the first place. Requiring minimum human force was ranked near the top because people will not purchase such a device if it requires more effort to use than manually crushing cans.

The next two goals or features listed were "affordable for the intended market" and "operates quickly," listed for the same reason as "requires minimum human force." It was found that most people consider price and speed less important than ease of use.

In each box in the decision matrix in Figure 4.10, the number at the top is the rating the team gave that design alternative's achievement of the indicated goal on a scale from 0 to 10, with 10 indicating the best rating. The number at the bottom in each box is that rating multiplied by the goal's value. Only these bottom numbers are totaled at the base of the decision matrix. The highest possible total was two thousand. The design team took the top three ideas (Designs 2, 7, and 8) to a manufacturing engineer and a tooling technician who work in a manufacturing plant near Chicago. They thought all three were good ideas; however, they found a major problem with the lever-and-toggle solution (Designs 2 and 7). Although the toggle provides much force, it has little throw; that is, the lever has to travel great distances to crush each can, making it ergonomically impractical (not well designed for human comfort). They also tested the force required to crush a can in different ways and the volume that resulted in each case. They were surprised to learn that crushing a can sideways by denting the center and folding in the ends required the least

Figure 4.11 Preliminary design solution.

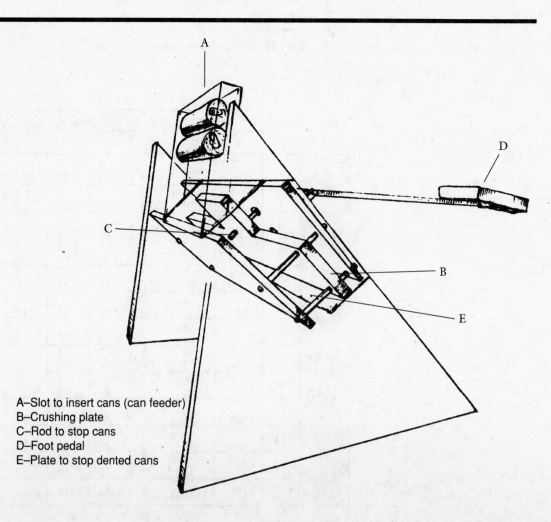

A–Slot to insert cans (can feeder)
B–Crushing plate
C–Rod to stop cans
D–Foot pedal
E–Plate to stop dented cans

1. Place can in feeder.

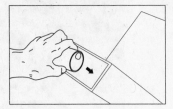

2. Can drops into chamber #1.

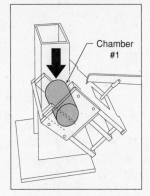

Chamber #1

3. Step on foot pedal to dent can.

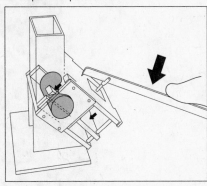

4. Release foot pedal. Dented can into chamber #2. New can falls into chamber #1.

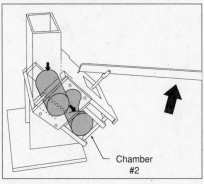

Chamber #2

5. Push on foot pedal. Dented can is crushed. New can is dented.

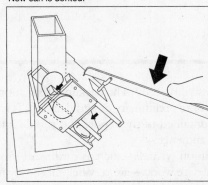

6. Release foot pedal. Flattened can drops out. Dented can falls into chamber #2. New can falls into chamber #1.

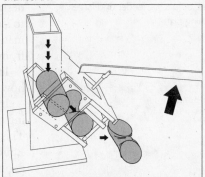

Figure 4.12 The Crusher operating procedure (see also actual prootype in Figure 4.13).

force and achieved the smallest volume. This made the foot-powered, can-flattening design (Design 8) appear to be more practical than it seemed earlier. Finally, the two engineers decided that Design 8 would be much less expensive to develop than the other two designs.

4.2 PRESENTATION OF THE FEASIBILITY DESIGN STUDY

In the preceding sections, we covered the typical contents of a design feasibility study. However, designers are usually required to make an oral presentation of their initial design solution sometime after they have delivered the feasibility report. For this occasion, the design team needs to be ready with slides, transparencies, videotape, or even a rough prototype showing the design solution.

The presentation usually includes **backup information** not contained in the

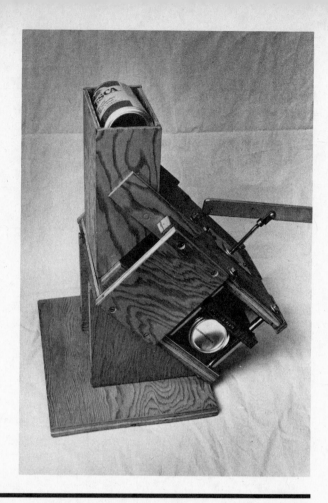

Figure 4.13 Crusher prototype: Can Compactor feeder and large crushing plate.

design feasibility study. The backup information consists of up-to-date material to support the preliminary design decision. It is used to clarify the design information contained in the report and should address any anticipated questions from the audience.

In addition, **visuals**—such as cardboard prototypes or diagrams illustrating how the device works—are very helpful conveying the proposed design solution.

It is also important to have preliminary information concerning manufacturing and production processes and the costs incurred in building the prototype. This information is necessary because the design process is concurrent and designers need to deal with multiple concerns—such as issues of function (FRs), geometry (shape), and manufacturing—as the design evolves, rather than wait until the design is complete (Cutkosky, 1991).

| Example 4.5 |

The Aluminum-Can Crusher: Oral Presentation

Once the design group delivered the completed design feasibility study, they were asked to prepare an oral presentation. The following comments were prepared for the occasion:

"If you have had a chance to look at our design feasibility study, you know that our goal is to design a simple device to reduce the volume of empty aluminum cans safely before taking them to a recycling center. This transparency (Figure 4.11) shows the preliminary design solution for this aluminum-can–crusher problem. This is a modification of design alternative #8 (Figure 4.9). Note that the primary change made was in the crushing mechanism. Although we felt that the original design would crush cans with minimum force—an opinion our consultants agreed with—the design proved to be inefficient at crushing cans when we built a wooden prototype. Therefore the new design changed the crushing into a two-step process (Figure 4.12). We also changed the foot pedal and frame for two reasons. First and foremost was the cost and size of the frame. It was found that a structure of that size would either have to be very costly or very unstable, both of which we wanted to eliminate. We also found that we could increase the power applied to the can more easily by extending the length of the pedal, something that would have been impractical in the original design because of the limited leg room beneath the ramp.

"The design is operated using the following step-by-step process (Figure 4.12):

1. Place the back of the unit against a wall.
2. Insert several cans into the can feeder.
3. A single can will drop into the first chamber and be stopped by a descending rod.
4. Step on the foot pedal to dent the can.
5. Release the foot pedal and the dented can falls into the second chamber, stopping when it hits a plate that descends from the crushing plate. A new can falls into the first chamber.
6. Step on the foot pedal again in order to flatten the can in the second chamber and dent the can in the first chamber.
7. Release the pedal and the flattened can falls out of the machine. The dented can falls into the second chamber, and a third new can falls into the first chamber.
8. Repeat steps 6 and 7 to crush all the remaining cans.

"We will now demonstrate this operation process with our design prototype (Figures 4.13 and 4.14). We should mention that there are very few ways to misuse this preliminary solution; however, there are some. For example, users may attempt to crush items other than aluminum cans in the crusher. As the entire crushing area will be enclosed, there would be little chance of injury occurring to the operator. However, attempting to crush such items as glass and steel would damage the crusher.

Figure 4.14 Crusher prototype showing that one can is dented while the can that was previously dented is crushed.

"This design solution is intended primarily for family garages or outdoors, as these are the main locations in which collected aluminum cans are stored before they are taken to the recycling center. Either of these locations should work well with the design solution, since virtually the only thing needed to operate the crusher is a wall against which to place it. However, it is recommended that the crusher be stored indoors to protect it from the elements.

"Many of the major components of the crusher may be purchased and used either 'as is' or with minor modifications. One item that can be used 'as is' is the die spring, which is used to return the pedal and crushing mechanism to the 'pre-crushing' position. The resistance on the spring must be strong enough to lift the handle and mechanism but weak enough to minimize the additional force required to crush the cans. These springs are relatively easy to obtain, yet they are somewhat more expensive than originally expected.

"The guide posts are simply ½-in. pipe cut into 5½-in. sections. The posts keep the crushing mechanism from moving around loosely inside the crusher. Bearings keep the mechanism from binding on the guide posts as it is raised and lowered. Our design team had originally planned on using plastic sleeve bearings, but these proved troublesome on our prototype, so we have opted for higher quality metal bearings.

"Several of the main components of the unit are the pieces of plywood for the frame and the top and bottom of the crushing unit. The bottom piece is an 8" by 8¾" piece of ½" plywood with four ³⁄₁₆" holes drilled for support rods. The top is the same size, with five ³⁄₁₆" holes and one 1" hole drilled into it. The sides are made of a 2-feet-square piece of ½" plywood cut diagonally into two triangles.

"The lever would be made out of a ¼-in.-by-1-in.-by-20-in. bar of aluminum with three holes punched in it. The crushing plate is a ⅝-in.-by-8-in.-by-8¾-in. piece of filled phenolic resin (Bakelite) with four holes punched in it for the bearings and guide rods and one smaller hole to bolt the metal bracket to it. This is by far the most expensive component of the entire crusher.

Two of the primary needs of the device's parts are strength and durability. With these in mind, and with the assistance of our consultants, it was decided to make the crushing plate out of Bakelite because it is extremely strong and easy to manipulate. The crushing plate must be sturdy enough not to dent or wear when crushing cans. We experimented with a wooden plate with a steel sheet screwed to its bottom to prevent this type of wear, but we encountered problems with the wood cracking near the bearings in even the slightest binding situation. It was also found that it would be too expensive to bend steel and punch holes into it. Therefore, we decided to make this part out of Bakelite, a material suggested by the resource people, which has worked very well.

"It was decided to make the top and bottom of the crusher and the framework from wood because wood is sturdy enough for our needs, easy to work with, and inexpensive. The design team thought that the bottom of the crusher might have to be made of metal, but it was found that the cans remained flat against the bottom as they were crushed, leaving few or no dents on the surface.

"Plexiglass was the original choice for the shields and can feeder because it is sturdy enough for our purposes and is transparent. However, it was found that Plexiglass is more costly than anticipated and is dangerous to work with, so it was decided to look into wireform for our feeder, for which, at the time of this report, the design team had not found an accurate cost. Finally, the stopping shield was be made from ¼-in. plywood."

The design team continued their oral presentation by displaying a bill of materials transparency (Table 4.1). The bill of materials contains the following information: part names, materials, specifications, quantity needed, and costs.

"These prices are for the prototype only. Our source estimated that forty percent could be taken off these prices if the crusher were mass produced.

PART NAME	MATERIAL/SPECIFICATIONS	QUANTITY	COST
Crushing Plate	5/8" filled phenolic resin (Bakelite)–6 punched holes	1	$7.00
Lever	20" x 1" x 1/4" aluminum bar 3 punched holes	1	2.50
Stopping Shield	1/4" plywood	1	.50
Guide Posts	5 1/2", 1/2"dia. steel pipe	4(@.35)	1.40
Auto. Feeder	wireform (cost not available, estimated cost shown)	1	3.00
Base & Top of Crusher & Frame	1/2" plywood top – 8" x 8 1/2" – 6 holes base – 8" x 8 1/2" – 4 holes frame – 2' x 2' cut in half diagonally	1	3.00
Pedal	wood – 2" x 4" x 4"	1	.50
Support Rods	6 1/2", 3/16" dia. – threaded	4(@.69)	2.76
Stopping Rod	4 1/2" rod, 3/16" dia. one end threaded	1	.49
Piston Rod	4 1/2" rod, 3/16" dia. both ends threaded	1	.59
Die Spring	1" dia., 3" long	1	1.79
Bearings	oil-impregnated thermoplastic (Oilon PV-80)	4(@.15)	.60
Wood Screws	3/4" x 3/16" dia.	10(@.06)	.60
Steel Bolt	3/4" x 3/16" dia.	2(@.10)	.20
Nuts & Washers	3/16" inside dia.	7 sets(@.06)	.42
Washer	1 1/4" outer dia.	1	.09
Clevices	1/4" dia. steel	3(@.49)	1.47
Cotter Pin	3/4" x 3/16" dia.	1	.04
Metal Bracket	four 3/16" holes	1	1.50
			$28.45
Labor (estimate)			10.00
			$38.45

Table 4.1 Bill of materials.

"Much of the testing occurred before building the prototype, usually with cardboard and wooden models. Further tests were made to determine which parts should be made from wood and which from steel. The group concentrated on the two parts that crushed the can in the second chamber. It was found that wood used for the crushing mechanism was easily damaged by the sharp edges of the can, but such was not the case with the bottom piece.

"Once the prototype was built, much testing occurred at and during the two days immediately before a preliminary design presentation. The prototype was not in its frame for the presentation; rather, it was clamped to a tabletop and used as a hand-powered model. To make the interior more open for viewing, the prototype also did not have the can feeder or any shields in place.

"These transparencies (Figures 4.15, 4.16, and 4.17) show detail-drawings of dimensioned orthographic projections of the prototype. The prototype is considered a preliminary design solution and is not the final product ready for manufacturing and marketing.

"Before proceeding with manufacturing, the design team would like to do some consumer testing to see what, if any, problems arise with common usage. We especially want to examine how tedious the average consumer finds crushing cans this way as compared to crushing cans using the traditional stomping method. The design team suspects that it would be much less tedious because the

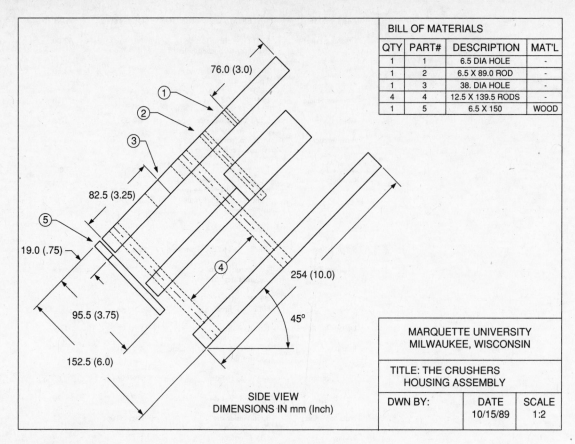

BILL OF MATERIALS			
QTY	PART#	DESCRIPTION	MAT'L
1	1	6.5 DIA HOLE	-
1	2	6.5 X 89.0 ROD	-
1	3	38. DIA HOLE	-
4	4	12.5 X 139.5 RODS	-
1	5	6.5 X 150	WOOD

SIDE VIEW
DIMENSIONS IN mm (Inch)

MARQUETTE UNIVERSITY
MILWAUKEE, WISCONSIN

TITLE: THE CRUSHERS
HOUSING ASSEMBLY

DWN BY:	DATE 10/15/89	SCALE 1:2

Figure 4.15 Crusher detail drawings:
Side view of housing assembly.

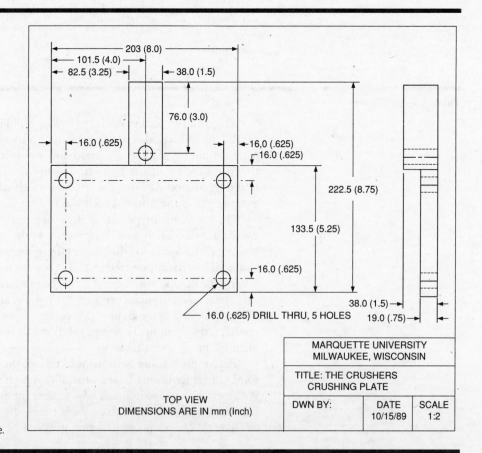

TOP VIEW
DIMENSIONS ARE IN mm (Inch)

MARQUETTE UNIVERSITY
MILWAUKEE, WISCONSIN

TITLE: THE CRUSHERS
CRUSHING PLATE

DWN BY:	DATE 10/15/89	SCALE 1:2

Figure 4.16 The Crusher detail
drawings: Top view of crushing plate.

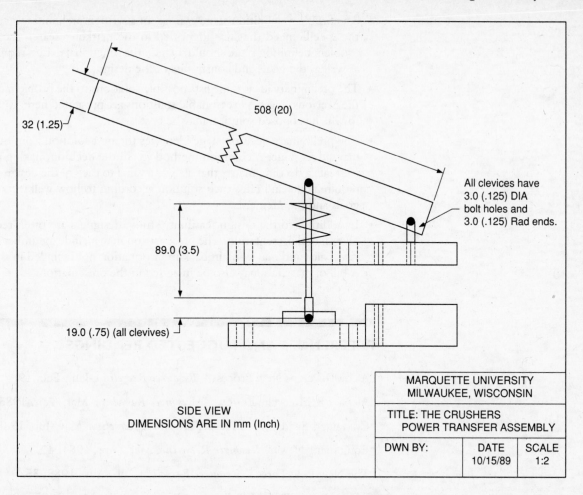

508 (20)

32 (1.25)

All clevices have
3.0 (.125) DIA
bolt holes and
3.0 (.125) Rad ends.

89.0 (3.5)

19.0 (.75) (all clevives)

SIDE VIEW
DIMENSIONS ARE IN mm (Inch)

MARQUETTE UNIVERSITY
MILWAUKEE, WISCONSIN

TITLE: THE CRUSHERS
POWER TRANSFER ASSEMBLY

DWN BY:	DATE 10/15/89	SCALE 1:2

Figure 4.17 The Crusher detail drawings: power transfer assembly.

lever greatly reduces the amount of force required and because the feeder and lever allow people to complete the task much more quickly. However, we would like to obtain concrete data on this question to confirm this. Also, the market study needs to be revised and updated, since the cost is higher than the original retail estimate of forty dollars because of the increased number of metal parts.

"We feel that our design is a vast improvement over current commercial crushing devices. It is much safer and faster than any model researched. It is assumed that the product would do well in the marketplace, since it provides most of the features the public is looking for in such a device. We have met all the initial design's FRs and goals. However, much remains to be done in terms of market research, engineering analysis (modeling and simulation), material testing, and the manufacturing concerns previously mentioned."

Chapter Summary

Chapter 4 detailed the following points:

- A design feasibility study encapsulates, in written form, the four stages of the ideation phase of the design process: market research, problem definition, preliminary ideas, and preliminary decision.

- The object of the market research section of the design feasibility study is to analyze market survey results, brainstorm about market needs, and identify an urgent and specific market need.

- The problem definition stage consists of a written preliminary statement of the specific need that was identified in the market research section. The problem definition stage should include the functional design requirements, as well as the goals and constraints of the design.

- The preliminary ideas stage lists possible solutions to the problem defined in the previous stage. All reasonable solutions are presented here, without bias to which proposed solution may be best.

- The preliminary decision stage identifies the best solution from the preliminary ideas stage. A common method to aid the decision-making process is to create a decision matrix that assigns a value to each of the design goals and requirements and rates each solution according to how well it meets those goals and requirements.

- In addition to the design feasibility study, designers are often required to give an oral presentation. The presentation may include a number of audio-visual aids and may contain backup information not included in the report. A bill of materials may also be included in the presentation.

REFERENCES AND SUGGESTED READINGS

"Alcoa Develops New Process." *Resource Recycling*, Jan./Feb. 1987, 15–16.

"Alcoa UBC Recycling Grows." *Resource Recycling*, Mar./Apr. 1985, 29.

"Containers Switching to Plastic." *Resource Recycling*, May/Jun. 1985, 15–17.

"Equipment News." *Resource Recycling*, Mar./Apr. 1984, 42.

"The New Poly Three." *Resource Recycling*, Jul./Aug. 1985, 35.

"Reynolds Sets Records." *Resource Recycling*, Mar./Apr. 1985, 29.

Cutkosky, M. "Next Cut: A Concurrent Design System." *Spatial Relations*, Jun. 1991, 2.

Emerich, R. H. *Troubleshooters' Handbook for Mechanical Systems*. New York: McGraw-Hill, 1969.

Grafstein, P. *Pictorial Handbook of Technical Devices*. New York: Chemical Publishing Company, 1971.

Javnarama, J. *The Recycler's Handbook*. Berkeley, Calif.: EarthWorks Press, 1990.

Keen, M. L. *How It Works*. New York: Grosset and Dunlap, 1974.

Lodewijk, T. *The Way Things Work*. New York: Simon and Schuster, 1973.

Newell, J. A. *Ingenious Mechanisms*. New York: Industrial Press, 1967.

EXERCISES

4.1 Define and/or determine the problem statement, FRs, goals, and constraints for the following market need: People need to dispose of house trash once or twice a week. The garbage truck usually picks the trash from the curb at the front of the house. You have been assigned the task of devising a way to dispose of various types of recyclable trash such as paper, glass, plastic, and aluminum.

4.2 Many people are making a tremendous effort to recycle paper products. However, in the U.S. alone, people throw away 44 million newspapers everyday—that is, the equivalent of 30 million trees each year (Javnarama, 1990). Conscious of these statistics, your neighbors have decided to collect as many newspapers as possible once a week. After defining the problem, propose alternate design solutions to store and collect the newspapers in your neighborhood before taking them to a recycling center. Submit a partial design feasibility study containing only two sections: problem definition and preliminary ideas.

4.3 Investigate and prepare the market research section of a design feasibility study arising from the following situation: After recycling centers collect glass bottles, they break them into smaller pieces, called "cullet." The recycling center then ships the cullet to the glass factory. When the cullet arrives at the factory, a device is needed to remove from the glass pieces the metal rings left on the necks of the bottles after the caps were unscrewed by the bottles' users. (For additional information on glass recycling, write to: The Glass Packaging Institute, 1801 K St. N.W., Suite 1105-L, Washington, D.C. 20006.)

4.4 Prepare a brief feasibility study for the following problem: After people finish moving from one house to another, they have many corrugated cardboard boxes left over after unpacking. You have been asked to design a device to store, transport, and dispose of this kind of corrugated cardboard material. Consider requesting the free fact sheet "Reducing Corrugated Cardboard Waste," Office Waste Reduction Services, Michigan Department of Commerce, P.O. Box 30004, Lansing, MI 48909 (517) 335-1178.

4.5 Draw an image and/or write a short statement that describes or defines each of the key terms, listed below, used in this chapter:

Backup information	Preliminary decision
Bill of materials	Preliminary ideas
Design feasibility study	Problem definition
Market research	Visuals

CHAPTER 5 Design Shape-Analysis

Using a two-dimensional geometric description of a product, how can we visualize it three-dimensionally? The first step is to analyze the product's shape using the available orthographic multiviews (in the case of a device) or the construction plans (in the case of a building or a large system). Then we need to determine all the spatial relationships not explicitly provided on the drawings (for example, nondimensioned oblique planes, inconsistencies, and missing lines and angles). This information is needed to manufacture the part or construct the building. The techniques for finding the information constitute what engineers call descriptive geometry. An engineer, architect, or builder may spend several days "reading," or analyzing, a set of construction plans in order to determine all the distances, angles, material quantities, costs, and operations involved in a project. In the same way, a manufacturing engineer must understand and fully visualize every single detail of a new product or device before beginning the production process—and at this point, he or she rarely has the opportunity to meet with the designer. The designer might have provided a building model or a device prototype, but this is the exception rather than the rule. Usually all that is provided to the construction engineer, the manufacturing engineer, or the machinist is a set of two-dimensional, or 2-D, drawings. (It should be noted that as more companies adopt concurrent engineering design strategies, both the designer and the builder or manufacturer work together from beginning to end.)

This chapter presents techniques in descriptive geometry for analyzing and visualizing the shape of objects. Since the advent of CAD modeling, descriptive geometry has been deemphasized. Many educators agree, however, that the skills learned from descriptive geometry enhance the student's visualization skills. In addition, two-dimensional shape-analysis techniques (for example, determining the intersection between two planes, given a set of orthographic multiviews) are still used in engineering design projects.

5.1 GEOMETRIC DESCRIPTION: 2-D TO 3-D VISUALIZATION

The principles studied in the traditional field of **descriptive geometry** facilitate shape-analysis and three-dimensional, or 3-D, visualization. Descriptive geometry involves the construction of precise drawings to determine unknown design dimensions such as the true lengths and angles of the oblique planes of a part. These drawings provide 2-D descriptions, as well as information about 3-D objects. Gaspard Monge (see Chapter 1) invented descriptive geometry to solve problems in the design of fortifications. He was the first to propose substituting simple descriptive geometry techniques for the complex mathematical calculations used to solve design problems. Using simple drawing instruments like triangles, compasses, and dividers—and Monge's descriptive-geometry principles— designers can determine the true shapes and angles of oblique surfaces and draw the unfolded shape, or development, of physical objects without the use of computers.

Descriptive geometry is based on logical reasoning. The visualization of an object from multiview drawings is derived from observation and accurate analytical thinking. Students frequently say "I can't visualize what this missing view should look like; how can I draw a pictorial of it?" However, such a situation, however frustrating at first, may be preferred, because the students then have no preconceived ideas and therefore can draw a pictorial or determine missing information without prejudice (Wellman, 1957).

The winning combination is to use both logical analytical visualization and constructive imagination (which is intuitive) to assist in the visualization and shape-analysis of objects.

5.2 ANALYTICAL VISUALIZATION: DEFINITIONS, CONDITIONS, AND AXIOMS

The process of analytical visualization is aided by axiomatic theory, which consists of definitions, conditions, and axioms. **Axioms** are postulates and propositions generally recognized as true. In the context of this discussion, they are used to describe general rules that allow you to infer a solution to a visualization problem—that is, to think (both analytically and imaginatively) in terms of the logical relationships between the orthographic multiviews of an object.

The following material describes some of the definitions, conditions, and axioms necessary for analytical visualization. These principles apply to multiview orthographic projections and are based on ANSI Y14.3 (American Society of Mechanical Engineers, 1975). In descriptive geometry, multiviews are generally named by the plane onto which they have been projected, for instance, Frontal (F), Horizontal (H), and Profile (P) multiviews.

Figure 5.1 Relationships among views. Note that the multiviews of point A (i.e., A_H, A_F, A_P) are aligned to each other.

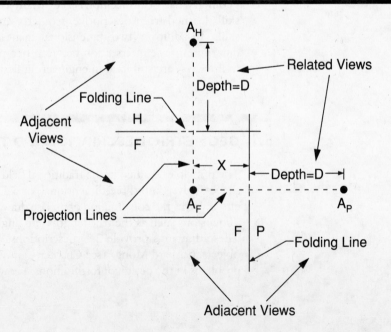

Definitions

- Definition 1: Aligned views are orthographic multiviews placed side by side, so that their corresponding points can be placed on the same projection line. For example, note that the horizontal and profile multiviews of point A are perfectly aligned with the frontal multiview of the point. In other words, a vertical projection line from A_H intersects A_F, and a horizontal projection line from A_F intersects A_P (see Figure 5.1).

- Definition 2: Adjoining views are views that share a common boundary. Note that the horizontal and frontal adjoining multiviews in Figure 5.1 share the same folding line or boundary.

- Definition 3: Adjacent views are aligned adjoining multiviews (Figure 5.1).

- Definition 4: Related views are two multiviews bordering a common intermediate multiview. In other words, two related views are adjacent to the same view (Figure 5.1).

Conditions

- Condition 1: Lines of sight are at right angles with the projection plane. (Refer to Figure 2.2 in Chapter 2.)

- Condition 2: Lines of sight of adjacent views are perpendicular to each other. (Refer to Figure 2.2 in Chapter 2.)

- Condition 3: All adjacent and related views are aligned to each other, following the standard (ANSI or ISO) orthographic multiview arrangements. (Refer to Figures 2.9 and 2.11 in Chapter 2.)

Axioms

- Axiom 1: The location of a point on a multiview is determined by its adjacent and related views. For example, to position point A we need the following: (1) the depth D between A_P and folding line F/P (which will be the same as the distance between A_H and folding line H/F—since P and H are related views); and (2) the distance (X) between A_F and folding line F/P (which gives the horizontal position of point A_H, since F and H are adjacent views).

- Axiom 2: Two bordering plane surfaces on a view are not on the same plane. Bordering surface areas on orthographic multiviews are separated by visible lines. These visible lines indicate a change in the direction of the plane or the curved surface. Therefore, two bordering surfaces are at a different depth, elevation, or inclination relative to each other.

- Axiom 3: Surfaces that are not parallel to the orthographic projection planes (for example, oblique or curved surfaces) appear foreshortened on their multiview projections.

The following example shows the application of these axioms in the analytical visualization of a simple object. The same principles would apply to a more complex 2-D to 3-D visualization problem.

Example 5.1

Analytical Visualization of a Simple Object

Visualize the relative position of two bordering surfaces for a set of multiviews. Figure 5.2 (a) illustrates H, F, and P multiviews of an object. Note that both H and F display two bordering surfaces (shown with different shades for illustration purposes). From the horizontal view, surface abcd appears to share a border with surface efgh. Note, however, that the visible line cd, or ef, separates the surfaces. Based on Axiom 2, surfaces abcd and efgh must be at a different elevation or inclination relative to each other. The frontal view shows a third surface, edef, which separates abcd from efgh. The profile view provides the relative height or elevation of all three surfaces (Axiom 1). In this case, surface abcd is

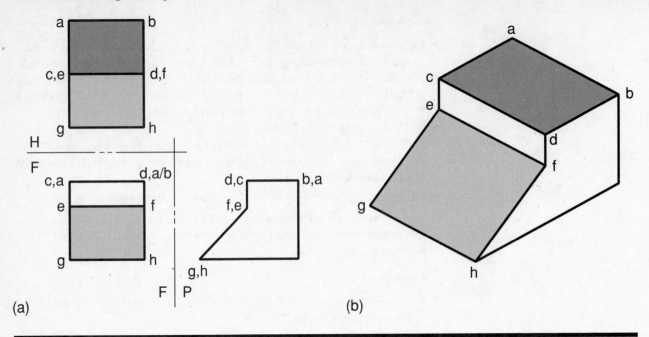

(a)   (b)

Figure 5.2 (a) Relative position of two bordering (contiguous) surfaces, (b) isometric showing how the surfaces are visualized.

above *efgh*. Note also that *efgh* is inclined relative to *abcd* even though both surfaces appear to have a similar shape from the frontal and horizontal views (Axiom 3). Figure 5.2(b) depicts the resulting image from the preceding visualization analysis.

5.3 AUXILIARY PROJECTIONS

Auxiliary projections are orthographic multiviews inclined to at least one of the **principal planes of projection**, i.e., the frontal, horizontal, and profile planes. They are used to display the true shape of an object's feature that is not parallel to any of the planes of projection.

Primary auxiliary projections are constructed by drawing an imaginary auxiliary plane of projection parallel to the inclined surface and projecting its features onto that surface. This process is similar to that used to draw multiviews. In Figure 5.3, the primary auxiliary projections have been generated by projecting points from a profile view.

Figure 5.3 An example of two primary auxiliary projections generated from a single profile view. (Courtesy of ASME and ANSI)

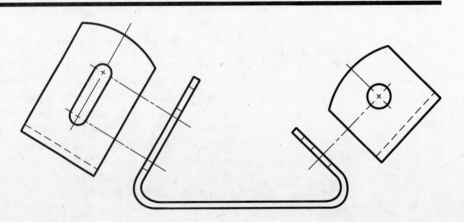

Secondary auxiliary projections can be constructed if a surface of an object is inclined and does not appear as a line (an edge of the surface) in any of the principal planes of projection. These views are sometimes used in working drawings to provide additional true-size dimensions of complex parts (see detail-drawing labeled "SECTION B-B," Figure 5.4). Secondary auxiliary projections are drawn relative to the primary auxiliary projection (see detail-drawing labeled "SECTION A-A," Figure 5.4).

5.4 MISSING VIEWS AND LINES

Sometimes it is difficult to visualize the three-dimensional shapes that will be manufactured or built. To make things worse, it is not unusual to find that working drawings are complicated by missing views and missing lines that may have been inadvertently omitted. However, one can visualize these incomplete missing elements by using the analytical principles of descriptive geometry and the power of constructive imagination.

Figure 5.4 The drawing labeled "Section B-B" is a secondary auxiliary projection of a tool sharpener base. This drawing shows the true size and shape of the hole. The drawing labeled "Section A-A" is a primary auxiliary projection. (Courtesy of Prof. E.G. Paré)

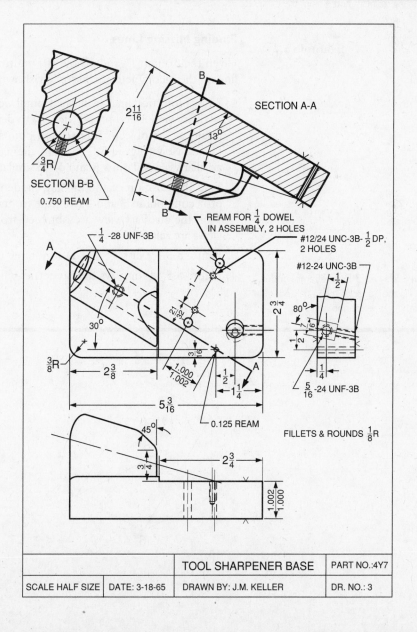

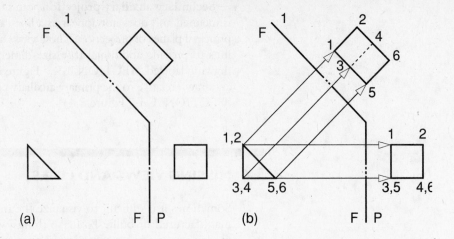

(a)   F | P   (b)   F | P

Figure 5.5 (a) Find the missing line for the given frontal, profile and auxiliary views. (b) The missing line is plotted in the auxiliary view by projecting points 3 and 4 from the frontal view.

Example 5.2

Finding Missing Lines

Given the frontal (F) and profile (P) multiviews of an object, find the missing line on the incomplete auxiliary view shown in Figure 5.5 (a).

1. Draw projection lines from the frontal view to the two related views (that is, auxiliary view 1 and profile view P) to determine the corresponding aligned points at the object's intersection points. Note that points 1 and 2 in the frontal view (Figure 5.5 (b)) are aligned with 1 and 2 on the profile and auxiliary views. Points 5 and 6 are similarly aligned.

2. Find the position of the missing hidden line 3–4 on the auxiliary view by projecting points 3 and 4 from the frontal view. The depths of points 3 and 4 on the auxiliary view are obtained from the profile view (because those views are related).

3. Figure 5.5 (c) displays a 3-D wireframe model of the visualized object.

4. Figure 5.5 (d) displays the isometric drawing of the visualized object.

Figure 5.5 (c) 3-D wireframe model showing the edges of the visualized object. (d) See caption attached.

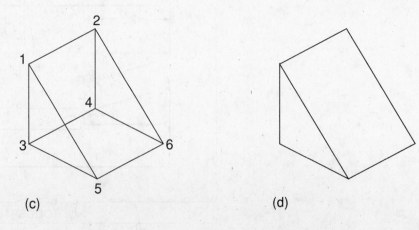

(c)   (d)

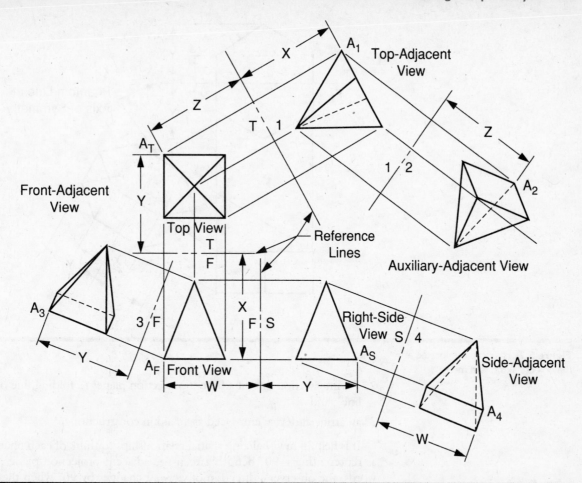

Figure 5.6 Standard use of phantom lines between views. (ANSI Y14.3-1975)

5.5 SPATIAL GEOMETRY*

Spatial geometry uses the principles of descriptive geometry to analyze and solve problems involving spatial distances and relationships. The most popular and practical method of solving such spatial-relationship problems involves the construction of orthographic multiviews supplemented by auxiliary views. Four basic view-construction techniques will be discussed in this section:

1. True-length view of a line
2. Point view of a line
3. Edge view of a plane
4. True view of a plane.

Before defining the techniques used to solve spatial-relationship problems, we must review the terminology used in spatial geometry. First, the **phantom line**—usually shown between adjacent views—is defined as:

1. an edge view of a plane of projection;

---

*The following paraphrased material has been extracted from the ANSI Y14.3 manual (ASME, 1975) with permission of ANSI/ASME. It is included for those who desire to review or expand their understanding of geometry.

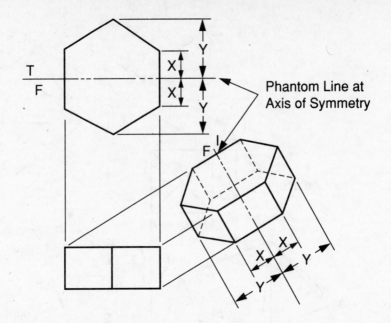

Phantom Line at
Axis of Symmetry

Figure 5.7 Phantom line located at
the object's axis of symmetry.

2. the intersection line of adjacent projection planes (a folding line or a hinge line); and

3. an artificial device employed as an aid in construction.

It is helpful in visualizing spatial relationships to think of each phantom line as representing a 90° bend between the adjacent projection planes; in other words, the observer's direction of viewing changes by 90° when the observer goes from one view to the adjacent view. It is standard practice to represent the phantom line with two short dashes and one long dash, alternately (see Figure 5.7). The line may be labeled with letters or numerals as desired.

In the construction of auxiliary views, the consistent and accurate transfer of distances from one related view to another is facilitated by the use of phantom lines. Several phantom lines (or reference lines) are shown in Figure 5.6. A height dimension, such as X, measured from the phantom line must be the same in both the front view and the related top-adjacent view. Similarly, distance Y in the right-side view must be the same in all views that are adjacent to the front view, and the side-adjacent view must show the same width dimension W as that shown in the front view. Likewise, in the auxiliary-adjacent view (a secondary auxiliary projection) distance Z must correspond to distance Z in the related top view.

In spatial geometry, the letters T, F and S shown beside the phantom lines and as subscripts for points signify Top, Front, and Side multiviews from which the auxiliary views are developed (T, F, and S thus signify the same views as H, F, and P do in Figures 5.1 and 5.2). The numbers 1, 2, 3, and 4 signify the auxiliary views projected from the top, front, or side views or from other auxiliary views.

For symmetrical objects, the phantom line may be on an axis of symmetry (in the middle of the object), as shown in Figure 5.7.

True-length view of a line: The true length of a line segment is the actual straight-line distance between the line's two end points. The projection of a line will be in true length (abbreviated TL in Figure 5.8) if, in the adjacent view, the projection of the line is parallel to the phantom line between the views. A line that is in true length in a principal view is called a **principal line** (in Figure 5.8, lines AB in the top view and CD in the front view).

Oblique line: Like line BC in Figure 5.8, an oblique line is not in true length in any principal view. Its true length is found in a primary auxiliary view, such as view 1 or view 2 in Figure 5.8, if the phantom line is parallel to the oblique line in its adjacent view.

Point view of a line: A view with the direction of sight parallel to a straight line in space provides a point view of the line. A point view of a line is adjacent to a true-length view, and the phantom line is perpendicular to the true-length projection of the line. See line B_1C_1 and point B_3C_3 in the upper-right corner of Figure 5.8: note that the point view (B_3C_3) of line BC appears in the secondary auxiliary view (view 3) because the line (B_1C_1) is in true length in the primary auxiliary view (view 1).

Edge view of a plane: A view with the direction of sight parallel to a plane in space gives the observer a straight line, or edge view of the plane. If any line in the plane is in true length in one view, then a point view of that true-length line will also show the plane as an edge (see Example 5.3).

True view of a plane: A true view is the direction of sight perpendicular to a plane. A true view of a plane is adjacent to an edge view, and the phantom line is parallel to the edge view.

Example 5.3 shows how to determine the true view of a plane.

Determining the True View of a Plane

Example 5.3

Determine the true view of plane ABC (Figure 5.9 (a)).

1. As stated in the previous paragraphs, we need first to obtain the edge view of plane ABC. To do that, we must identify or construct a line inscribed in the plane ABC that appears in true length. In this case, we must construct an

Figure 5.8 True-length and point views of lines.

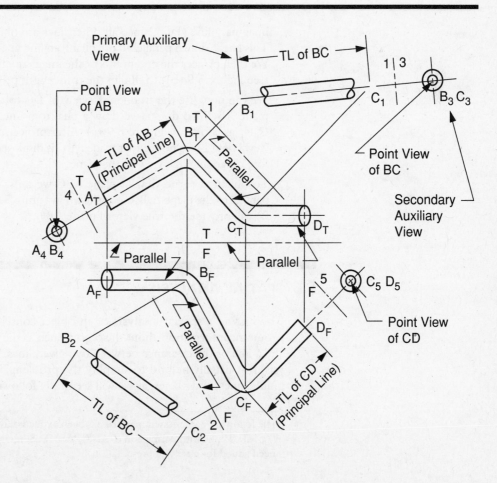

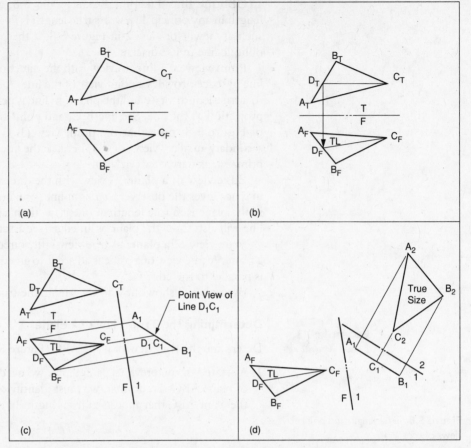

Figure 5.9 (a) Obtain edge and true-size views for the given plane. (b) Find the true length of a line inside plane ABC by constructing a line from C to AB (D_TC_T), that is parallel to the phantom line (T/F) and projecting the line into the adjacent view (D_FC_F). (c) Draw a phantom line (F/1) perpendicular to line D_FC_F to obtain a point view of line D_1C_1 and the edge view of plane ABC. (d) Draw a phantom line (1/2) parallel to A_1B_1 to obtain the true view of the plane.

imaginary line (DC), since all other lines are oblique (not in true length). This line is drawn parallel to the phantom line in either the top or front view. We then project the end points of the imaginary line onto the adjacent view (see Figure 5.9 (b)) to obtain the true-length projection of the line DC.

We can now use the true-length view of DC to construct the edge view of plane ABC. To do so, we draw a phantom line perpendicular to the line C_FD_F as shown in Figure 5.9 (c). After projecting all the points onto this view (view 1) we notice that plane ABC is displayed as a line. View 1 is therefore called an edge view of the plane.

2. To obtain the true view of plane ABC we must draw a new phantom line parallel to the plane $A_1B_1C_1$, as shown in Figure 5.9 (d). This new view (view 2) will provide the true view of plane ABC.

5.6   SPATIAL ANALYSIS*

Conducting a **spatial analysis** of an object consists of determining specific geometric information about the object, such as the clearance between a point and a line or the clearance between two given lines. To conduct a spatial analysis, it is usually helpful to simplify the problem by reducing it to terms of points, lines, and planes, as we will see in the following examples.

---

*The following paraphrased material has been extracted from the ANSI Y14.3 manual (ASME, 1975) with permission of ANSI/ASME. Several examples and drawings have been added for clarity of presentation.

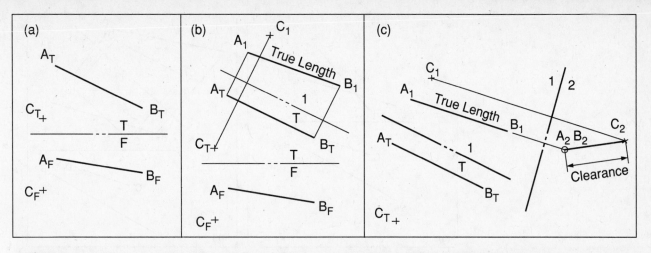

Figure 5.10 (a) Determine the clearance between the given point (C) and line (AB) (b) Construct a phantom line (T/1) parallel to A_TB_T to obtain the true-length view of AB. (c) Construct a phantom line (1/2) perpendicular to A_1B_1 to obtain the point view of the line. The clearance between line AB and point C is the distance between A_2B_2 and C_2.

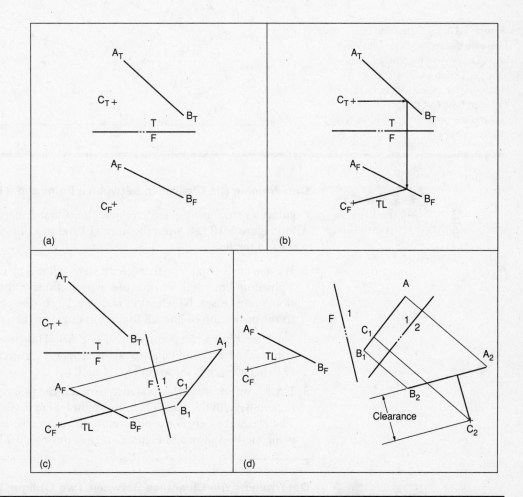

Figure 5.11 (a) Determine the clearance between point C and line (AB) (PLANE METHOD). (b) Find the true-length of a line inside plane ABC by constructing a line from C to AB that is parallel to the phantom line (T/F) and projecting the line into the adjacent view. (c) Find the edge view of plane ABC by constructing a phantom line (F/1) perpendicular to the true-length line and projecting A, B, and C into the auxiliary view. (d) Obtain a true view of plane ABC by constructing a phantom line parallel to the edge view of the plane and projecting line AB and point C into the secondary auxiliary view. The clearance between the point and the line can be measured as the perpendicular distance between the two in the true view of plane ABC.

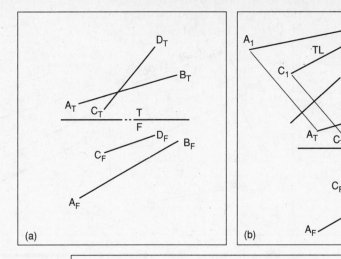

Figure 5.12 (a) Determine the clearance between oblique lines AB and CD. (b) Find the true-length of CD. (c) Obtain the clearance by measuring the perpendicular distance between the point projection of line CD and the projection of line AB in auxiliary view 2.

Example 5.4	**Determining the Clearance Between a Point and a Line**

Conduct a spatial analysis to determine the clearance between point C and line AB in Figure 5.10 (a), given the front (F) and top (T) view projections of the point and the line.

1. We must first obtain the true-length view of line AB. This is done by making a phantom line parallel to any of the projections of the line AB (top projection, in this case). Note that in Figure 5.10 (b) the phantom line is parallel to the projection of line AB in the top (T) view (i.e., $A_T B_T$).

2. Next, we obtain the point view of line AB. This time the phantom line is constructed perpendicular to the true-length projection of line AB (i.e., $A_1 B_1$). This step is shown in Figure 5.10 (c).

3. Finally, we measure the clearance between the point projection of line AB (i.e., $A_2 B_2$) and the point C_2, as shown in Figure 5.10 (c) in auxiliary view 2. The clearance between a point and a line can also be obtained using the plane method shown in Figures 5.11 (a) through 5.11 (d).

Example 5.5	**Determining the Clearance Between Two Oblique Lines**

Through spatial analysis, determine the clearance between the oblique lines AB and CD, shown in Figure 5.12 (a).

1. We must first construct a view of the two lines that shows one of the lines as a point. This procedure is outlined in steps 1 and 2 of Example 5.4 and is demonstrated again in Figure 5.12 (b) and Figure 5.12 (c).

2. To obtain the clearance, we measure the perpendicular distance between the point projection of line CD (C_2D_2) and the projection of line AB in view 2 (A_2B_2).

<table>
<tr><td>**Example 5.6**</td><td>

Determining the Clearance Between a Point and a Plane

Determine the clearance between point X and plane ABC, shown in Figure 5.13 (a).

1. We obtain the edge view of plane ABC by following the procedure outlined in step 1 of Example 5.3. The procedure is demonstrated again in Figures 5.13 (b) and 5.13 (c).

2. We then measure the clearance between plane ABC and point X. Note that in an edge view of the plane, the clearance between the point and the plane is in true length (the perpendicular distance from the point to the edge).
</td></tr>
</table>

<table>
<tr><td>**Example 5.7**</td><td>

Determining the Point of Intersection Between a Line and a Plane

Find the point of intersection of line XY and plane ABC, shown in Figure 5.14(a). (Note: The point of intersection is referred to as the **piercing point**.)

Let's imagine first that we are looking at these planes from the top view and that we are illuminating the scene with a hand light. We cannot see the shadow that the line XY projects on the surface of the plane ABC because our visual rays are parallel to the light, but someone looking at this scene from the front view will be able to see that shadow. That person will also notice that the shadow
</td></tr>
</table>

Figure 5.13 (a) Determine the clearance between point X and plane ABC. (b) Find the true length of a line on the plane. (c) Construct a phantom line perpendicular to the true-length line D_FC_F to obtain an edge view of plane ABC. Measure the clearance between point X and the plane ABC in auxiliary view 1.

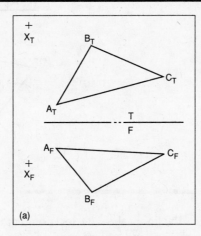

(a)

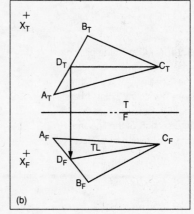

(b)

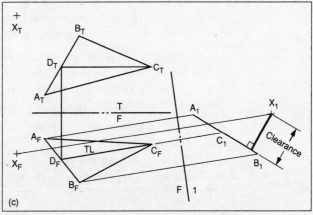

(c)

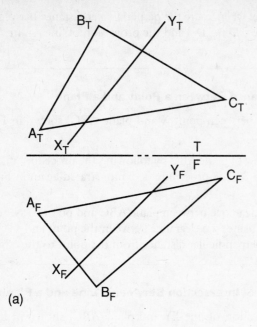

(a)

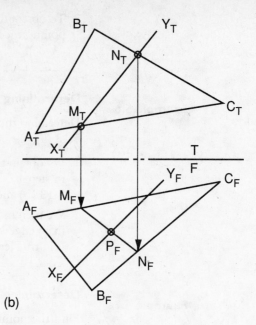

(b)

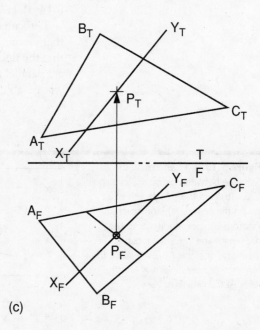

(c)

Figure 5.14 (a) Obtain the piercing point for the given plane and line. (b) Find the "shadow" of XY in the front view by projecting points M and N from the top view. (c) P_F is the point of intersection of the line and the plane. P_T is obtained by projecting P_F onto the top view.

intersects the line at the same location that the plane does. Therefore, the intersection of a line and a plane can be found if the shadow projection of the line onto the plane can be obtained from one of the orthographic views.

The steps that follow explain the process for obtaining the piercing point.

1. First we find the points where the line XY crosses the edges of the plane ABC in the top view. These intersections are designated by M_T and N_T (see the top view in Figure 5.14 (b)).

2. We then project these points onto the front view and find their location by placing them on the appropriate plane edge (i.e., point M_F is on edge AC, and N_F is on BC).

3. Next, we join the points M_F and N_F with a line. This line is the shadow projection in the front view, and it intersects line $X_F Y_F$ at point P_F (see Figure 5.14 (b)).

4. The location of the intersection point P in the top view may be easily obtained by projecting point P_F onto the top view to obtain P_T (Figure 5.14 (c)).

In some cases, the preceding method will not work. Sometimes the line and its shadow do not intersect at all, in which case the line is parallel to the plane. It is also possible that the two may intersect outside the plane, in which case the line intersects the plane outside its boundaries. Finally, the line and its shadow projection can overlap if the line is actually inscribed on the plane.

Figure 5.15 (a) Find the line of intersection of the given planes. (b) Find the point of intersection for plane ABC and lines DE and GF by projecting the vertically-cast shadows of the lines on the plane (lines 1-2 and 3-4) and plotting the intersections of the shadows with DE and GF. (c) Project the points of intersection back onto the top view. Eliminate any part of the line of intersection that lies outside the boundaries of plane ABC. (d) Eliminate the hidden surfaces and shade.

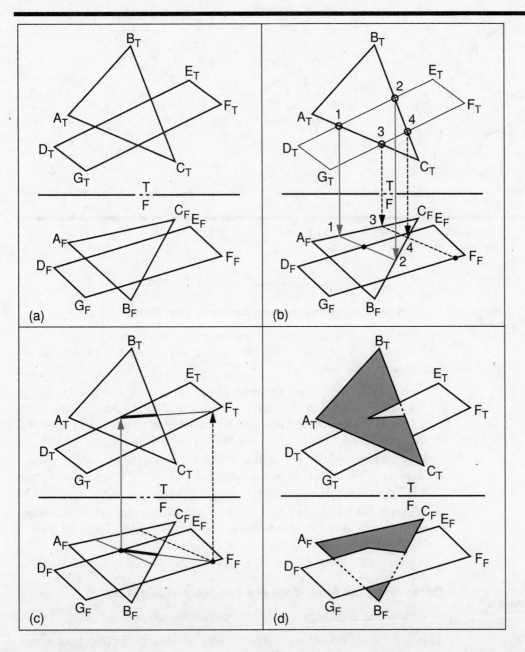

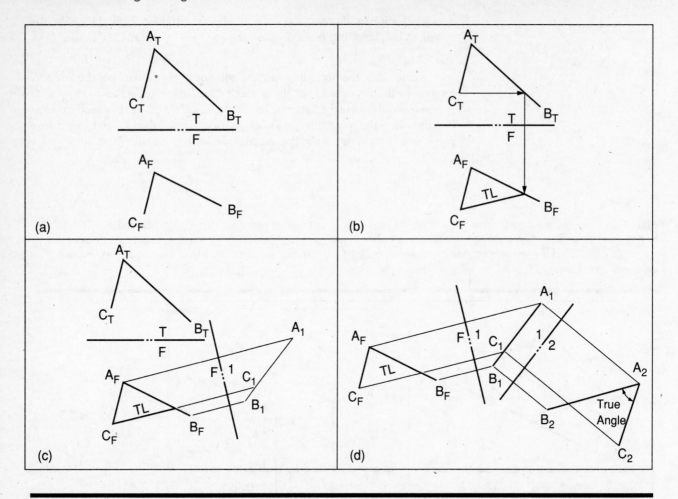

Figure 5.16 (a) Determine the angle between two intersecting lines. (b) Find the true length of a line inside ABC. (c) Find the edge view of plane ABC (d) Measure the true angle between the two lines.

| Example 5.8 | **Finding the Line of Intersection Between Two Planes** |

Find the line of intersection of two planes, shown in Figure 5.15 (a).
This problem is very similar to the one shown in Example 5.7. In this case the procedure is done twice.

1. First, we find the point of intersection of plane ABC and line DE in the front view by plotting the shadow of DE on ABC and marking the intersection of the shadow and line DE (see steps 1–4 in Example 5.7). Find also the point of intersection of plane ABC and line GF (see Figure 5.15 (b)).

2. We then project the points of intersection back onto the top view. Trim any segment of the line of intersection that falls outside the boundaries of plane ABC as shown in Figure 5.15 (c).

3. We finish the problem by determining which surfaces are hidden according to the position of the points in both projection views. This is shown in Figure 5.15 (d).

| Example 5.9 | **Determining the Angle Between Two Intersecting Lines** |

Determine the angle between two intersecting lines, shown in Figure 5.16 (a).

1. First, we use the plane method to obtain a view that shows both lines in true

length (refer to Figure 5.11). This is shown in Figures 5.16 (b), (c), and (d).

2. We then measure the angle between the two lines as shown in Figure 5.16 (d).

Example 5.10

Finding the Angle Between a Line and a Plane

Find the angle between a line and a plane, shown in Figure 5.17 (a).

1. We obtain the true-size view of plane ABC as illustrated in Figures 5.17 (b), (c), and (d).

2. We find the true-length view of line XY using view 2 as the adjacent view so that plane ABC is again seen as an edge (see Figure 5.17 (e). We can now obtain the true angle between the line and the plane in view 3.

Figure 5.17 Find the angle between a line and a plane. (b) Find the true length of a line inside ABC. (c) Find the edge view of ABC. (d) Find the true size view of ABC. (e) Find the true length of XY and obtain the true angle between the line and the plane (view 3).

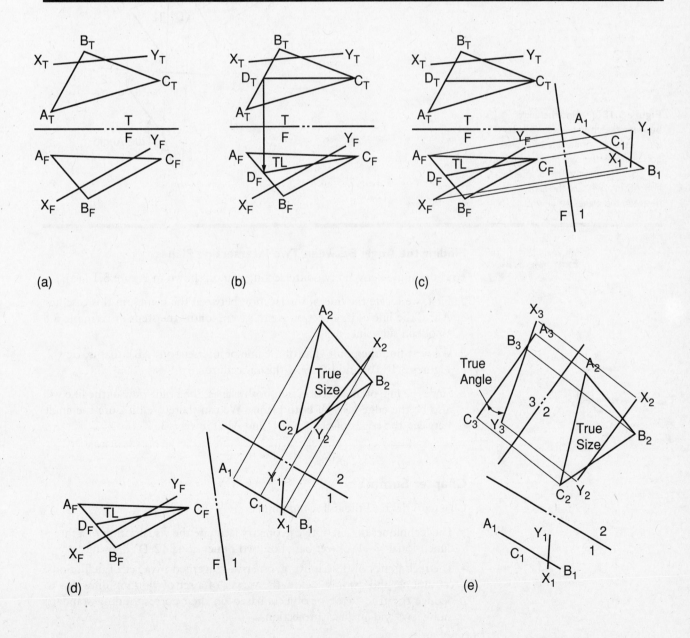

(a) (b) (c)

(d) (e)

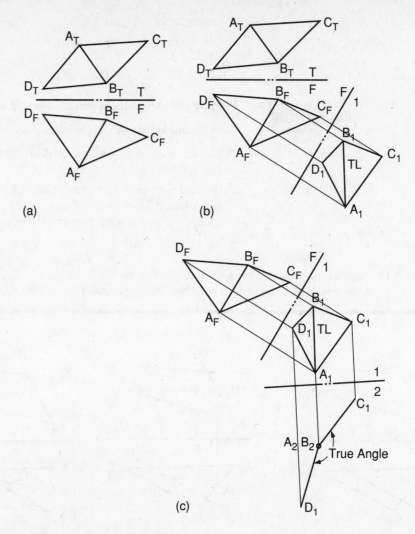

Figure 5.18 (a) Find the angle between the given planes. (b) Find the true length of the line of intersection between the two planes. (c) Find the point view of the line of intersection AB and measure the angle between the planes in View 2.

Example 5.11	**Finding the Angle Between Two Intersecting Planes**

Find the angle between two intersecting planes, shown in Figure 5.18 (a).

1. First, we locate the line of intersection between the planes, in this case line AB. If the line of intersection is not given, follow the steps in Example 5.8 to obtain such line.

2. We next find the point view of the line of intersection (AB), that is, view 2. Figures 5.18 (b) and (c) show this procedure.

3. Since the line of intersection is in both planes, the point view of the line will also be the edge view of both planes. We can therefore measure the angle between the edges of planes ABC and ABD in view 2.

Chapter Summary

Chapter 5 detailed the following points:

- The techniques of descriptive geometry facilitate the visualization of a three-dimensional (3-D) object based on two-dimensional (2-D) drawings.

- The techniques of descriptive geometry—governed by a set of definitions, conditions, and axioms—allow the viewer of a set of working drawings to deduce the true shape of objects based on their corresponding standard multiviews and auxiliary projections.

• Some problems that arise when trying to analyze drawings require the techniques of spatial geometry, which are based on the principles of descriptive geometry. These techniques allow the true shape and spatial position of objects to be determined, even when the entities comprising an object are not parallel to the projection plane in any of the original projections provided. Such shapes and positions are determined by construction of additional primary or secondary auxiliary views.

• Certain types of geometric information regarding an object require conducting a spatial analysis of the object, based on its multiviews. Such information includes the clearance between a point and a line, the clearance between two oblique lines, the clearance between a point and a plane, the point of intersection of a line and a plane, the line of intersection of two planes, and the angles between two intersecting lines, between a line and a plane, and between two planes.

REFERENCES AND SUGGESTED READINGS

American Society of Mechanical Engineers (ASME). ANSI Y14.3—1975. New York: American Society of Mechanical Engineers, 1975.

Paré, E. G., et al. Descriptive Geometry. New York: Macmillan, 1965.

Rodriguez, W. E. "Axiom-Based Spatial Analysis and Visualization." Journal of Theoretical Graphics and Computing, 1(1).

Wellman, B. L. Technical Descriptive Geometry. New York: McGraw-Hill, 1957.

EXERCISES

5.1 Figures 5.19 through 5.24 consist of multiview projection sets that are incomplete (that is, have missing lines). Determine the missing lines and sketch a logical isometric drawing that corresponds to each of the completed multiview sets. (Optional: Since more than one correct solution is possible for each multiview set, sketch all viable solutions.)

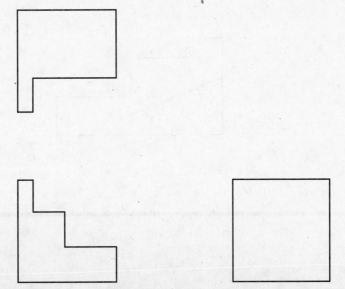

Figure 5.19

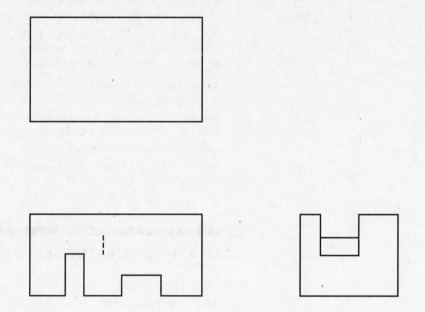

Figures 5.20

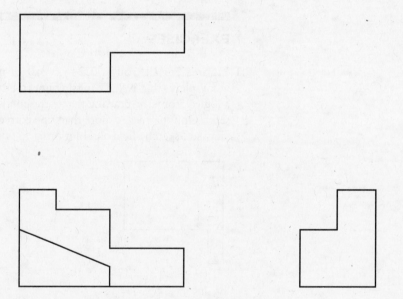

Figures 5.21

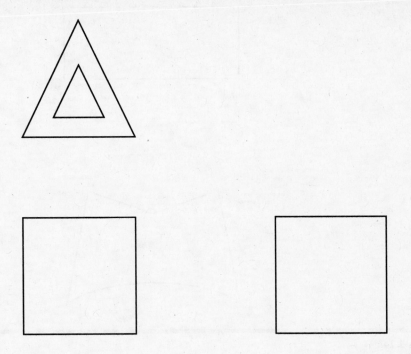

Figure 5.22

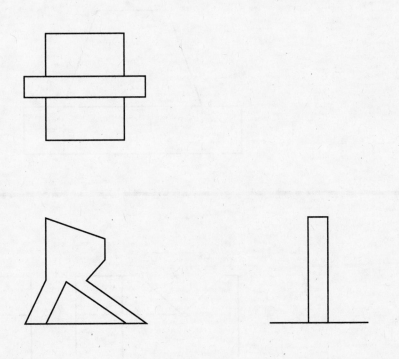

Figure 5.23

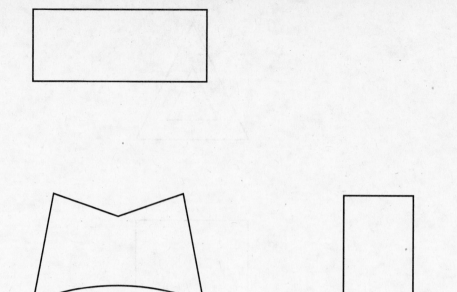

Figure 5.24

5.2 Given the frontal and right-side views in Figures 5.25 and 5.26, sketch the missing top view and the isometric drawing for each set.

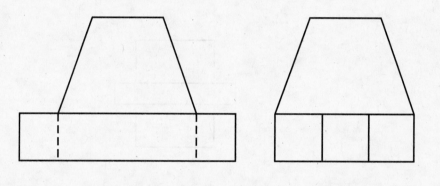

Figure 5.25

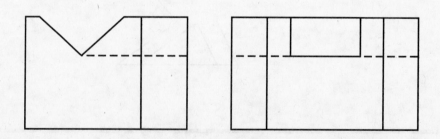

Figure 5.26

5.3 Find the true size of the guide wires for the tower shown in the front view in Figure 5.27. Use a 1" = 100' scale.

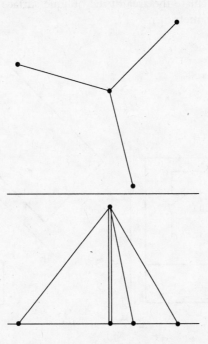

Figure 5.27

5.4 Obtain a true view of one side of the truncated pyramid shown in Figure 5.28 by drawing the necessary auxiliary views. Determine the angle between each of the planes of the pyramid.

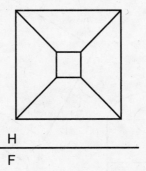

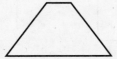

Figure 5.28

5.5. Complete the missing lines in the auxiliary view, and sketch the isometric drawing for the sets of multiviews given in Figures 5.29 and 5.30. (Optional: Calculate the area of the oblique surface and the volume of the object [scale 1:1, metric].)

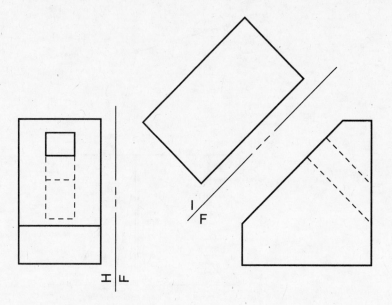

Figure 5.29

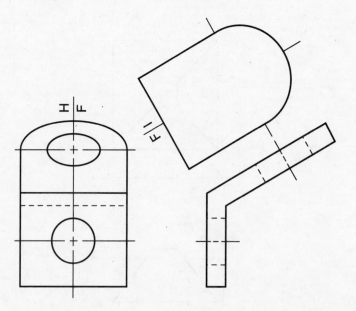

Figure 5.30

5.6 Based on the given multiview sets in Figures 5.31 and 5.32, perform the necessary spatial geometric analysis to do the following:

a. Complete the missing lines.

b. Draw the secondary auxiliary view.

c. Determine the angles between all the surfaces.

d. Calculate the area of the oblique surface(s) (scale 1:1, metric).

e. Sketch the isometric drawing.

f. Calculate the volume of each object (scale 1:1, metric).

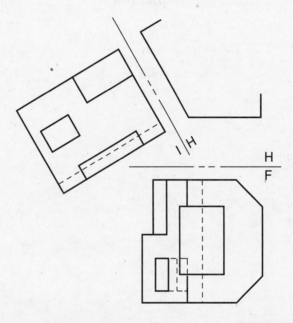

Figure 5.31

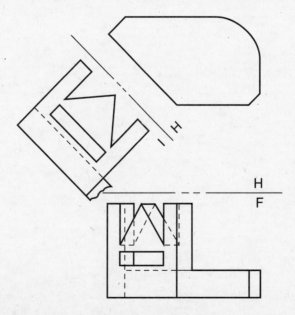

Figure 5.32

5.7 Draw an image and/or write a short statement that describes or defines each of the key terms, listed below, used in this chapter:

Adjacent view	Point view of a line
Adjoining view	Primary auxiliary projection
Aligned view	Principal line
Auxiliary projection	Principal plane of projection
Axiom	Related view
Descriptive geometry	Secondary auxiliary projection
Edge view of a plane	Spatial analysis
Oblique line	Spatial geometry
Phantom line	True-length view of a line
Piercing point	True view of a plane

CHAPTER 6 The Design Workstation

Many designers use computers to model and analyze their proposed design solutions. However, not all computers are able to run the types of CAD-modeling, analysis, animation, and visual-simulation programs used in the design process. Designers today use a powerful desktop computer called a workstation. Before workstations were developed, designers used less powerful microcomputers. One drawback of the earlier microcomputers was that they did not have the tremendous amounts of memory required to display and manipulate CAD-generated models, making the design process slow and inefficient. Consequently, the full potential of CAD, as a design tool, was not realized until microcomputers were upgraded (enhanced) to become the powerful workstations that designers use today.

This chapter discusses the design workstation's principal components and the specifications of these components needed to do engineering design work. A designer must be familiar with the components of a design workstation and understand what the components are used for. A designer must also understand the differences between comparable workstations to choose which workstation configuration is best suited to the job.

6.1 DESIGN WORKSTATION BASICS

A **design workstation** (also called an **engineering workstation**) is a set of integrated computer components assembled for an individual designer. It is used to perform very fast calculations and to produce and present information helpful to the designer, such as geometric models, simulations, or working drawings. Design workstations operate through a combination of **hardware** and **software**. A computer's hardware is the physical computer equipment. Software is the program that tells the computer's hardware what to do and when to do it. Given the right combination of hardware and software, called the system's **configuration**, much of today's typical information processing work can be performed by a workstation. Designers can now electronically "sketch," input 3-D data and instructions directly at the workstation, and make on-the-spot changes without having to spend several days or weeks doing tedious calculations or revising manual drawings. Modern workstations are sold by many different manufacturers including Adage, Apollo, Ardent, Control Data, Digital Equipment, Hewlett-Packard, IBM, Intergraph, Prime, Silicon Graphics, SUN Microsystems, Stellar Computer, and Tektronix.

Workstations that do not need to be connected to any other computers in

Figure 6.1 An example of a design produced using a standalone workstation. (Courtesy of Adage, Inc.)

order to work are called **standalone** workstations. In many applications it is desirable for users to share data, and it is generally possible to connect many standalone workstations together in a **network** so that they can communicate with one another. Figure 6.1 shows a design being created on a standalone workstation. Figure 6.2 shows the hardware components of a typical design workstation.

6.2 WORKSTATION HARDWARE

To use any workstation effectively, you need to understand its hardware components and how they interface with one another. This section provides a description of the main hardware components used in a design workstation.

6.2.1 Processing

Workstation hardware is categorized by the four basic operations that it performs: processing, input, output, and storage. **Processing** entails the numerical and character manipulation activities that transform data into information.

Processing is handled by the **central processing unit** (**CPU**), which is mounted on the **motherboard** inside the **system unit** (the computer's main housing). The CPU is a microprocessor, a chip with microscopic electronic circuitry that analyzes every instruction and directs computational activities. The CPU is often referred to as the brain of the computer and is divided into two major units and several minor units. The first major unit is the **arithmetic logic unit** (**ALU**), which performs mathematical and logical operations. The second major unit is the **control unit**, which organizes the operations of the ALU and, consequently, the functions of the entire computer. Small **registers**, also part of the CPU, provide temporary data storage necessary to the function of the computer. The registers also advance a **counter**, which tells the computer to execute the next program line after the current program line has been executed.

Read-only memory, random-access memory, the system clock, and other coordinating chips are mounted on the motherboard along with the CPU. The **system clock** coordinates computer circuit responses. **Read-Only Memory (ROM)** is the permanent memory residing within the microcomputer on a set of silicon chips. Stored in the chips are very basic instructions essential to the operation of the computer. Without the instructions contained in ROM, the computer would not know what to do when first switched on or how to interpret certain types of input. Most ROM information tells the computer to look to a certain input device or a certain place in memory where the computer will get additional information. Because it is so basic to the computer's operation, this memory can only be read by the computer and never can be erased or written over.

Random-Access Memory (RAM), also called read-and-write memory, is the memory space within the computer that holds programs and data needed immediately for processing. This memory is called random access because the computer can access any one part of it without having to examine all of it. RAM chips hold information in the form of electrical charges, and store it in particular locations in the chip called **addresses**. RAM is volatile memory; that is, its contents are not retained when the computer is turned off, because the electrical charges that represent the information stored by the chip are maintained by the computer's power supply. In addition, because of the temporary nature of the information stored in the RAM chip, information in RAM can be modified, written over, or erased.

Also contained in the system unit along with the motherboard are the power supply, which converts alternating current to direct current, and **ports**, which are used to connect other hardware components to the system unit, such as a keyboard or a printer. Figure 6.3 shows the typical system unit's main elements.

6.2.2 Input

A workstation cannot process data unless it is provided by the designer. This is the function of the **input devices** of the design workstation.

There are several devices available to the user to input data into a workstation. The **keyboard** is the most commonly used input device. Although there is no standard keyboard layout, most computer keyboards share the same set of

Figure 6.2 Components of a typical workstation.

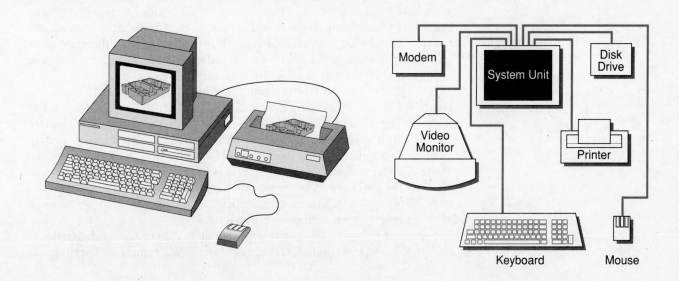

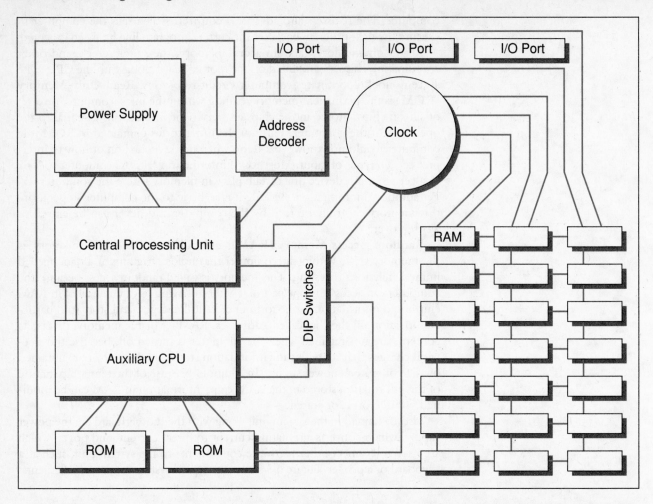

Figure 6.3 System unit components. The CPU, ROM, RAM, and system clock are mounted on the motherboard.

128 alphanumeric characters found in IBM-compatible keyboards. These characters are letters of the alphabet, numbers, and special function characters.

Another useful and popular device for data input is the **mouse**, which can be used to move a cursor on the workstation's screen, to specify locations for data entry, and to select menu commands. The cursor is moved by sliding the mouse around a flat surface. Once the cursor is in the proper position, objects on the screen are selected with the buttons on the mouse. Some mice have only one button, some have several; a three-button mouse is most common (Figure 6.4). Most mice are mechanical and have a ball on their bottom surface that rotates in a socket when the mouse is moved. These types of mice can be used on any surface. Optical mice, in contrast, have no moving parts and are therefore more reliable. They must be used on a special surface, a small pad that reflects the light emitted by the mouse back into detectors in the mouse.

A **digitizer** is another type of input device useful to designers and engineers. Figure 6.5 shows a digitizing tablet and stylus. When the stylus touches the surface of the digitizer, the command associated with that area on the digitizer is executed. A digitizer enables the designer to read in data from an overlay menu or a document map or chart by first placing the document on the surface of the digitizer and marking the boundaries of the document with the stylus. The user then uses the stylus to indicate the desired points within the boundaries. Although digitizers are quite expensive, their value becomes obvious when dealing with large irregular documents.

A **scanner** is a useful input device that is able to read images or design documents into a workstation. A scanner operates like a camera, converting the

Figure 6.4 A mouse. (Courtesy of IBM)

image of a photograph or drawing placed in it into information the workstation can accept. Scanners are helpful when converting drawings into models on the computer.

6.2.3 Output

A designer also needs **output devices** to use a workstation to perform a design task. Input from the designer is processed by the workstation, and the results of the processing must be available to the designer in an easily understood form. This is the function of output devices.

The screen's **monitor**, or **video display**, is the most prominent output device of the workstation system. The monitor is connected to the system through a video card, often purchased separately from the computer. This card is installed in the workstation, and the monitor is plugged into the card, which transforms the computer's output into information the monitor can understand. Some cards are designed to display high-quality, high-resolution graphics, and some inexpensive cards are designed for lower resolution display. Some video graphics cards can display millions of different colors, some only a few colors, and some can display only black, white, and gray. The monitor connected to the video card must be compatible with it. High-quality monitors are usually compatible with lower-quality cards, but a high-quality video card cannot be used with a low-quality monitor. The wide selection of video cards offers the designer a chance to customize the computer to his or her needs. The VGA or Super VGA video cards and monitors are the most popular for IBM-compatible design workstation applications.

Although there are several types of video monitors, the **cathode ray tube** (**CRT**) is the most widely accepted design in the workstation environment (Figure 6.6). The CRT closely resembles a small TV screen. It is a versatile output device and typically is able to display both text (alphanumeric characters) and graphics (pictures or graphs generated by computer programs). The **refresh CRT** device consists of electron guns, a focusing device, horizontal and vertical deflection plates, and a screen coated with thousands of individual phosphors. The electron gun contains a filament that, when heated, emits a stream of electrons. The electrons are focused with an electromagnet into a sharp beam and directed to a specific point on the face of the picture tube. The front face of the screen is coated with small phosphor dots, which the electron beam causes to glow for a short length of time. The phosphors are arranged on the screen in a matrix of points, or **pixels** (a shortened word for picture elements). By illuminating some of the pixels with the electron beam, or by illuminating the pixels at varying levels of intensity, an image is formed on the screen. The image is "refreshed" to keep phosphors glowing by repeatedly illuminating the pixels with the electron beam.

Two types of refresh CRTs are **raster scan** and **random scan**. The raster-scan CRT operates by sweeping the electron beam across every row of pixels on the screen and varying the intensity of the beam as it sweeps. In other words, video raster devices display an image by sequentially drawing out the pixels of the **scan lines** (a row of pixels) that form the **raster** (a regular array of pixels). Raster-scan CRTs are best for displaying solid-shaded areas, since all pixels must be illuminated by the electron beam. Random-scan CRT video monitors handle the pixel display task by directing the beam only to specific pixels on the screen, rather than sweeping across all the pixels in succession. Random-scan monitors are more efficient for drawing lines on the screen, since only the pixels required to draw the line need to be illuminated.

Video displays are classified as either **monochrome**, which display only a single color, or **color**. Monochrome displays are classified according to the number of intensity levels that can be set at an individual pixel. On color displays, each pixel is actually a combination of red, green, and blue phosphors and the intensity of the red, blue, and green phosphors determines the color at each pixel. For example, yellow can be specified by giving high values for red and green phosphors and a low value for the blue. Color displays are classified according to the number of colors that can be specified at each pixel.

Another valuable output device of the workstation system is the **printer**. Most printers fall into one of three main categories: dot-matrix, letter-quality, and laser printers. Dot-matrix printers are inexpensive and fast and are usually able to print graphic output. Their disadvantage is that their print quality may not be acceptable for some jobs, especially when they are operated at top speed.

Figure 6.5 Digitizer and stylus. (Courtesy of HP)

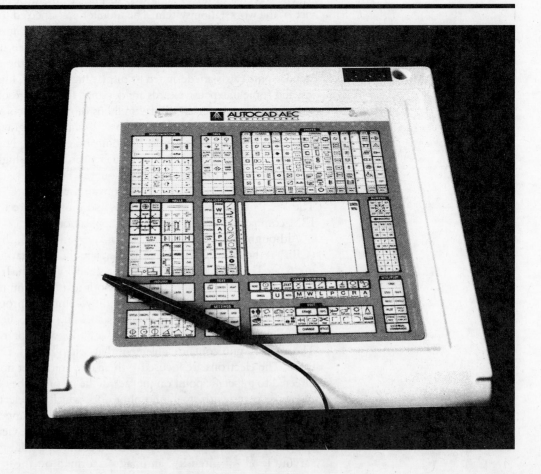

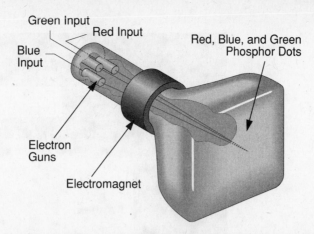

Green Input

Red Input

Blue
Input

Red, Blue, and Green
Phosphor Dots

Electron
Guns

Electromagnet

Figure 6.6 Schematic drawing of a color cathode ray tube. (Courtesy of Larry Hodges)

Letter-quality printers work much like a typewriter, producing high-quality text, but they cannot print the graphics required for computer-aided design. Laser printers are well worth their sometimes higher cost, since they are quick, quiet, and capable of producing quality graphic output. Most of the CAD drawings in this book were produced originally with the laser printer shown in Figure 6.7.

Plotters, unlike printers, draw by using small ink pens of as many as fourteen different colors and pen widths. The computer tells the plotter to choose a certain pen, move it to a certain point, and press the pen against the paper. Flat-bed plotters operate by holding the drawing surface fixed on a flat bed and moving the print head on the surface to create the desired picture. Drum plotters function by rolling the drawing surface over a revolving cylinder and moving pens back and forth across the direction of flow. Figure 6.8 shows two large-format drafting plotters. Large-format drafting plotters are capable of printing up to A0-size paper (841 x 1189 mm) or E-size paper (34" x 44").

Plotters are faster than most laser printers, but they are noisy. The plotter has the ability to draw intricate shapes and designs on paper, vellum, mylar, or transparent film, providing output that resembles high-quality manual ink drawings. Maps, graphs, blueprints, and other charts can be generated on the plotter easily and with very high quality. They are expensive but perform detailed printing and drawing tasks very well.

Figure 6.7 Laser printer. (Courtesy of HP)

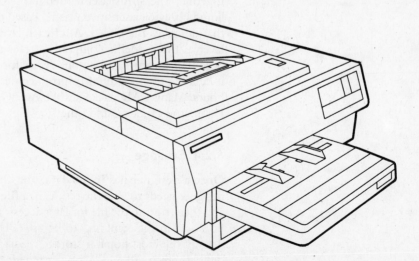

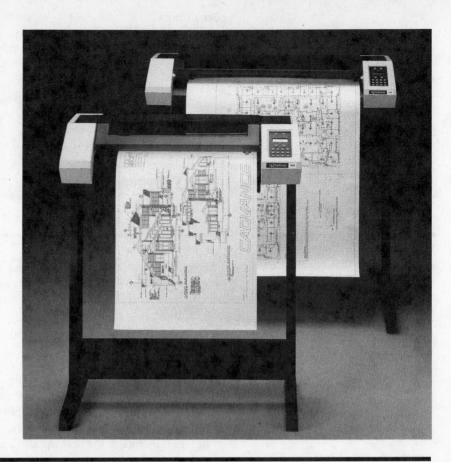

Figure 6.8 Pen Plotter.
(Courtesy of Houston Instruments)

A new output device available to the designer is the **stereolithography apparatus** (**SLA**). Stereolithography is a patented process developed by 3D Systems, Inc., that creates a plastic prototype model from a computer graphics geometric model. This process eliminates the need for machining or tooling when building prototypes of devices. By using a laser beam that hardens layers of ultraviolet-sensitive plastics, the SLA is capable of hardening cross sections of plastic in layers, one at a time, to form the three-dimensional shape of the object, much like cutting thin slices of a real solid model and gluing them together. The SLA's laser hardens cross sections of the object on the surface of liquid ultraviolet-sensitive plastic, based on the solid modeling CAD database that describes the object. After each layer hardens, it adheres to the previous layer as the model is completed (refer to Figure 6.9). Stereolithography is becoming a very useful output device for designers and manufacturers because it cuts the time required to produce design prototypes from weeks down to hours. Many CAD packages like AutoCAD I-DEAS, CADKEY, Intergraph, Parametric Modeler, and others have interfaces that work with the SLA.

6.2.4 Storage

Once a designer has input data, and the workstation has processed it, the designer needs to save the results in a **file**, which is a collection of related data, and then to store the file for later access; the workstation's software, too, must be stored in the computer to be used. This is the function of storage devices. Two of the most popular storage media are **hard disks**, which are aluminum disks covered with microscopic magnetic particles, and **diskettes** (floppy disks), which are thin plastic disks covered with magnetic particles. Both types of disk storage require the installation of a **disk controller card** in one of the workstation's slots, which assists the computer in transmitting or accessing data from a disk.

Hard disks are standard in all workstations. They are preferred because of their ability to store large quantities of data and recall that information quickly. From time to time, however, the data on a hard disk can be lost (often due to user error); therefore, hard disks are often backed up, by copying their information onto floppy disks or tape cassettes. Hard disk drives are also referred to as fixed disk drives, since the disk is usually sealed.

Diskettes, or floppy disks, are very popular among engineering designers and come in three sizes: 8", 5¼"(5.25"), and 3½" (3.5"). Eight-inch disks are becoming obsolete because of the large size of the disk and the increasing efficiency of the smaller disks. The middle 5.25" size is a flexible double-sided/double-density (DS/DD) disk, with a typical capacity of 360K bytes (remember that one K byte, or kilobyte, equals 1,024 bytes). The 5.25" disk is also available as a double-sided/high-density (DS/HD) diskette that will store 1.2 M bytes (one M byte, or megabyte, equals 1,024 K bytes, or 1,048,576 bytes) of data. The small, 3½" diskette, used first in portable workstations, has gained popularity since it can hold more information (as much as 1.44 M) on a smaller, better-protected diskette encased in hard plastic.

It is important to keep in mind that information is stored on a magnetic storage device by changing the polarity of a very small section of magnetic film that has been applied to either a plastic or metal base. This means that any device that generates a magnetic field has the potential to erase the information in storage. Also, over the life of the storage device, the polarity of the particles of metallic oxide will wear off, and the stored data will gradually be lost. Consequently, it is a good idea to have a **backup disk** or tape made so that information will not be lost. You should also back up your CAD files often by copying the files onto a disk other than the original.

Another form of information storage media is the **optical disk**. Optical disks often are used for multimedia design presentations involving text, images, photos, animations, sound, and video. At present, optical disks are rarely used in actual design work. However, it is expected that designers will use this powerful storage technology more in the future to access design databases such as CAD symbol libraries and material specifications. A compact disk ROM

Figure 6.9 Schematic drawing of a stereolithography apparatus. (Courtesy of 3D, Inc. and Dataquest)

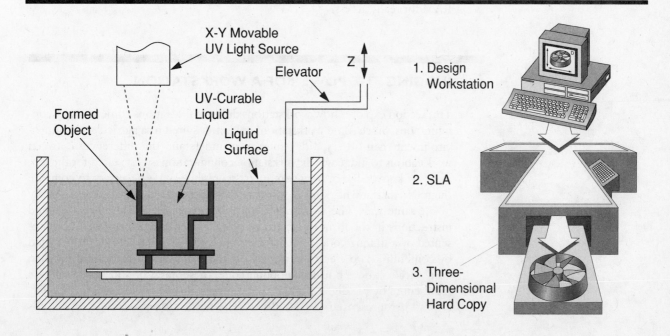

X-Y Movable UV Light Source

Elevator

Z

Formed Object

UV-Curable Liquid

Liquid Surface

1. Design Workstation

2. SLA

3. Three-Dimensional Hard Copy

(CD-ROM), the most common optical disk in use today, may exceed 600 MB of storage capacity—enough to hold more than 100 copies of a thick book—while a single 3.5" diskette can store a maximum of 1.44 MB. CD-ROMs, unlike diskettes or hard disks, can only be read—the data on them cannot be changed or new information added to them by the workstation user.

6.2.5 Communications

Communication devices are the fifth type of hardware component used by many design workstations. Communication between workstations allows designers to share information and ideas almost instantly. Communication devices also allow designers to pass their ideas directly to computers that control machining tools, thus allowing a product to be created by a machine without a single plan being drawn.

The oldest communication device still common today is the **modem**, a shortened term for MOdulator-DEModulator. This is a device that enables a computer to communicate with another computer through telephone lines. In addition, the modem allows designers to access computer information services, such as CompuServe, which maintain large telecommunications network that provide access to on-line assistance and tutorials. A modem on one end of a telephone line takes the output from a computer and translates the digital information into audible signals, or modulates the output. On the other end of the telephone line, a modem in another computer translates the audible tones back into digital information, or demodulates the input. Modems come in two basic types: external and internal. Both must have a telephone jack for the phone line, and both must have some form of interface with the computer. The major difference between them is that the external modem sits alongside the computer and is connected to the workstation through a communications port, while the internal modem is connected inside the system unit and does not require an external port. Software, included with the modem or purchased separately, enables the workstation to take advantage of the modem's capabilities.

Another method of communication involves using **local area networks** (**LAN**s) that permit connecting design workstations with other workstations and **file servers**. File servers handle the network administration in systems of computers connected through a LAN. They are used for backing up files from a central location, stacking plotting requests in order of their entry (called "queueing") sending administrative messages, and temporarily placing files in RAM for ready access.

6.3 JUDGING THE POWER OF A WORKSTATION

This section explores how workstations differ. Workstations come in many configurations. Since some workstations are better suited to a particular design environment than others, a designer must understand the differences between workstations to judge which workstation configuration is best suited for the job.

Some knowledge of how computers represent data is necessary to compare them. No matter what kind of workstation you purchase, they all work basically in the same way. The workstation accepts, processes, and outputs data and instructions in the form of electronic signals. Each character of data is represented by a unique code, which is a set of electronic pulses. Codes are created by combining two electronic states: on and off. "On" means a pulse ocurs; "off" means it does not. In computer code, these states of "on" and "off" are represented by the digits 1 and 0. For example, in one coding scheme, the letter "a" is represented as 01000001. The workstation's storage capacity is measured by how many of these digits can be stored.

The term **binary** means made up of two parts. The digits 1 and 0, which refer to the two states of "on" and "off," are called binary digits, or **bits**. One bit is either a 1 or a 0, a **byte** equals 8 bits, a **kilobyte** (K or **KB**) equals 1,024 bytes, and a **megabyte** (M or **MB**) equals 1,024 kilobytes, or over one million bytes.

In judging the power of a workstation, the designer is most interested in how a workstation's processing, input, output, storage, and communications capabilities differ.

6.3.1 Processing

One characteristic used to describe the capabilities of a design workstation is its **RAM capacity**. RAM capacity is measured in kilobytes or megabytes; for simplicity, one byte equals one character. For example, if you type a short memo with 2,000 characters in it, it would require around 2 kilobytes, or 2K of RAM, to hold it in memory. Most design workstations require at least 4 MB to 8 MB of RAM, but 16 MB or 32 MB of RAM is common.

Workstations are often described on the basis of their CPU **word size**. These "words" are not words such as the ones you are now reading; instead, they are groups of bits that represent letters or numbers or any type of keyboard character. There are three main microprocessor word sizes: 8 bits, 16 bits, and 32 bits. Each microprocessor picks up the largest number of bits that it can handle, manipulates them, and returns them to the computer's memory. The larger the word size, the fewer cycles it takes for the microprocessor to perform program instructions. For example, a 32-bit microprocessor will be able to process data faster than a 16-bit microprocessor.

Another characteristic often used to describe the capabilities of a design workstation is the rate at which it can perform functions, or its **clock speed**. The clock speed of the CPU is measured in **megahertz** (**MHz**). A microprocessor's clock is much faster than the clock used to tell time. On Intel's 80286 microprocessor, it functions at 4.77 to 16 MHz. On the 80386 or 80436 microprocessor, it functions at 20 to 50 MHz. The higher the clock speed, the quicker the microprocessor does its job. Consequently, the larger the word size and the higher the clock speed, the faster the microcomputer.

In some workstations, a chip called a **math coprocessor** speeds up math calculations, and therefore will allow most CAD programs to run faster. Both of Intel's 286- and 386-class machines are based on integer arithmetic (they do not handle fractions or decimal numbers efficiently). Therefore, they are not classified as workstations, and CAD programs will run slowly on these machines. If a math coprocessor has been installed on a 286 or a 386, the math coprocessor works with the CPU to do the math requiring fractions and decimals. For the 80286 machine the math coprocessor is the 80287, and for the 80386 it is the 80387 coprocessor. However, unlike the 286 and 386 microprocessor chips, Intel's 486 microprocessor does not require an additional math coprocessor. The 486 chip is a 386 microprocessor with a 387 math coprocessor assembled onto the same piece of silicon as the CPU, along with other features that increase its efficiency. If the CAD package you are using is written to take advantage of these coprocessors, they will increase the execution speed of your software.

A final way to judge workstations is by their graphics display efficiency. The efficiency is usually given in terms of the number of lines (or vectors) that the system can draw per second and the number of smoothly shaded polygons that can be displayed per second.

6.3.2 Input

There are many input devices available for the design workstation, and each is suited to a particular task. Keyboards, digitizers, scanners, and mice all differ, and the designer must be able to distinguish between them to judge which one is suitable for the design task at hand.

Workstation keyboards come in many configurations. Although they all have the standard letter and number keys, they differ in other ways. Most keyboards include **function keys** which allow the user to execute functions or commands with one keystroke. Some keyboards have function keys along the top of the keyboard, others have them along the left side of the keyboard, and others have function keys along both the top and the left side of the keyboard. Some CAD packages require these keys to access immediate commands used for executing quick geometric construction operations. Keyboards may also have an additional set of number keys, a set of editing keys, and cursor positioning keys. Some keyboard keys click when they are pressed, and others do not.

Digitizers mainly differ in their resolution. A typical resolution for a design workstation's digitizer is 480 lines per centimeter, and a positioning accuracy of within 0.5 millimeter.

A scanner's characteristics are similar to a video display's. Some scanners are monochrome, and others are color. Scanners are also specified by how many intensities they are capable of resolving. A monochrome, 256 intensity level scanner is satisfactory for most applications, but a full-color scanner may be useful if multimedia presentations are desired.

Mice come in many varieties. A three-button mechanical mouse is satisfactory for most CAD applications. Optical mice, however, are more reliable than mechanical mice and are included with most higher-performance workstations, such as the SUN Microsystems SPARCstation and the Silicon Graphics IRIS.

6.3.3 Output

Input from the designer is processed by the workstation, and the results of the processing must be available to the designer in an easily understood form. This is the function of output devices. The capabilities of available output devices, such as the video display and the printer, are therefore significant in judging the power of the workstation.

The quality of the generated picture on a video display depends on the **resolution**, that is, the total number of pixels (picture elements or definable locations) on a display screen. Screen resolution is given by the number of pixels per centimeter vertically and horizontally, or by the total number of pixels in the horizontal and vertical directions. The resolution can also be defined as the width of a single row of pixels drawn on the CRT screen. A resolution of 1,024 pixels horizontally by 768 pixels vertically is the most popular today. The older standard of 640 pixels by 480 pixels is also widely used by designers using IBM-compatible workstations.

The simplest monochrome monitors display each pixel as either on or off. The illusion of shading different areas is obtained by using different patterns of on and off pixels. Monochrome displays that allow more variety in the pixel intensity are described by the number of bits of information that can be specified per pixel. The number of intensity levels is equal to the number of binary numbers that can be expressed by the bits, which is calculated by two raised to the power of the number of bits. For example, a two-bit display allows four gray levels to be displayed per pixel, or two to the second power, with the levels associated with the binary numbers 00, 01, 10, and 11. A four-bit display allows sixteen levels to be displayed, and an eight-bit display allows 256 levels to be displayed.

As with monochrome displays, color displays are also classified by the number of bits of information that can be specified for each pixel. Most color displays can potentially display any combination of 256 intensities of red (R), 256 intensities of green (G), and 256 intensities of blue (B), for a total of 16,777,216, or 256 x 256 x 256, potential combinations. The number of combinations that can potentially be displayed is referred to as the **palette** of the display. For an eight-bit display, only 256 of the possible combinations can be displayed at a time. The system may preassign the combinations that are available, or it may allow the user to choose which combinations are available. In a twenty-four-bit display (eight bits each for R, G, and B), any of the 16,777,216 combinations can be displayed at each pixel. Twenty-four-bit displays are sometimes referred to as "full color" or "true color" displays.

As with video output, the quality of printed output also depends on the resolution. Laser printers can print at a 300-dots-per-inch (dpi) resolution or better (1,270 dpi is typical), providing crisp graphics and easy-to-read text. Laser printers work like copying machines, even using some of the same components. A laser printer with PostScript capability is also desired by some design workstation users. PostScript is a well-accepted and versatile printer language supported by many design workstations. To print highly detailed drawings or to accommodate printer languages such as PostScript, laser printers need memory. At least 4 MB of RAM is required to accommodate the needs of most designers.

6.3.4 Storage

Storage media vary in physical size and capacity to store information. The 3.5" diskette is preferred for portable storage of small amounts of information because of its small size and rugged plastic housing. A 3.5" diskette comes in two information capacities, double-density (DD) and high-density (HD). Double-density 3.5" diskettes store up to 720 KB, and high-density 3.5" diskettes store up to 1.44 MB.

In addition to one or two drives for floppy disks, a design workstation requires a hard disk that is fast and has large information capacity. Hard-disk speed is measured in milliseconds and is related to how fast a hard disk can access data. A typical speed for a fast hard drive is 18 milliseconds or better. Hard disks are available in capacities of 10 MB to thousands of MB. A disk drive that holds at least 220 MB is recommended for a design workstation, since the hard disk must hold both the workstation's software and its data. CAD modeling software is sophisticated and requires a significant quantity of memory to store it; also, design databases are usually extensive.

Hard drives also differ in the way they communicate with the computer. A designer only needs to know that the hard drive's way of communicating must match the card that controls it. Common communication formats for hard drives are SCSI, RLL, MFM, and IDE. SCSI (pronounced "scuzzy") is standard in Unix-based workstations.

A SCSI disk controller card is also usually required for a CD-ROM. CD-ROMs can store much more data than diskettes, but they are much slower. A design workstation requires a CD-ROM with a typical average access time of not more than 350 milliseconds. A feature of some CD-ROMs allows them to operate like a standard audio compact-disk player.

6.3.5 Communications

Modems permit workstations to exchange data, but some modems are better than others. The effectiveness of a modem is measured in its speed, or **baud rate**. This number, roughly equal to bits per second, ranges from 110 up to 9,600 baud and refers to the speed at which the modem can receive and transmit information along the phone line. A speed of 2,400 baud is the standard over phone lines, while 9,600 baud, although now also available for phone lines, is the standard for hard-wired transmission.

| Example 6.1 | **Sample Workstation Configurations: A Comparison** |

The configuration requirements of two design workstations described below are followed by some designers to achieve maximum graphics software performance. Here we list the components of an IBM-compatible workstation and a SUN Microsystems workstation.

An IBM-compatible design workstation might include the following:

1. An Intel 80436 (32-bit microprocessor) CPU with a minimum clock speed of 25 MHz and at least 8 MB of RAM.

2. Three storage devices: a 3.5"/1.44 MB and a 5.25"/1.2 MB diskette drive, plus a 16 millisecond, 220 MB hard-drive disk.

3. A standard or enhanced IBM-compatible keyboard.

4. A color VGA (video graphics adapter) card and 14" (diagonal) monitor with 1024 x 768 resolution (1,024 pixels high by 768 pixels wide).

5. A Microsoft three-button mouse.

6. One parallel and two serial ports.

7. A communication card, or modem.

A SUN Microsystems SPARCstation typically includes the following:

1. A 40 MHz SPARC integer unit and a SPARC floating-point unit (equivalent to a CPU and a math coprocessor).

2. 32 MB of RAM on the motherboard.

3. A 3.5"/1.44 MB diskette drive and a 14 millisecond, 424 MB hard disk.

4. Several communication ports of different formats, including ethernet, and an audio port for multimedia presentations.

5. A 19" 1280 x 1024 resolution color display, with 24-bit true color.

6. A three-button optical mouse.

7. A 107-key, low-profile keyboard.

Note that neither of the configurations listed above includes a printer or plotter, though these items are generally regarded as essential in a design workstation.

6.4 WORKSTATION SOFTWARE

A design workstation system has two main interdependent components: software and hardware. Software programs, such as CAD and geometric modeling packages, consist of coded instructions that direct the computer hardware. For software to be executed, it must be loaded from a storage device, such as the hard disk or diskettes, into RAM. The computer then follows the instructions in the software step by step to perform such tasks as asking the user for information, printing a response, or drawing a line on the video display.

Software does not process data and manage information on its own; human action or direction is required to make the software useful. The term **interactive** refers to the relationship between user and software. The workstation user directs the software running in the computer system to execute certain instructions, and the computer responds to the instructions with, for example, some output or a message displayed on the screen. Based on the user's perception of the output or the displayed message, he or she then issues more instructions. This interaction continues until a particular task is accomplished.

CAD modeling software packages are called **user-friendly** if they allow users to access options easily and to accomplish their goals with a minimum of com-

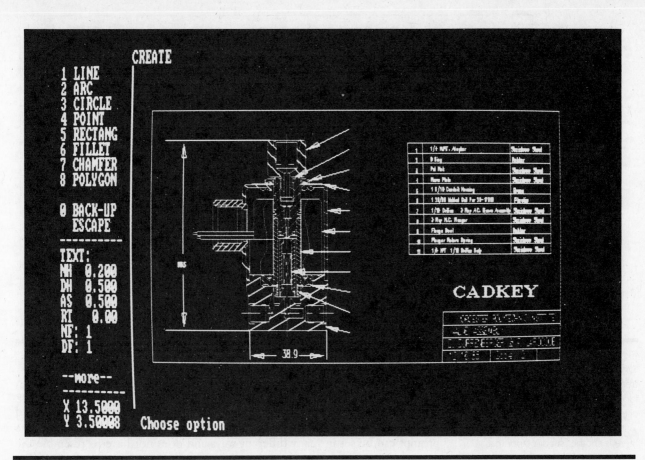

Figures 6.10 User-friendly menu. The user can create the shape listed in the left side of the menu by pressing a function key number on the keyboard that corresponds to the shape. (Courtesy of CADKEY)

plication. **Menus** are screen-displayed lists of options from which users select an operation to be performed by typing certain characters on the keyboard or by using a mouse to select the option. Figure 6.10 shows two user-friendly menu styles. Many CAD modeling software packages allow designers to customize their menus to include special functions. **Macros** are functions that the user can define to customize software and speed up frequently executed tasks. Menus and macros provide an efficient, user-friendly way of using the design workstation.

Software can be categorized into three groups by the job it does: operating systems, application software, and programming languages. The operating system (OS) of a workstation controls the way the computer utilizes its resources. Application software is what the operator uses to perform a task, such as designing a part, simulating how something works, or writing a report. A programming language is software that helps in **programming** or writing new software.

6.4.1 Operating Systems: DOS and Unix

Operating systems are computer programs that direct all disk operations and allow you to use peripheral devices such as a display monitor, a mouse, and a plotter. Operating systems control how you store and recover information, and they process the commands you enter from the keyboard or mouse. Operating systems are used to perform the following operations: formatting new disks, copying files, deleting old files, listing files, and backing up files for safekeeping. An operating system must be running in the system unit before a computer can begin any application program.

Formatting a new disk prepares it to store files. All disks need to be formatted before use, although some diskettes are available that have been preformatted at the factory. You can also reformat a used disk, but it will destroy any information that was on it.

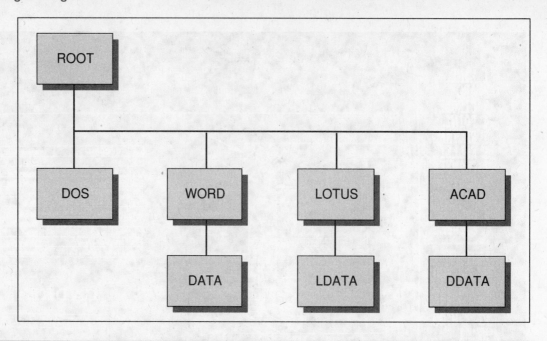

Figure 6.11 An example of a directory tree. The root directory in this tree contains four subdirectories, one for the operating system and three for different application software packages. Within each application subdirectory there is another subdirectory that contains data files specific to that application package. (Courtesy of Georgia Tech Education Extension)

If you turn on a workstation and see on your screen a combination of symbols such as: C> or /usr/people/guest>, it means that the operating system is ready to accept your commands. It is called the system's **prompt** and is used to let you know that the system is ready for input by the user. The prompt can be set in many different ways and does not have to resemble the examples shown here. However, users often use the prompt to display what directory they are in.

A **directory** is a list of files, in the same way that a telephone directory is a list of people's names and telephone numbers. Creating a set of directories on a hard disk or diskette is a way of logically organizing files to keep them together and make it easy to find them. In addition to files, directories can also contain other directories, called **subdirectories**.

A set of directories is often organized in a **tree**, which, like a real tree, has a root and branches (Figure 6.11). The **root directory** is the main directory, or starting point. The root directory can contain files and other directories. Those directories, in turn, can contain files and other directories. The branches of a directory tree are the **paths** you follow to find a file. For example, suppose Melba is a workstation user looking for a file called "data" on a disk that has a directory called "melba" in a directory called "people" in the root directory. From the root directory, she could go to the directory called "people," then to the directory "melba," where she will find her file called "data." The path to "data" is "/people/melba," where the "/" (slash) character is used to specify that the next name in the path is a subdirectory. The first slash specifies the root directory, because there are no directories listed before it. A file can be reached by following the path to it or by specifying the name of the path with the name of the file, such as "/people/melba/data." A particular hard disk or diskette can also be specified in a directory path. The name of the disk is usually put first in the path name before the slash. The **default drive** is the disk that will be searched if no specific disk is indicated in the path name.

Graphically-oriented versions of operating systems provide **icons** (symbols or graphic images) to perform many operations, such as loading a piece of application software into the system. When an icon is selected by using a mouse, the software associated with the icon is loaded. Icons depict the software graphically, reminding the user what software is available. Graphically-oriented operating systems also may provide highlighted bars or **pull-down menus** to help the user select the available options with either a mouse or the keyboard arrows. A pull-down menu only appears when you select a specific area of the screen with the mouse, as if you are pulling down a window shade with the menu options printed on it. An example of a graphically-oriented operating system, or **graphical user interface** (GUI, pronounced "gooey"), is Microsoft's Windows (see Figure 6.12), an operating system for IBM-compatible workstations. Microsoft Windows and other GUIs use **program managers**, or additional software, that allow the user to work with several programs on the screen at the same time. Common GUIs are MIT's X Windows, Apple Macintosh Finder, Microsoft Windows, OS/2 Presentation Manager, SUN's NeWS, and Silicon Graphic's 4Sight.

DOS (Microsoft's MS-DOS and IBM's PC-DOS and its derivatives) is the most frequently installed operating system in 386- and 486-class machines. As do other operating systems, DOS manages the flow of information between what is stored on the floppy and hard disks and the computer's active memory (RAM). Microsoft Corporation's MS-DOS has been the standard operating system for IBM-compatible workstations. However, OS/2 (Operating System/2), also developed by Microsoft for the IBM PS/2 workstation, has gained some popularity among CAD users because it has some additional capabilities, including **multitasking**. Multitasking is the capability of running several programs simultaneously.

Bell Labs developed another popular operating system, **Unix**, especially for the use of the engineering and scientific visualization fields. Unix is now used in fields ranging from architecture to zoology. A multitasking graphics interface is usually available for Unix. Unix, or a comparable operating system, is available for almost every brand of computer. According to *MicroCAD News* magazine, "Unix lives in many forms, all under license to AT&T. IBM has AIX, Hewlett-Packard has HP-UX, DEC has Ultrix, Apple has A/UX, and Microsoft has developed Xenix."

The Unix operating system, like DOS, is a set of programs that controls the workstation. Unlike DOS, Unix provides a multitasking, **multi-user** environ-

Figure 6.12 Microsoft Windows, a popular user interface for machines running under DOS. The creation of documents containing both text and graphics, like the one shown in the lower left, is made possible by Windows' ability to have more than one program on the screen at once. (Courtesy of Microsoft)

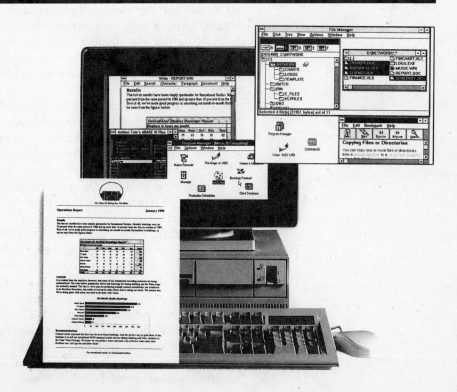

```
C:\: cd temp

C:\TEMP: dir
  Volume in drive C is VISUALIZATION
  Directory of C:\TEMP
  .              <DIR>           12-07-90      8:24a
  ..             <DIR>           12-07-90      8:24a
  DATA1            1234           9-10-91      8:34a
        3 File(s)    2990080 bytes free
C:\TEMP: copy datal data2
        1 File(s) copied

C:\TEMP: mkdir design

C:\TEMP: dir
  Volume in drive C is VISUALIZATION
  Directory of C:\TEMP
  .              <DIR>           12-07-90      8:24a
  ..             <DIR>           12-07-90      8:24a
  DATA1            1234           9-10-91      8:34a
  DATA2            1234           9-10-91      8:34a
  DESIGN         <DIR>           9-11-91       8:59a
        5 File(s)    2985984 bytes free
C:\TEMP:
```

Figure 6.13 Example 6.2: Using DOS.

ment. A multi-user system permits many users to execute software on a machine at the same time. A multi-user system must keep track of **user numbers** to distinguish between users, and **passwords** to tell who can and cannot access the system. To use a multi-user workstation, such as one running Unix, a user must know his or her user number and password. The process of telling the workstation who you are by your user number and password is called the **login**. A user number and password are not needed for DOS, as only one person can use the system at a time.

Case sensitivity is another difference between Unix and DOS important to the operating system beginner. Unix is **case-sensitive**; that is, upper and lower case characters are seen as different by the operating system. DOS is not case-sensitive. For instance, DOS does not distinguish between "a" and "A."

There are interactive tutorials available for most types of operating systems. Your institution CAD/CAE or computing facility manager can provide you with the access procedure for these tutorials. You are encouraged to learn more about Unix and DOS; although much of the designer's work is handled by the design software, a general knowledge of the operating system is required to perform certain operations, such as file deletion, moving files, or backing up files. You also may discover that an important file has become "lost," or you forgot where the file is on the disk. A knowledge of the operating system and directory structure will allow you to search for it.

The following examples illustrate a few of the similarities and differences between DOS and Unix. In these examples, the current directory will be changed to a subdirectory called "temp." The directory will be displayed to show the names of the files contained in it. The file "data1" will be duplicated, and the duplicate file will be called "data2." A subdirectory will then be created called "design." The directory will be displayed again to show that the new file is listed in the directory. Note how the system prompt changes when the directory is changed.

Example 6.2

Using DOS

This is an example of changing directories, copying a file, and creating a subdirectory in DOS. The command for changing to a directory is "CD," followed by the directory name. The command for displaying a directory is "DIR;" for copying a file, "COPY;" and for creating a directory, "MKDIR." These procedures are illustrated in Figure 6.13.

Example 6.3

Using Unix

This is an example of changing directories, copying a file, and creating a directory in the Unix operating system. The command for changing to a directory is "cd," for displaying a directory is "ls," and for copying a file is "cp;" the command for creating a directory, as it is in DOS, is "mkdir." These procedures are illustrated in Figure 6.14. (In case you are curious, "Mr. Burdell," whose name is given in the figure, is a fictional figure who was registered as a prank in a U.S. university a long time ago: only after "he" received his degree was his non-existence discovered.)

6.4.2 Application Software

While the operating system of a workstation controls the way the computer utilizes its resources, **application software** (sometimes just called software) is what the operator uses on the system to perform a task, such as word processing, drawing, geometric modeling, or simulation.

There are thousands of software packages available to the user to assist in almost any task, from balancing a checkbook to simulating construction or manufacturing processes. Generally, however, a software package is available for only a few types of computers. Before you buy a software package, be sure it can run on your computer. If you want to use a particular software package, then that package limits the choice of computers available to you. If you are interested in a particular type of computer, make sure the software available for it will satisfy your needs.

Figure 6.14 Example 6.3: Using UNIX.

```
/usr/people/burdell>
/usr/people/burdell>cd temp
/usr/people/burdell/temp>ls
total 1
-rw------- 1 burdell        6 Sep 11 02:11 data1
/usr/people/burdell/temp>cp data1 data2
/usr/people/burdell/temp>mkdir design
/usr/people/burdell/temp>ls
total 3
-rw-------   1 burdell        6 Sep 11 02:11 data1
-rw-------   1 burdell        6 Sep 11 02:12 data2
drwx------   2 burdell      512 Sep 11 02:12 design/
/usr/people/burdell/temp>
```

For the designer, the most important software is that designed for CAD modeling. The main functions of a CAD modeling package, such as AutoCAD, are the drawing editor, plotting functions, and several utilities. As an overview of CAD software, two programs popular with designers will be mentioned: AutoCAD and CADKEY.

AutoCAD is one of the most popular programs that provide CAD, modeling, and customized programming capabilities for workstations. Until the advent of AutoCAD, CAD capabilities were available only on larger computers. There are now hundreds of third-party software developers that have customized and developed AutoCAD-based applications such as automated manufacturing and cost estimating. AutoCAD was initially a two-dimensional–based graphics package. However, the latest versions have 3-D capabilities, solids modeling, and programming capabilities. In AutoCAD, commands are selected from a menu, and the software can be used by operators with a minimum of computer experience. AutoCAD is particularly well suited for mechanical, industrial, structural, and architectural work. AutoCAD is available for DOS- and Unix-based workstations.

CADKEY is a three-dimensional CAD and geometric modeling package with engineering analysis functions (that is, it allows you to determine stresses caused by loads, and so on). In CADKEY, a model is constructed as a 3-D wireframe model (see Chapters 7 and 8), instead of as separate orthographic projections. As in AutoCAD, a designer can generate an axonometric drawing, shade three-dimensionally, remove hidden lines, and calculate mass properties of mechanical parts. CADKEY is available for both DOS and Unix workstations.

When purchasing a workstation, a designer may wish to buy the workstation hardware by itself and then select a CAD or geometric modeling software package to use with it. For example, a designer might buy a Silicon Graphics IRIS workstation and then install the SDRC I-DEAs or the CADKEY package, or buy an IBM (386 or 486) or SUN Microsystems' SPARCstation and install AutoCAD. The advantage of buying the workstation and software separately is greater flexibility. The designer can assemble a workstation system to suit his or her particular needs by combining hardware and software that is most appropriate to the specific situation. Alternatively, a designer may choose to buy a workstation with software included, or bundled with it. For example, Computervision sells the CADDStation, which includes a SUN Microsystems workstation, graphics hardware developed by Computervision, and CADDS software. The advantage of a bundled system is that the user does not have to be concerned about software that may not be suited to the hardware. Also, the software included with the system is often customized to work efficiently on the hardware.

6.4.3 Programming Languages

Programming languages are a third type of software of interest to the design workstation user. With programming languages, new software can be written to perform any task that is not already performed by existing software packages.

A computer can only run software that it can understand, and computers only understand **machine code**, i.e., the codes that the CPU executes. Programming languages provide a bridge between machine codes and the language that we speak, thus making it easier to write software. Programming language software includes a **compiler**, which translates the programming language into machine code that can be run on the computer.

Computer programming languages can be classified as **general purpose** and **special purpose languages**. General purpose languages are designed so that the user can create a program to perform almost any task. As an overview, several of the more common general purpose computer languages will be mentioned.

BASIC, the Beginner's All-purpose Symbolic Instruction Code, has been a very popular language ever since its introduction at Dartmouth College in the mid-1960s. BASIC programming is easy to learn, since most of its commands are single-word commands taken from everyday English. FORTRAN stands for FORmula TRANslation and is a language developed for use by scientists and engineers. Its commands are very similar to those of BASIC, with more emphasis on numerical work. Pascal is widely used in computer graphics applications. COBOL, COmmon Business Oriented Language, programs are long, but they execute very quickly. Because of the memory requirements of COBOL programs, the language is rarely used on design workstations. Forth is a new language, designed to appeal to BASIC users, but is more efficient than BASIC.

The C programming language is one of the most popular languages among professional CAD/CAE and computer-graphics programmers. Its popularity is due in large part to its close association with the creation of the Unix operating system, though C is independent of any operating system or workstation.

Special purpose languages are only suitable to create a program to perform a specific type of task. Special purpose languages perform a limited number of commands or functions more efficiently than a general purpose language performs those same functions, but a special purpose language understands many fewer functions.

Certain CAD packages contain both special and general purpose languages. The special language features allow the designer to program certain sequential tasks such as macro programming, slide shows of images, and scripts ("canned" sequences of commands). General purpose language capabilities such as Auto CAD's AutoLISP and C, CADKEY's CADL and C, and VersaCAD's CPL can be utilized in all engineering and design fields and can augment, replace, or automate repetitive modeling, drafting, and design tasks.

Today's designer does not need to be an expert in computer programming, but some knowledge of special purpose languages is helpful. A knowledge of special purpose languages allows the designer to write custom software that is specific to his or her needs. Special purpose languages are becoming increasingly popular as they become better able to accomplish more and more with greater ease.

Chapter Summary

Chapter 6 detailed the following points:

- Many designers now run CAD modeling software on powerful desktop computers called design workstations or engineering workstations, to model, analyze, and render proposed or existing products.

- The hardware components of a workstation are categorized as processing, input, output, storage, and communications devices.

- The processing components of the workstation are contained on the motherboard within the system unit. The principal processing component, the central processing unit (CPU), is a microprocessor that acts as the brain of the computer. Other processing components include read-only memory, random-access memory, and the system clock.

- A workstation's input devices provide the designer with the ability to enter data into the computer. Common input devices include the keyboard, mouse, digitizer and stylus, and scanner.

- Output devices enable the computer to present information to the designer. The three most common output devices are the monitor (or video display), the printer, and the plotter. A new type of output device, the stereolithography apparatus (SLA), creates solid plastic models from geometric models within the CAD database.

- Storage devices are used to save information. The two most common types of storage device are the hard disk drive and floppy disk drive. Both are used in most workstations.

- Communication devices allow a workstation user to send and receive data to and from another workstation. Where two designers are in the same building, they are often connected through a communications system called a local area network (LAN). Where they are not nearby, they can use a modem, in conjunction with the telephone lines, to send and receive data.

- Processing components are judged by their amount of random-access memory (RAM) capacity, word size, and clock speed.

- Keyboards are judged by the number and type of keys they have, mice by the number of buttons or the way in which they detect movement, digitizers by their resolution, and scanners by their resolution and whether they read color or just shades of black and white, and the number of intensity levels that can be detected.

- Like scanners, monitors are judged by their resolution, ability to display color, and number of intensity levels or different colors that can be displayed. Laser printers are judged by their resolution.

- Storage media are judged by the number of bytes they can hold. Hard disk drives are also judged by the speed with which they can retrieve information.

- Modems are judged by the number of bits that can be communicated per second, called the baud rate.

- A workstation's software can be classified as operating system software, application software, or programming language software.

- DOS and Unix, the two most common operating systems, control how the workstation stores and recovers information and how the computer interacts with other pieces of software. Common operating-system functions include formatting disks, creating directories to organize files, and changing the default disk drive or directory.

- Application software allows the user to perform the task desired. On a design workstation, the most important piece of application software is the CAD modeling package. Each CAD package has a different user interface, different capabilities, and different limitations.

- Programming languages allow new software to be written by providing a link between the language we speak and the machine code that the computer understands. Common general-purpose languages include BASIC, FORTRAN, Pascal, and COBOL, although the most popular language among CAD users is C. Special-purpose languages are designed for creating certain types of software; they are more efficient, but more limited, than general-purpose languages.

REFERENCES AND SUGGESTED READINGS

Kernighan, B., and D. Ritchie. *The C Programming Language*. Englewood Cliffs, N.J.: Prentice-Hall, 1988.

Seymout, J. *PC Magazine*, 10(3),

"Viewing the OS Dilemma." *MicroCAD News*.

EXERCISES

6.1 Compare the hardware of the two workstations described in Example 6.1.

6.2 Compare the hardware of an IRIS Silicon Graphics workstation and a SUN SPARCstation.

6.3 Find the login procedure and the most popular operating system used at your institution's CAD laboratory (or nearest computer facility). How do the login procedure and operating system contrast with those used on an IBM-compatible desktop computer?

6.4 Research user preferences between any two leading CAD modeling packages, for example, AutoCAD, CADKEY, I-DEAS, Silverscreen, VERSACAD, and so on. (*Research sources*: DesignNet magazines such as *MicroCAD News* (MCN) and *CADENCE* in the U.S., *CADdesk* in Great Britain, *Harvest* in France, *AutoCAD* in Spain, *CAD Magazine* in Czechoslovakia, and *Personal Engineering: MCN* in Japan.)

6.5 The terms listed below are likely to appear in CAD literature without explanation. Draw an image and/or write a short statement that describes each of the key terms, listed below, used in this chapter.

Addresses	Diskette (floppy disk)
Application software	DOS
Arithmetic logic unit (ALU)	File
Backup disk	File server
Baud rate	Formatting
Binary	Function keys
Bit	General purpose languages
Byte	Graphical user interface (GUI)
Case-sensitive	Hard disk
Cathode ray tube (CRT)	Hardware
Central processing unit (CPU)	Icons
Clock speed	Input devices
Communication devices	Interactive
Compiler	Keyboard
Configuration	Kilobyte (K or KB)
Control unit	Local area network (LAN)
Counter	Login
Default drive	Machine code
Design workstation (engineering workstation)	Macros
Digitizer	Math coprocessor
Directory	Megabyte (M or MB)
Disk controller card	Megahertz (MHz)
	Menu

Microprocessor

Modem

Monitor

Processing

Programming Languages

Program managers

Prompt

Pull-down menus

RAM capacity

Random-access memory (RAM)

Random scan

Raster

Raster scan

Read-only memory (ROM)

Registers

Refresh CRt

Resolution

Root directory

Scan lines

Scanner

Software

Special purpose languages

Standalone

Stereolithography apparatus (SLA)

Storage devices

Subdirectory

System clock

System unit

Tree

Unix

User-friendly

User numbers

Video display

Word size

CHAPTER 7 Geometric Entities in 3-D Space

After studying a set of orthographic multiviews or detail drawings, it becomes evident that they consist mainly of points, lines, circles, and other basic elements, called geometric entities, as well as text. This chapter covers the fundamental graphical-user-interfaces, coordinate formats, coordinate systems, and methods available for constructing geometric entities in the design workstation's 3-D space. The objective of this chapter is to explain the generic (non-software specific) methods common to all CAD modeling systems. To provide a frame of reference however, we will compare the graphical-user-interfaces of two popular CAD modeling packages.

7.1 GRAPHICAL-USER-INTERFACES IN CAD

Figure 7.1 Types of menu systems. Tree-structured menu sequences are used by most CAD modeling packages, though some single menus and linear menus will be found within the overall tree structure. (Courtesy of Prof. Ben Shneiderman)

Most CAD packages provide a visual means, called the **graphical-user-interface (GUI)**, to access its geometric construction and modeling capabilities. GUIs provide menus and icons that can eliminate the need to memorize complex sequences of commands. GUIs provide the user with a visual framework that consists of a structured list of options, such as displaying objects, changing settings, or modifying geometric entities.

In most cases, a GUI's menu displays commands in a **tree-structured** format in which the user can see the main categories of construction commands at the

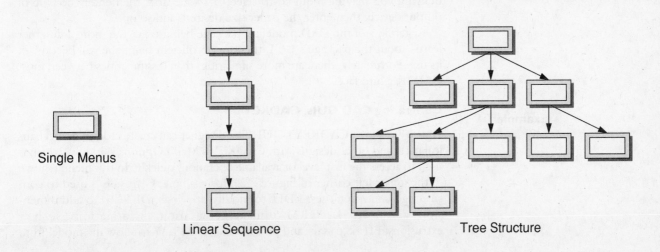

Single Menus

Linear Sequence

Tree Structure

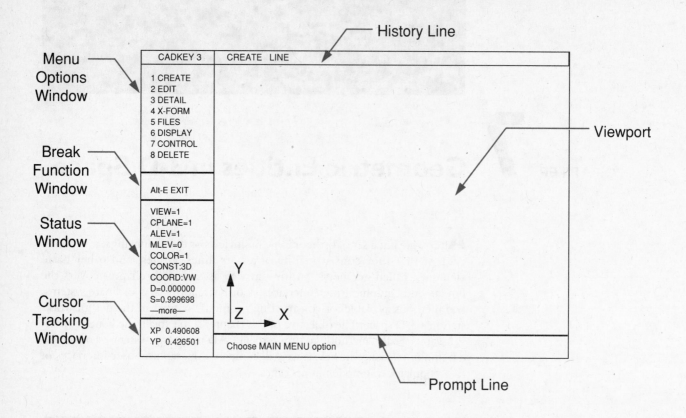

Figure 7.2 CADKEY's Graphical-User-Interface.

main menu level, and subcommands (or suboptions) at subsequent levels. Tree-structured menus are used to manage large collections of commands that belong to specific categories (for example, for geometric-entity construction or manipulation).

CAD modeling packages often use single menus and linear-sequence menus (see Figure 7.1) to process geometric-construction tasks, such as drawing lines or deleting lines. **Single menus** are used when one menu is sufficient to accomplish a task (for example, a single "plot" icon on the screen may be used for sending preformatted output to a laser printer). **Linear-sequence menus** are used to guide a user through a chain of menus. For example, in printing a drawing you may be required to select the scale first, then enter the type of output device, then enter the paper size desired, and so on.

Regardless of the CAD modeling package being used, the more a designer learns about the package's GUI, the more proficient he or she will become in its use. Fortunately, there are more similarities than dissimilarities between most CAD user-interfaces.

Comparing CAD GUIs: CADKEY

Example 7.1

Figure 7.2 shows CADKEY's GUI. The designer can create models of mechanical parts and other designs with CADKEY's Menu Options Window, which is used to access the first level of available operations quickly. In this menu (shown in the upper-left corner of Figure 7.2), for example, CREATE is used to construct geometric entities; EDIT to modify drawings; DETAIL to add dimensions and notes; X-FORM to make geometric transformations, such as extrusions; FILES to save and plot models; DISPLAY to show the model from different points of view; CONTROL to select coordinates and construction planes; and DELETE to erase entities. In addition to the main menu options, CADKEY's GUI preserves other areas of the screen to display other options and the characteristics of the current CADKEY session. CADKEY tells you the location of the cursor with the Cursor Tracking Window. It also lets you see, in the History Line, the sequence of commands that you have performed and in the Prompt Line, the requested input. You may exit the system at any time with the Break Function Window. The current settings are located in the Status Window. Finally, you can display the model in the Viewport.

Example 7.2

Comparing CAD GUIs: AutoCAD

AutoCAD's GUI uses a **menu-bar** that contains a series of **pull-down menus** (Figure 7.3 (a)). These menus appear on the screen in response to a click on the mouse button. Commands are made by selecting the menu-bar items using the mouse, thereby activating the pull-down menu, and clicking again on the selected command in the pull-down menu. The tree-structured menu bar thus provides an efficient way for a designer to access the many commands that are available (Figure 7.3 (b)).

As in most CAD modeling packages, AutoCAD provides a Drawing Area to display the geometric entities; a Command Prompt Area to access drawing functions by typing commands such as "line"; a Standard Screen Menu to access commands with a mouse or pointer; and a Status Line to remind you that you have selected special features and to indicate the position of the cursor (see Figure 7.4).

AutoCAD offers another way to perform CAD operations by providing a digitizing tablet overlay (Figure 7.5). You can see in the overlay that the options are grouped by topics, and that the most common selections occupy a larger area of the tablet than the less-used options.

The usual hardware setup of a CAD system includes either a mouse or a digitizing tablet. Therefore, the designer uses only one of the two approaches discussed (the GUIs or the digitizing tablet) during a specific CAD session.

Figure 7.3(a) AutoCAD's main menu screen with a single pull-down menu activated in the menu bar.

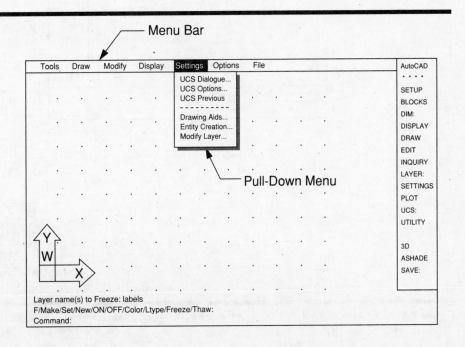

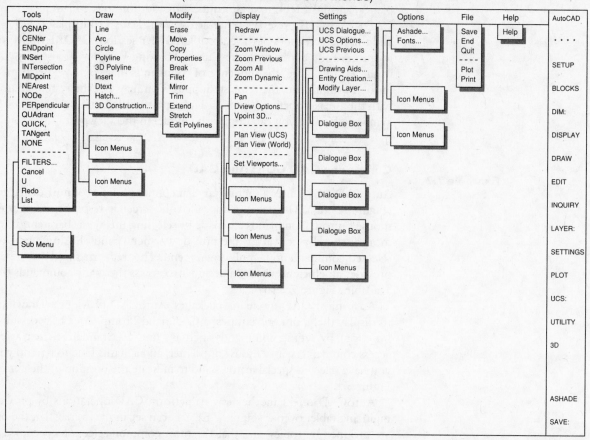

Figure 7.3(b) The full set of menus and submenus available from AutoCAD's menu bar. (Courtesy of Autodesk, Inc.)

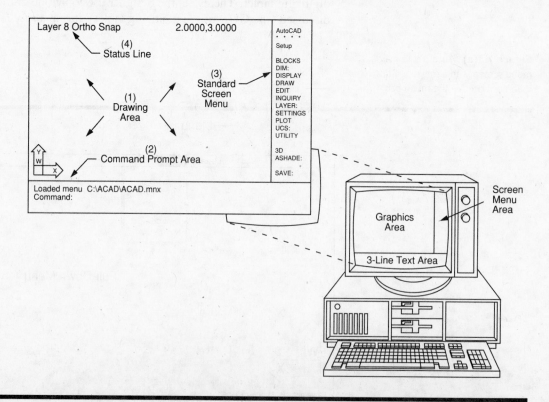

Figure 7.4 AutoCAD's user-interface showing the drawing area (1), command prompt area (2), the standard screen menu (3), and status line (4). (Courtesy of Autodesk, Inc.)

7.2 CAD COORDINATE FORMATS

There are many different ways of representing locations in 3-D (three-dimensional) space. In general, to specify a unique position in 3-D space, a designer uses an ordered set of three numbers (n_1, n_2, n_3). These three numbers differ depending on how the coordinate format is defined.

The following sections will cover several coordinate formats that are used widely in engineering and design. The Cartesian coordinate format is the most common in CAD user-interfaces. Other formats, such as cylindrical, polar, and spherical, are not supported by all CAD user-interfaces, though they are often used internally by the system.

7.2.1 Cartesian Coordinates

The **Cartesian coordinate format** was developed by René Descartes, the famous seventeenth-century mathematician. The term "cartesian" is derived from his name. Descartes developed the analytical-geometry concept of locating a point on a given plane by means of the distance from three mutually perpendicular axes. These three perpendicular axes are generally called X, Y, and Z (Figure 7.6 (a)). Hence, a point location in cartesian format is defined as an ordered set of values labeled X, Y, and Z, where each number represents the distance along its respective axis.

The location where all axes meet is called the **origin**. The origin is a reference location from which distances are measured, thus the coordinates of the

Figure 7.5 AutoCAD tablet overlay. (Courtesy of Autodesk, Inc.)

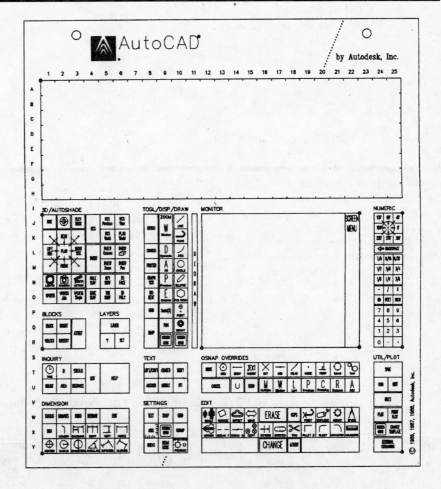

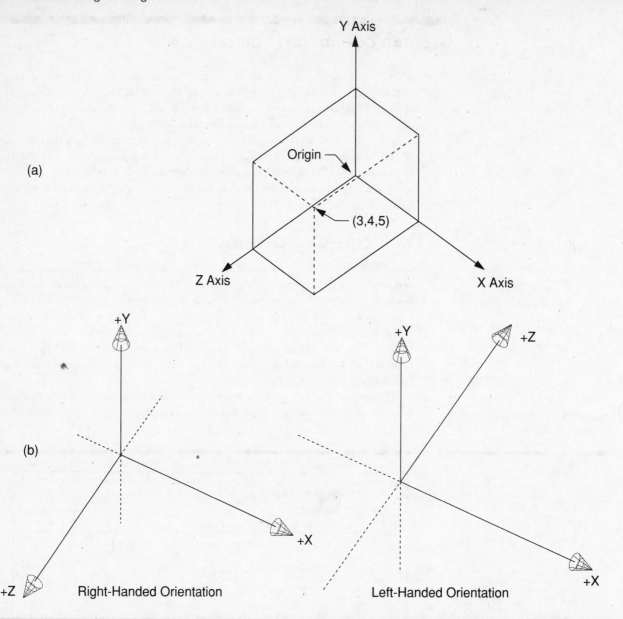

Figure 7.6 (a) Representation of the point (3, 4, 5) in a Cartesian coordinate system. (Courtesy of GE/Calma) (b) Comparison of the two prevalent orientations of axes. Any orientation is valid as long as it is maintained throughout the geometric construction process.

origin are (0,0,0). Some CAD modeling systems display a symbol at the origin at all times to orient the user in 3-D space (refer to Figures 7.2 and 7.3 (a), lower-left corner). If a CAD system does not specify the location of the origin, the user can create a point at that position for orientation purposes.

Since the three axes are mutually perpendicular by definition, there are only two major choices regarding their orientation (see Figure 7.6 (b)). The first orientation shown is refered to as "right-handed," and the second as "left-handed." Most commercial CAD modeling systems are based on the right-handed orientation. A designer may choose to use either orientation, but it is important that the same orientation be used throughout the geometric-construction process.

7.2.2 Cylindrical and Polar Coordinates

Another format for representing a position in 3-D space is using **cylindrical coordinate format**. A unique location is defined in cylindrical coordinates using the ordered set {r,θ,z} (see Figure 7.7). The first term, r, is the radius or distance

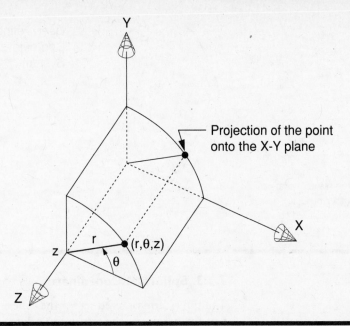

Figure 7.7 Representation of the point (r, θ, z) given in the cylindrical coordinate format.

from a reference location to the specified point. The second term, θ, is the angle between the positive X-axis and the projection of the point onto the X–Y plane. The last term, z, is the distance along the Z-axis from the origin to the point.

Polar coordinates can be considered a subset of cylindrical coordinates. They represent a 2-D (two-dimensional) location on a defined plane instead of a 3-D location in space. Hence, the ordered set for polar coordinates, {r,θ}, has only two numbers. Polar coordinates are the same as cylindrical coordinates, except that in polar coordinates the value of z is implicit, usually zero.

Most CAD modeling systems that support cylindrical and polar coordinates use the angle bracket symbol (<) to specify the angle component of the coordinates. For example, the point (r,θ,z) in cylindrical format is input as r<θ,z and the point (r,θ) in polar format is input as r<θ.

Figure 7.8 Representation of the point (r, θ, Φ) given in the spherical coordinate format.

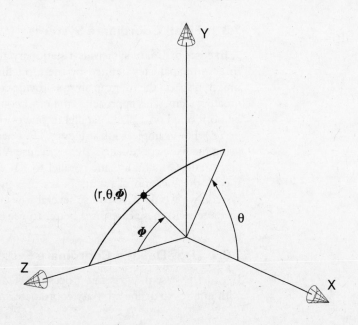

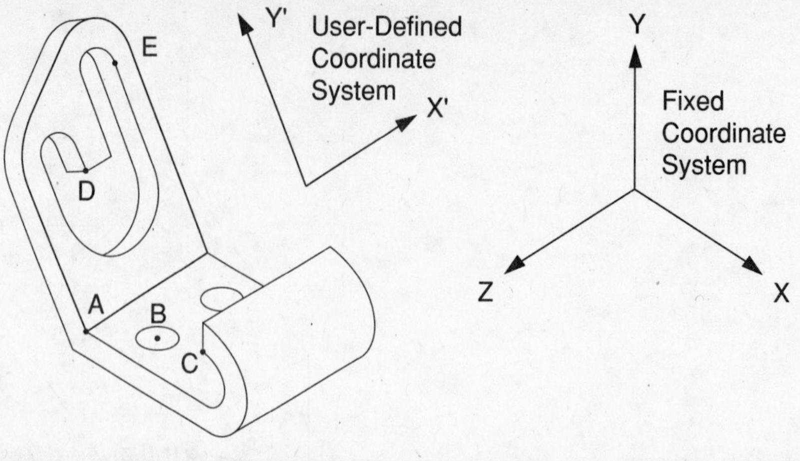

Figure 7.9 Locations A, B and C can be specified using the fixed coordinate system, because they lie on planes parallel to the three planes. Locations D and E, on the other hand, are easier to define using a user-defined coordinate system.

7.2.3 Spherical Coordinates

The three-term ordered set for the spherical coordinate format is (r, θ, Φ). The first two terms are the same as in cylindrical and polar coordinates. However, the last term, Φ, is the angle between the positive Z-axis and an imaginary line between the origin and the point (see Figure 7.8).

Most CAD modeling systems that support spherical coordinates use the angle bracket symbol (<) to specify these coordinates. For example, the point (r, θ, Φ) in spherical coordinates is in put as r< θ < Φ, where r is a distance, θ is an angle, and Φ is another angle.

7.3　COORDINATE SYSTEMS

The term **coordinate systems** refers to the specific arrangement of the three principal axes (X, Y, and Z) in space. A CAD modeling package will provide one fixed coordinate system that is constant for each model created. In addition, the user can specify and create his or her own coordinate systems in order to ease the construction process of a computer-based model. If a CAD Modeling System is designed to follow the right-handed orientation convention for defining coordinate systems, then all the coordinate systems should follow it.

7.3.1　Fixed Coordinate Systems

A **fixed coordinate system** is a stationary and permanent arrangement of the three principal axes defined by the modeling package. When positioning an object in space, the user can always provide coordinates based on the fixed coordinate system. This approach is the most convenient one when the object must be positioned on a plane parallel to one of the three principal planes (XY, XZ, or YZ). For example, look at Figure 7.9. Locations A, B, and C can be specified using the fixed coordinate system, because A and B lie on a plane parallel to XZ, and A and C lie on a plane parallel to XY. On the other hand, if we want to specify the location of points D and E, relying on only the fixed coordinate system, we would have to use several trigonometric functions to define them accurately. In these cases, it is better to use user-defined coordinate systems.

7.3.2　User-Defined Coordinate Systems

In order to ease the drawing process, CAD modeling systems provide the user with utilities to define arbitrary coordinate systems. This gives the user the flex-

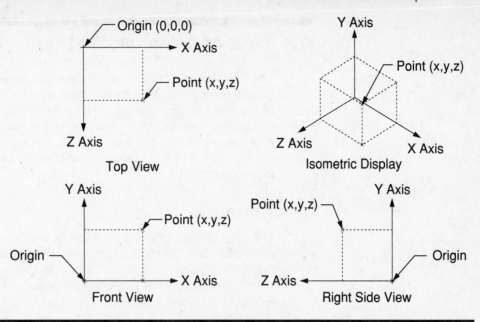

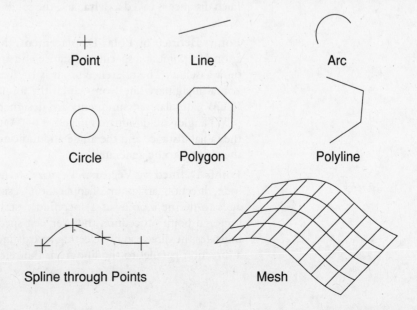

Figure 7.10 Changing orientations of the coordinate axes in orthogonal multiviews.

Figure 7.11 Sample of geometric entities. (Courtesy of S. Otero)

ibility needed to model inclined planes, such as the plane containing the points D and E in Figure 7.9. **User-defined coordinate systems** allow the designer to rotate the object's reference axes to accommodate features not parallel to any of the principal planes. Unfortunately, the user-defined capabilities of CAD modeling are software-dependent and vary with the system being used.

7.3.3 Coordinate Systems Conventions in CAD Systems

Most CAD modeling systems will display on the screen some kind of visual aid that will tell you the orientation of the three principal axes (refer to Figure 7.4, lower-left corner of projected screen). Normally, the origin in 3-D space is located at the lower-left corner of the display or monitor screen. The user can, however, change the view being displayed. As the user changes the point of view, the system displays the new orientation of the axes.

Figure 7.10 shows the four views of the Cartesian coordinate system on a CAD system. Notice how the position of the origin changes in the four views.

7.4 TYPES OF GEOMETRIC ENTITIES

The most fundamental element of computer-generated drawings or models is the geometric entity. Most models created with CAD modeling systems consist of the following geometric entities: points, lines, circles, arcs, polygons, and other curves and surfaces, such as splines and meshes (see Figure 7.11). In the next few subsections, you will find a description of how these geometric entities are created in CAD modeling systems, and what restrictions, if any, are imposed on them.

7.4.1 Points

Points are defined by indicating a specific location in space. In CAD modeling, a designer may create points using several procedures. For instance, he or she may create a point by typing its location in Cartesian coordinate format; he or she may define the point location in relation to other preexisting entities in the model; or he or she may define a point arbitrarily in space by pointing with a mouse or stylus.

When modeling a design product in a CAD system, the designer starts by creating entities at key locations, such as the entities that intersect the origin. From then on, the designer may use the entities already created as reference locations for all other entities.

Before specifying point locations, it is necessary to indicate the type of coordinates being entered. Generally, the default coordinates are understood to be **real-world coordinates**; that is, the computer assumes that the coordinates represent the actual size of the object. After the designer types in the real-world coordinates, the system converts them to **device coordinates**, so the generated points will fit on the screen.

Although the first points on a model must be entered using real-world coordinates, designers frequently find it convenient to specify subsequent points relative to the entities they have already created.

The following are some of the methods available for entering point coordinates.

Points Defined by Delta, or Relative, Displacement. A simple way to designate a point location relative to another point is to use **delta**, or **relative, displacements**. With this procedure, each new point is created by entering the distance along the X, Y, and Z axis from the reference point to the new point. Each distance is called a **delta**, and the set of delta displacements is ΔX, ΔY, and ΔZ.

Points Defined by Polar Displacement. Many CAD packages allow the creation of a point at a specified distance and angle from a certain reference point on a baseline. The reference point is the vertex, and the baseline is the horizontal imaginary line from which the angle is measured. Counterclockwise (CCW) angular measurements are designated positive (+) angles; clockwise (CW) angles are designated negative (−). With this procedure, the user inputs the radial distance and the angle and indicates the reference entity from which the point is to be generated.

Points Defined by Vectors. **Vectors** are normally described by their magnitude, direction, and point of application. A similar concept is used in CAD packages to define a point at a specified distance from a base point. With the vectored-point procedure, the user first specifies the point of origin and then indicates the direction by selecting an existing line. The new point is defined in a direction parallel to the line from the reference point. If a positive value is

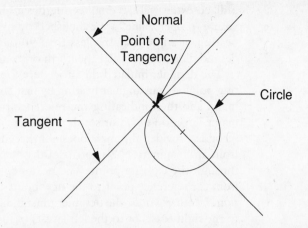

Figure 7.12 A tangent and normal to a circle.

entered for the distance to be traveled from the reference point parallel to the indicated line, then the new point will be created in the positive direction of the X axis from the reference point (looking at the XY plane, the new point will be further to the right than the reference point). A negative distance tells the system to create the point towards the negative X direction from the reference point.

Points Defined by the Center of a Circle. Many packages allow the user to create a point that corresponds to the center of an existing circle or arc. The method for generating such a point consists of indicating the arc or circle whose center is to be defined, and issuing the proper command.

Points Along a Circumference. If available, this option lets the user draw a point at a specified angle on the edge of a selected arc or circle. The user selects the arc entity using the pointer and then enters the angle at which the point is to be defined. A positive value signals the system to create a point measured counterclockwise from a line that passes through the center of the circle, parallel to the horizontal axis. Subsequent points can be specified along the circle's edge in the same fashion without having to select the circle again.

Points on a Line. A designer can also create points on an existing line at a certain displacement along the horizontal, vertical, or depth axes. The user selects the line and enters a displacement along one of the axes.

Points at the Intersection of Curves. Sometimes it is helpful to be able to create a point at the intersection of two curves or lines. To create such a point, each curve must be selected individually. The definition of a curve in this case includes lines, arcs, conics, and splines. Of course, if no intersection is found, the system will indicate so by displaying a message such as "no intersection found."

Normal and Tangent Points. A **tangent** to a circle is a line that intersects the circle in only one place. The **point of tangency** is illustrated in Figure 7.12, where the line makes contact with the circle. The line perpendicular to the tangent is defined as the normal.

Certain systems allow the user to select either a screen position or an existing point and then select a curve to define the point on the curve where the normal to the curve would pass through the selected position or point. Various CAD packages would let the user define a true three-dimensional-curve normal point by selecting a screen position and current depth or by selecting an existing point and curve. In each of these cases the selection procedure is managed by "indicate point" or "indicate curve" prompts.

Points Defined by the Bearing of a Line. The direction of a line with respect to the north/south axis is called the **angular bearing** of a line. This concept is utilized extensively in engineering design practice. For example, in land surveying, property lines are established by specifying line bearings. The angular bearing of a line is always less than 90 degrees, since you can reference the desired direction to either the north or south axis (as depicted in Figure 7.13).

The designer initiated the procedure for defining a point based on an existing point and an angular bearing by first choosing a "bearing/distance" command and then indicating the reference point. The designer then picks the major direction north or south and enters any angle in degrees, minutes, and seconds, provided the angle does not exceed 90 degrees. The angle is measured from an imaginary N-S (north-south) line parallel to the Y-axis and passing through the existing point. The next steps consist of keying in the distance from the reference point to the new point and indicating the east/west direction. In other words, the designer must indicate whether the new point is to be to the right (east) or to the left (west) of the existing point.

Parametrically Defined Points. A **parameter** is a variable whose value determines a position on a preexisting geometric entity. By using parameters, the designer can often specify a point by using a single number, which is the basis for generating 2-D and 3-D coordinates. Since CAD curves are measured parametrically, a given parameter will give a unique definition for a point on a curve.

Generating Points on a Surface. Points can be generated on a surface by such methods as finding a normal to a surface, finding a piercing point to a surface, and specifying parameters. For instance, on a sphere a point can be generated relative to the normal that connects a point outside the sphere to the sphere's center.

7.4.2 Lines

A **line** is an entity defined by two points or locations. Therefore, in order to create a line on a CAD modeling system, a user must specify at least two sets of coordinates in 3-D space or in a 2-D plane.

CAD modeling systems can draw lines of finite length, called **segments**, or lines of infinite length. Therefore, it is necessary to specify the type of line desired. However, the system default is usually set for drawing line segments. If a user needs an infinite line but is not certain of how to create it, he or she can simply create a line that has a very long finite length and then trim it to the proper size as the model is created.

Figure 7.13 Point "A" is 60° west of the north axis.

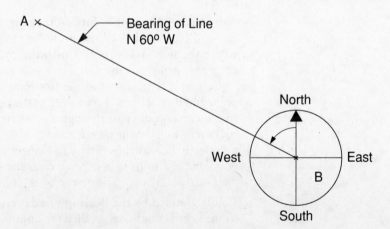

7.4.3 Circles and Arcs

Circles are a special case of **arcs** in which the included angle is 360 degrees. In order to define arcs or circles in a CAD modeling system, the user must input the location of the center, the radius, and the starting and ending angle of the arc. In most CAD systems, arcs and circles can be created only in planes parallel to the principal planes of a defined coordinate system. Drawing circles in any plane is thus made possible by employing the user-defined coordinate capabilities of the system.

7.4.4 Polygons and Polylines

Polygons and **polylines** are collections of lines and arcs that are defined as a single entity. For instance, an octagon, even though it is comprised of eight lines, is considered by the system to be a single geometric entity (refer to Figure 7.11).

7.4.5 Splines

Another type of entity that you can create in CAD modeling systems is a **spline**. A spline is a smooth curve defined by a collection of **control points** (refer to Figure 7.11). A control point is a location in 3-D space that influences the shape of the curve. In most CAD modeling systems, all control points have equal influence over the curve. There are many types and ways of calculating the shape of splines mathematically, given the control points. For simplicity, most CAD modeling systems limit the number of methods available.

CAD modeling systems usually have two main sets of splines: those that go through the points specified, and those that are only influenced by the control points. For a spline that goes through the control points, the user inputs at least three different positions in space. The system in this case will create a smooth curve that goes through those points. In the same fashion, the user can specify that the inner control points should influence the curve but not go through the point location. In this case, the spline will not go through the second point (the inner point), though the first and last point will define the locations of the start and end of the curve.

Interestingly, in the same way that a spline is defined by point locations, we can define points along an existing two- or three-dimensional spline—at the original points used to define the spline. This allows you to re-create the original spline locations even after you have deleted them.

7.4.6 Meshes

Meshes are similar to splines, with the difference that they lie on a surface and are defined in two different directions (refer to Figure 7.11). The main purpose of a mesh is to subdivide a surface into smaller pieces for further calculations. Meshes are widely used in engineering in order to calculate different characteristics of a surface area. For example, the stress characteristics of a thin-walled structure, such as an airplane wing, change along its surface area. Consequently, using a mesh to subdivide a surface area permits generalized calculations in a given section, or "patch," of an area.

7.5 METHODS OF DATA INPUT IN CAD

In addition to defining the orientation of the coordinate system, data input is the most important activity for constructing geometric entities on a design workstation. The most common method of defining positions in space is to use the keyboard. This section provides an overview of the other methods available for entering geometric data in 3-D space. It includes methods for specifying positions, and methods for importing data from other systems.

7.5.1 Using a Pointer

Selection of entities by screen position or pointing consists of specifying a point using an input device (for example, a stylus with digitizing tablet, a light pen, a puck, a mouse, or a joy stick). Please note that some users prefer to use the term locator rather than pointer.

To generate a point in this fashion, the user moves the pointer on the tablet surface or mouse pad until the crosshairs on the screen are at the point desired. The user then presses the stylus against the tablet or presses the mouse button. The position is read, and coordinate values are recorded and stored for that point. A lighted point, x, or + appears on the display.

Because the screen is a two-dimensional surface, positioning a point using a mouse, stylus, or other pointer provides the computer with only two-dimensional data. Unless a depth value is specified for the point, the computer assumes that a position specified with a pointer lies on the **work plane**. For most packages, the default work plane is either the XY or XZ plane of the fixed coordinate system. The work plane can be changed from the default by indicating a new depth, by switching views, or by establishing a user-defined coordinate system.

To make the use of a pointer more efficient, the designer can also work with a **grid** to provide a frame of reference that is displayed on the screen. A grid consists of a series of construction dots, called **grid dots**, which are independent of the drawing file; they will not show when the file is plotted (grid dots are visible on the projected screen in Figures 7.3 (a) and 7.4). The user sets the grid by invoking the proper command and then makes the necessary changes that will suit the drawing.

A designer can set the spacing of the grid dots so that the grid works to the designer's greatest advantage. For example, when modeling a large part or a building, grid dots given at intervals of a millimeter would not be appropriate, because the display would be too cluttered. On the other hand, grid dots spaced at intervals of a kilometer would be too far apart. For such a model, a designer might set grid dots to show every foot or every meter.

In addition, a designer can increase the accuracy of a pointer by telling the system to use only locations that lie on the grid dots. This feature is usually called **snap**. If the snap setting is on, the cursor selection system will be forced to select locations on the grid dots.

7.5.2 Importing CAD Data

Sometimes it is necessary to read graphical data that were originally created on paper or on other CAD modeling packages. Scanning and data transfer are the two major techniques for importing data into a CAD model.

Scanners are devices that allow the designer to convert a paper drawing into a 2-D image that can be displayed by the CAD modeling system. Some systems allow the designer to delete or modify specific entities within the scanned drawing. In this way, it is possible to make corrections to paper drawings and store them in a computer file.

In addition to the benefits of creating geometric entities in 3-D space, many CAD packages also offer the ability to communicate with other packages. For example, data generated by the designer's computer can be used by the machinist's computer to produce a design prototype. Thus, a drawing or model

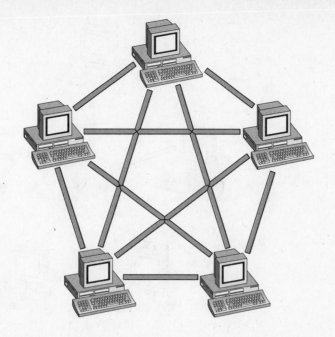

Figure 7.14 The Direct Translation Method: Each CAD modeling package develops translation software to convert data from *each* of the other competing CAD packages. When a new CAD package is introduced, the manufacturer of the new package must develop software to translate from each of the existing CAD packages. Each of the competing CAD packages must then add new translation software to accommodate the new CAD package.

developed on one CAD modeling package can be sent to a workstation using a different software package. In this way, designers are able to share their ideas and pool their resources.

However, a drawing or model created in one system can not be used directly by another system, because each individual package uses a unique representational scheme for storing the data that defines the model (Short, 1989). Getting two unrelated systems to understand each other is the job of data transfer, or data translation, software.

The difficulty of communication between CAD systems rests in how many geometric entities are not shared by both systems. For example, if one system uses curves but another system uses only lines, some way of converting a curve to a collection of lines is necessary. A translation can only be approximated in many cases. There are two approaches to graphic data transfer or exchange: direct translation and translation through a mediating neutral format such as the Initial Graphics Exchange Specification, or IGES.

The first attempts at data translation were **direct translators**, a schematic drawing of which is shown in Figure 7.14. These are single programs dedicated to translation between two specific systems, such as AutoCAD and CADKEY. Direct translators are usually written by the manufacturer of the target system, i.e., the system that is receiving the information. Creation of direct translators allows previous work done on a rival system to be imported into the manufacturer's own system, making the new system more appealing to the consumer. The manufacturer of a direct translator knows its own system's representational scheme well; however, knowledge of the rival system's data structure may be sketchy, which can cause problems in communication between systems. Direct translators, though once convenient for CAD users, have become cumbersome. As more CAD software hit the market, the need for direct translators grew geometrically. Only two translators are needed between two systems, one program for each of the two possible data directions. For three systems, six translators are required; for four systems, twelve; and so on.

A more recent approach to the problem of data translation is the **neutral file format**, described in Figure 7.15. In this method, a CAD modeling system

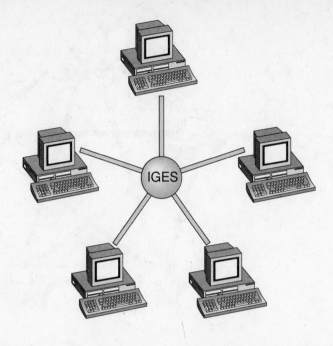

Figure 7.15 The Neutral File Format (for example, IGES and DXF): Each CAD modeling developer provides software to convert to and from the neutral file specification. When a new CAD package enters the market and supports IGES or DXF translation software, compatibility between all systems is maintained.

has the ability to convert to and from an industry-specified file format. The most common neutral file format is the **Initial Graphics Exchange Standard**, or **IGES**. IGES grew out of the need for quick compatibility between many different systems. For a CAD system to be IGES compatible, only two programs need to be written: the IGES **preprocessor** and IGES **postprocessor**. The preprocessor reads an IGES file and converts it into the system's format. The postprocessor converts the system's data back into the IGES format.

Chapter Summary

Chapter 7 detailed the following points:

- Designers generally access a CAD modeling package's capabilities through a graphical-user-interface, or GUI, which typically lists commands in a tree-structured format.

- Points in space can be represented in various coordinate formats, including Cartesian, polar, cylindrical, and spherical.

- The Cartesian coordinate format is the most common, positioning points by measuring linear distances along three mutually perpendicular axes that all intersect at the origin.

- The cylindrical format also uses the three perpendicular axes, but only the first and third coordinates give linear distances; the second stipulates an angle to be measured from the X axis in the X-Y plane.

- Polar coordinates are a special case of cylindrical coordinates in which the Z coordinate is omitted (polar coordinates are a two-dimensional format).

- The spherical coordinate format is similar to cylindrical format, except that the third coordinate, like the second, is given as an angle rather than as a length.

- When using a CAD package, coordinates can be given according to either the fixed coordinate system, which is permanent for each model created, or a user-defined coordinate system, which can be changed at any time to accommodate features not parallel to any of the principal planes (i.e., not perpendicular to any of the fixed coordinate axes).

- The simplest geometric entity is the point. When using CAD software, points can be entered in a number of ways: using real-world coordinates, relative displacements, polar displacement, vectors, centers of circles, circumferences of circles or arcs, distances along lines, intersections of curves, normals and tangents, line bearings, parameters, and distances along surfaces.

- Other common geometric entities that can be created on the basis of point location include lines, circles and arcs, polygons and polylines, splines, and meshes.

- In addition to using the keyboard to input coordinate positions, a designer can use a pointer, such as a mouse or digitizing tablet, with or without the aid of grid dots and a snap feature.

- A designer can import information directly from preexisting documents with a scanner.

- Modern CAD packages can use information from, or provide information for, another CAD package by translating from or to a neutral file format.

REFERENCES AND SUGGESTED READINGS

Brown, J. "CADAM to AutoCAD and Back Again." *MicroCAD News,* August, 45–46, 1989.

Initial Graphics Exchange Specification (IGES), Version 4.0, Final Report, NIST, Gaithersburg, MD, 1988.

LaCourse, D. "Clearing the Way for Modeling." *MicroCAD News,* March, 23–24, 1989.

Shneiderman, B. *Designing the User Interface: Strategies for Effective Human-Computer Interaction.* Reading, Mass: Addison-Wesley, 1987.

Short, D. "The Transfer of Data Between Dissimilar Systems." *Engineering Design Graphics Journal,* ASEE, 53(2), 1–9, 1989.

EXERCISES

7.1. Research the types of geometric entities supported by your institution's CAD modeling system. How do they compare with the generic entities discussed in this chapter?

7.2. Research the characteristics of the fixed and user-defined coordinate systems supported by your institution's CAD modeling package. How do they compare with the generic coordinate systems discussed in this chapter?

7.3. Figure 7.16 shows an unfinished drawing (model) of a part being modeled on a CAD modeling system. You have been asked to:

A. Sketch the corrected orthographic multiview projections for the part.

B. Arrange and position a right-handed fixed coordinate system suitable for the given multiview display.

C. Using the coordinate system you developed in B, above, determine the Cartesian coordinates of the points A, B, and C.

D. Assuming that the origin is located at point O, determine the cylindrical coordinates of point D.

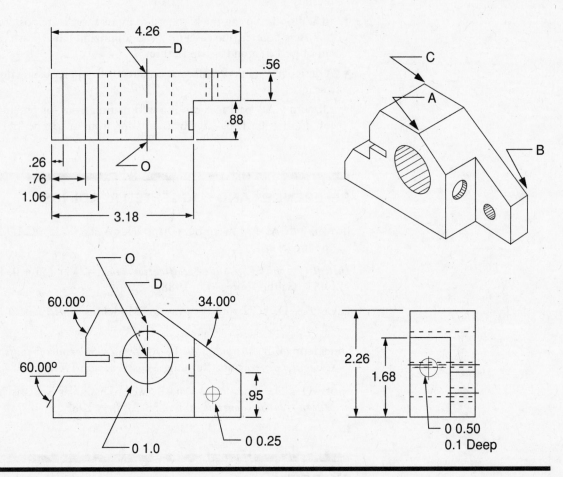

Figure 7.16 Exercise 7.3: unfinished drawing.

7.4. Research and write a report about transferring data with IGES. (*Hint:* You may request information from the National Technical Information Service, 5285 Port Royal Road, Springfield, VA 22161. To receive the IGES Newsletter, you may contact the IGES Coordinator, National Bureau of Standards, Room A-353, Building 220, Gaithersburg, MD 20899.)

7.5. Draw an image and/or write a short statement that describes or defines each of the key terms, listed below, used in this chapter.

Angular bearing	Origin
Arc	Parameter
Cartesian coordinate format	Point
Circle	Point of tangency
Control points	Polar coordinates
Coordinate systems	Polygons
Cylindrical coordinate format	Polylines
Delta	Postprocessor
Delta displacement or relative displacement	Preprocessor
	Pull-down menu
Device coordinates	Real-world coordinates
Direct translators	Scanner
Fixed coordinate systems	Segment
Graphical-user-interface (GUI)	Single menu
Grid	Snap
Grid dots	Spherical coordinate format
Initial Graphics Exchange Specification (IGES)	Spline
Line	Tangent
Linear-sequence menus	Tree-structured
Menu-bar	User-defined coordinate systems
Meshes	Vectors
Neutral file format	Work plane
Normal	

CHAPTER 8 3-D Geometric Modeling

In the design of products such as structures, mechanical devices, and electrical components, shape is one of the most important pieces of information needed to visualize the product and determine possible interferences between related components. Designers use **geometric modeling** to describe the physical shape of a product in the computer workstation. Depending on the capabilities of the CAD modeling software used, geometric modeling has the potential to represent fully the product design, including all the information needed to analyze and simulate the product's operation.

Designers use **geometric models** because they are an economical and convenient substitute for the real object (Mortenson, 1985). Since geometric models have the potential of completely defining both the interior and exterior of the product being designed, ambiguities in viewing and interpreting the object are minimized. With the 3-D electronic database generated by geometric modeling, the designer can produce a complete set of design documents, present renderings of the designed product to a client, and even provide most of the information needed to manufacture or build the product.

This chapter covers the three types of geometric models: wireframe, surface, and solid models. Wireframe and surface models combine geometric entities in 3-D space to construct a model's edges and surfaces. These types of models can be rendered to look like a solid model of the real object, such as the object shown in Figure 8.1. Solid models use a combination of strategies, including predefined 3-D volumes that are used as building blocks to construct the object. In this chapter, we will focus most of our attention on solid models, since this type of model is currently dominating the field.

Before we discuss the creation of the different types of geometric models, however, we need to understand the general use of models in engineering and design.

8.1 USING MODELS IN ENGINEERING AND DESIGN

Normally, designers and engineers cannot work in their office with the actual physical product that they are designing or analyzing. While designing a new product, or working on improving an older one, the product's components may be too big, too complex, or too cumbersome to bring into the work place. Designers find that it is more convenient to work with the model of a product being developed than with the real thing (Turner, 1978).

In design work, a **model** is an accurate representation of an actual device, system, or process. In general, models can be classified as iconic, analog, or

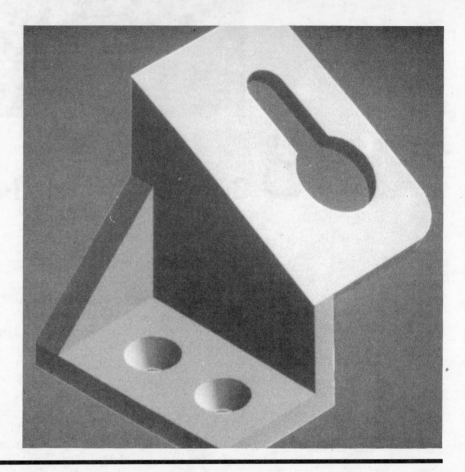

Figure 8.1   A solid geometric model.

symbolic. An **iconic model** is a scaled prototype of the real object that looks similar to the object being represented. You are probably familiar with scaled models, such as small plastic replicas of toy cars and airplanes. An iconic model can be either 2-D (for example, photos, drawings) or 3-D (plastic toy cars). The aluminum-can-crusher design prototype that we studied in Chapter 4 is another example of an iconic model.

Analog models substitute one property in the representation of an object for another and thus allow the problem to be solved in a substituted state. Analog models do not have to look like the object being represented, as long as the model follows the same physical principles or simulates the real system. Graphs and charts, for example, can be classified as analog models because they can represent magnitudes of physical quantities as distances (Dieter, 1983). Usually, the solution derived from an analog model is then translated back to the original dimensions or characteristics.

Symbolic models, also called **mathematical models**, are abstract representations of the system, process, or product being portrayed. Since geometric models are defined by mathematical functions, they are usually classified as symbolic. Symbolic models are characterized as either prescriptive or descriptive models. **Prescriptive models** dictate (prescribe) a certain course of action. For example, a program that tells a robot or tower crane in a building what to do to solve a problem in a given situation is a prescriptive model. On the other hand, **descriptive models** characterize (describe) the behavior of the system, process, or device being portrayed. From the mathematical point of view, all geometric models—wireframe, surface, and solid—are classified as symbolic-descriptive models. However, when these models are rendered to resemble closely an actual object, they can be classified as iconic-descriptive.

8.2 TYPES OF 3-D MODELS

In designing physical devices, we use analog, iconic-descriptive, and symbolic-descriptive models to describe the unique characteristics of the product being designed. Since geometric modeling may describe the product both mathematically (symbolic) and visually (iconic), it is the most useful and comprehensive modeling technique available for developing new physical products.

Geometric models may be classified as 2-D or 3-D. A 2-D model is always a wireframe model. A 3-D model may be classified as wireframe, surface, or solid (see Figure 8.2). We shall discuss wireframe, surface, and solid models in the following sections.

8.2.1 Wireframe Modeling

Wireframe models are the earliest type of geometric model; dating back to 1960, when Ivan Sutherland was working on Sketchpad at MIT (see Chapter 1). The technique for creating 2-D wireframes was originally called computer-aided drafting, because of its similarity to drawing on a drafting board.

Both 2-D and 3-D **wireframe models** represent objects by the edge lines, curves, and points on the surface of the object (Weiler, 1989). You may think of wireframe models as skeletal descriptions of the product being designed (Santelle, 1989). Note that there are no visible surfaces on the wireframe model shown in Figure 8.3; only geometric entities such as lines and curves. Although wireframe models do not look like a solid object, they do contain an accurate geometric description of the object being modeled.

Wireframes are practical because of the speed with which they can be displayed. Since a design workstation does not need a sophisticated color video monitor to display complex wireframe models, it is inexpensive to model objects using the 3-D wireframe technique. And in many cases the design results are the same as with more sophisticated representational techniques, such as solid modeling.

Figure 8.2 Classification of geometric models. (Courtesy of Drs. Barr & Juricic)

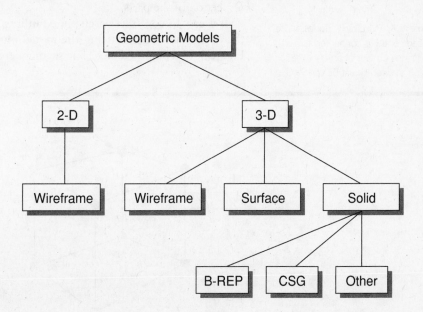

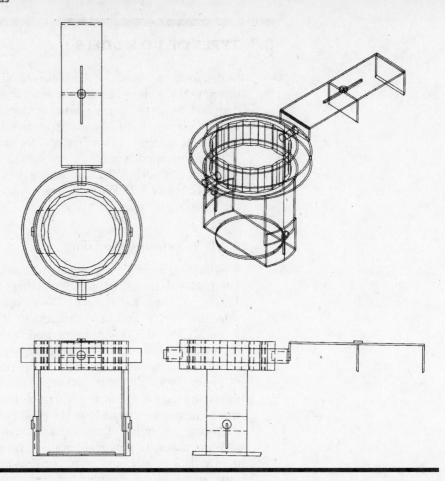

Figure 8.3 Wireframe model of a drink holder device showing the top, front, and right-side 2-D multiviews, plus an isometric view.

Figure 8.4 Wireframe nodes. Note that each entity is connected to its neighboring entities at a node, the location of which must be specified.

As shown in Figure 8.3, the designer can display wireframe orthographic multiviews, which are 2-D, and modify the display so that non-visible lines appear as hidden (dashed) lines instead of visible (solid) lines. On the other hand, if the designer wanted to see what is behind an object, he or she can use a 3-D wireframe model like the isometric view shown in the upper right of the figure. Thus, if the designer wants to see if two parts in a certain design assembly interfere with each other, a wireframe of the assembly allows an inspection of the parts.

It is easy to construct wireframes, but it is also tedious, because every one of the edges and nodes defining the model must be specified. The wireframe in Figure 8.4 is composed of 12 line segment entities, which form the edges of the

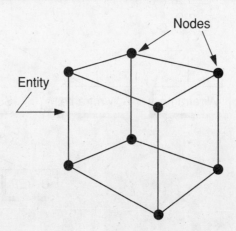

cube. The figure uses heavy dots to emphasize the **nodes**—locations where geometric entities are connected to each other. Within the computer's memory, a wireframe is represented by "tables" of data that define the edges and nodes on the model. For instance, the start node and the end node of each edge—where an edge may be either a line or a curve—are stored in the edge table. In addition, the coordinates of each node are stored in the node table (Chiyokura, 1988).

The display of a wireframe model is often an **ambiguous representation**, because it can be impossible for the viewer to determine which lines are in the foreground and which are in the background. Since wireframe models do not contain any information about the space between the edges, it can be difficult to determine, for instance, if two objects will interfere with each other. Also, it is possible to create a wireframe model of a **nonsense object**—that is, an object that is a physical impossibility.

Despite their limitations, however, wireframes can be very useful. For instance, a designer can use a wireframe model to determine the shortest distance between two points (refer to Chapter 2, Minimum Path Problem); to do visual interference checking to see if two moving parts collide; and to create orthographic views for detail-drawings and visualizing the internal space of an object.

Some designers prefer to use wireframe rather than other types of geometric models, because they feel that wireframes help enhance their visualization skills. Their reasoning is that it requires a greater visual mental effort to visualize an object on the basis of a wireframe than to visualize an object on the basis of a surface or solid model rendered on a computer screen.

However, most designers prefer the realism of rendered models (surface or solid models). One easy way to render a wireframe model is to remove the background (hidden) lines and shade the curved features of the object. This technique was used to render the object shown in Figure 8.5.

Figure 8.5 Rendering a wireframe model.

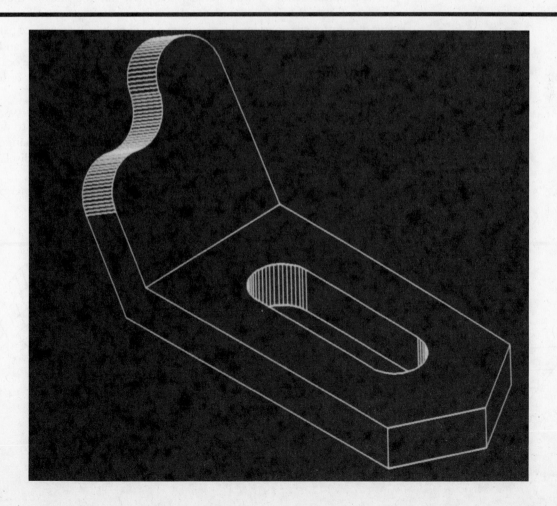

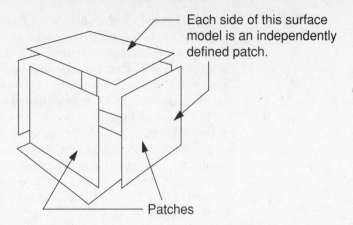

Each side of this surface
model is an independently
defined patch.

Patches

Figure 8.6   Surface model.

8.2.2 Surface Modeling

The second type of 3-D model, the **surface model**, was first developed in the early 1960's. Surface models, unlike wireframes, provide both visual and mathematical descriptions of the surface shapes of the object. You may think of a surface model as an infinitely thin shell corresponding to the shape of the object being described. Surface models are generated by placing flat and curved patches together to form the shell that surrounds the object (Santelle, 1989). The term **patch** is used by CAD modeling software developers to designate a limited region on a larger surface. Patches are mathematically defined by a curve-bounded collection of points whose coordinates are given by continuous, two-parameter functions.

The simplest example of a patch is a flat plane like the sides of the cube shown in Figure 8.6. The second simplest surface patch is a sphere, where a locus of points is at a constant distance from a fixed point. Other surface patches include the cylindrical surface, the ruled surface, a bicubic surface, and the Bezier surface. When using a CAD modeling package that employs one or more of these patching techniques, you would have to look very closely in order to note any difference in the way the surface has been modeled.

Geometric modeling (or 3-D CAD modeling) packages like AutoCAD, CADKEY, and I-DEAS can also generate polygonal surface meshes to define complex surfaces. As shown in Figure 8.7, a designer can even change the density of the mesh in these surfaces to achieve greater accuracy in displaying curved surfaces.

An advantage of surface models is that they are easy to construct by creating

Figure 8.7   A complex surface defined by polygonal surface meshes. (Courtesy of Autodesk, Inc.)

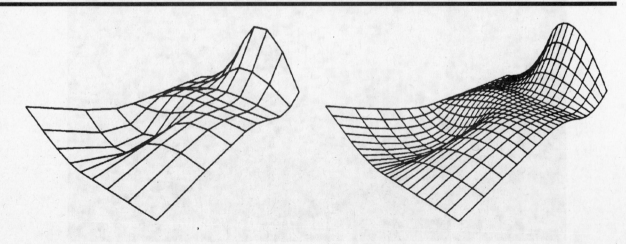

plane surfaces, as well as by sweeping, revolving, or extruding entities. In addition, a designer can use patches to create a transition between adjacent surface edges. Surface models are also useful for finding the intersection of surfaces in space, calculating volume and estimated mass, and creating models for shaded renderings.

One reason that surface modeling is flawed as a representational technique is that the polyhedral geometry lacks the analytical link back to the surfaces from which the patches were created (Santelle, 1989). Surface modeling's main fault, however, is that it cannot represent the interior of the model as solid. Therefore, surface models cannot represent properties needed to analyze a product's internal structure.

8.2.3 Solid Modeling

Solid models (commonly referred to simply as "solids") were developed in the early 1970's. Solid models are an unambiguous and informationally complete description of the object being represented. An example of a rendered solid using solid modeling techniques is shown in Figure 8.8.

The construction procedure for solid modeling is different from that for wireframe and surface modeling. Instead of having to generate specific lines, curves, and surfaces that define the object, the designer uses mathematically predefined **solid primitives**, such as blocks, cylinders, cones, wedges, spheres, and so on. The designer can define a particular primitive by specifying the desired shape, and then entering parameters such as size, position, and orientation. For example, a designer can specify a parallelepiped (a block primitive), and then enter its length, width, height, and initial position.

Most CAD modeling packages have a limited number of primitives available, but the designer can use them creatively to model very complex shapes.

Figure 8.8 Solid model.

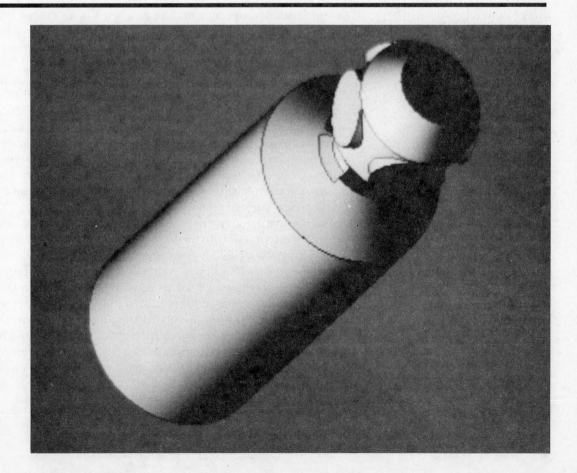

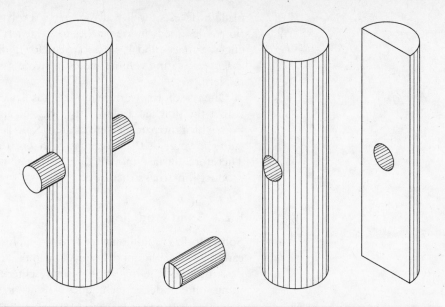

Figure 8.9 Some possible results of combining cylindrical solid primitives using Boolean operations. (CADKEY)

To create complex shapes, the designer can combine primitives using the **Boolean operations**: *union* (the sum of two primitives), *intersection* (the common mass shared by two primitives), and *difference* (subtracts a primitive from another). The Boolean operators used in solid modeling are derived from **Boolean algebra**, the mathematical system used formulating logical statements symbolically. The system was named for George Boole (1815–1864), an English logician and mathematician. As an example of the shapes made possible with Boolean operations, we can obtain all of the shape designs shown in Figure 8.9 by combining just cylinder primitives.

More than one operator may be combined in an expression allowing the user to use more complex results. These expressions are evaluated from left to right, as in algebra. To insure that expressions are evaluated properly, the liberal use of parentheses is recommended.

In addition to combining solids using Boolean operators, the designer is able to manipulate solid primitives with unary operations. In CAD modeling software, the **unary operations** control the manipulation of the selected solids and allow the designer to modify the selected solids. A typical unary menu contains operations such as move, scale, mirror image, duplicate, delete, separate, and so on. For example, the move operation is used to move a selected solid a specified distance along an axis or at an angle relative to an axis; the separate operation divides a solid model created with Boolean operations into its component parts or primitives.

The Boolean and unary operations used in solid modeling are powerful, but sometimes it is necessary to use other techniques such as sweeping. **Sweeping** consists of creating two-dimensional contours and moving them along a curve or revolving them along an axis. A simple case of a sweeping operation is **extrusion**. Extrusion allows a solid to be generated from a 2-D image that is stretched a specific distance along an axis. **Rotation** is another sweeping operation, in which a 2-D object is rotated around an axis to create a solid.

Since solids contain more information about the closure and connectivity of shapes than wireframes and surface models, they have become the most important type of model for designing, analyzing, and manufacturing products. Solid models offer a number of advantages over surface models, including the ability to calculate mass properties such as weight and center of gravity, and guarantee (to a greater extent) the structural integrity and accurate physical production of the model (Weiler, 1989).

Most of the commercial 3-D CAD modeling packages available today employ a combination of the techniques used in wireframe, surface, and solid modeling. In engineering design, we use the term "solid modeling" freely to refer to state-of-the-art modelers that can produce an image resembling and describing an object, whatever the technique used to create the image.

8.3 TECHNIQUES FOR CONSTRUCTING SOLID MODELS: CSG AND B-REP

Two solid-modeling representational techniques have dominated the 3-D CAD modeling field: constructive solid geometry and boundary representation. **Constructive solid geometry** (CSG) is characterized by defining solids in terms of Boolean combinations of solid primitives as we discussed in the previous section. To facilitate the construction of solids with the CSG technique, designers use a diagram called a **CSG tree**. Figure 8.10 shows the CSG tree for an L-bracket shape with a drilled hole. The CSG tree serves to divide the shape into simpler predefined shapes or primitives, thus providing a plan for constructing an object with solid primitives and Boolean operators. This approach is called the **divide-and-conquer strategy**, because it attacks complex problems (in this case, shapes) by decomposing them into smaller, simpler problems whose solutions can be combined to obtain a solution for the original problem. CSG trees and the divide-and-conquer strategy are particularly useful for modeling complex prismatic shapes like the object shown in Figure 8.8, but not as useful for modeling free-form curvilinear shapes like the surface shown in Figure 8.7.

Figure 8.10 CSG tree for modeling an L-bracket. (Courtesy of Dr. J. Miller)

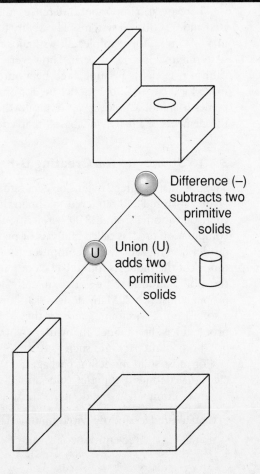

Difference (−) subtracts two primitive solids

Union (U) adds two primitive solids

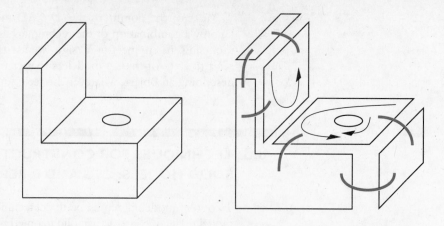

Figure 8.11 Boundary scheme for modeling an L-bracket. (Courtesy of Dr. J. Miller)

The other popular representational technique describes the faces, edges, and vertices of a solid that form the boundaries of a solid object. This representational technique is called **boundary representation**, or **B-Rep**. Figure 8.11 shows the L-bracket of Figure 8.10 represented as a B-Rep.

In terms of the usefulness of the finished product, CSG is well suited for analysis operations that require that objects be partitioned into sets that are inside, outside, or on the surface of other objects. Common examples of this include the partitioning of a line with respect to a solid while calculating volumetric properties and the realistic generation of shaded color images. The B-Rep approach on the other hand, is ideally suited for operations that require an orderly traversal of the outer boundary of an object, such as the generation of instructions for numerically controlled milling machines. From a model construction point of view, neither representation is clearly better than the other.

There are also important differences in the editing capabilities available in B-Rep and CSG-based systems. The ability to modify, replace, or delete primitives in a CSG tree, for example, allows major modifications to be made to a model with minimal input. There are, however, powerful B-Rep–based methods that cannot reasonably be supported by a pure CSG approach. Here the ability to make local changes to a model by, for example, chamfering edges and vertices comes to mind. Moreover, it is typically the faces, edges, and vertices—precisely the elements of a B-Rep database—that a designer wants to view and manipulate.

8.3.1. Strategies for Creating B-Rep Solids

The boundary strategy begins by generating a wireframe model. This wireframe is then analyzed and rendered to obtain the solid model. However, the change to a solid model from a 3-D wireframe is not trivial. This change involves a computation process called **analysis** or **processing**, in which the 3-D wireframe model is analyzed by the computer to check if it is a completely bounded model. If the model is found to be completely bounded, it is then rendered. If the model is found to be not completely bounded, the designer must make the proper adjustments. Many designers follow all the necessary steps for rendering a solid from a wireframe, and yet they still get errors during processing. This problem has discouraged many users who, unfortunately, give up too soon on good modeling packages such as AutoSolid and CADKEY Solids.

For most solid modeling packages, a solid is a collection of flat, or planar, faces that defines a completely bounded model. To ensure that the model is bounded completely, the designer must check on the following conditions:

- that all the faces of the wireframe model are planar,
- that at least three entities come out of each junction location of the model,

- that the respective endpoints of the entities (the nodes) share the same coordinates, and

- that lines do not overlap.

Let's say, for example, that a designer tries to create the object shown in Figure 8.12, which has some curved surfaces. While processing the wireframe model, the CAD modeling program will try to divide all the curved faces of the solid object into small polygons until the curved boundaries are smoothly defined. The degree of smoothness is given by the **segmentation value** set under the modeler configuration. The higher the segmentation value, the smoother the shape.

Sometimes a CAD modeling package will show errors on a face, even when all the entities that bound that face exist in the correct location. In this case, the designer must check that all those entities are part of a single plane. Refer to the faces in Figure 8.12. For this object the designer needs to verify that locations a, b, c, d, and e all lie on the same plane. The failure to do so may create a problem during the processing phase that produces the rendered solid.

There are two quick methods to examine the **planarity of a face**. The method used depends on whether the plane is or is not parallel to one of the three principal planes (X-Y, Y-Z, or X-Z). If the plane is parallel to a principal plane, the coordinates of both endpoints of each entity must be verified. They all should have one coordinate the same. Even a small variation between these values will cause errors in the processing of that face. If the face is oblique, as in Figure 8.12, the designer should examine the planarity in a different way. The designer can create a new view by setting the projection plane parallel to the plane in question. Working with the new user-defined coordinates, the designer can verify the coordinates at the endpoint of each entity on that plane by checking to see that they all have the same Z value.

Figure 8.12 Solid model created by rendering planar and curved faces.

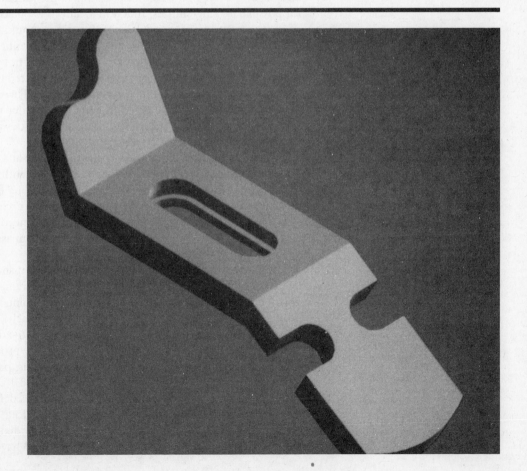

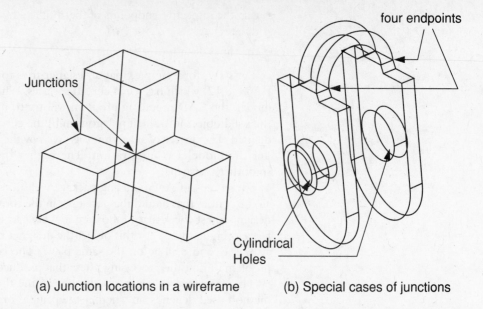

(a) Junction locations in a wireframe   (b) Special cases of junctions

Figure 8.13 Examples of junction locations on 3-D wireframes.

If a face in a solid model has one or more points off its intended location, the face will be distorted, even though it will look fine to the viewer's eyes. Sometimes this distortion may cause a "graphical user's error." If the error file created by the solid modeler postprocessor indicates that it finds an error in a face, checking for planarity will be a good idea.

If the designer receives error messages after ensuring the planarity of each face, he or she must now take a closer look at the **junction locations**, searching for possible missing entities. Junction locations are places where the endpoints of entities meet (see Figure 8.13 (a)). Junctions should always be the endpoint of at least three entities. For instance, if one line entity lies by itself without sharing its endpoints with any other entity, it does not contribute to the definition of a face. If there are only two entities connected to a junction, these two entities may define a face, but not a solid object. Therefore, there must be at least three entities at each junction location in order to completely define a solid model. A junction having less than three entities attached to it indicates that the solid object is not completely bounded.

In most cases, three entities will enclose the space at a junction. Occasionally, however, a junction will be shared by four or more entities. In Figure 8.13 (a), for example, the middle junction has six lines extending from it. In this case, the designer must be careful to see that the endpoint of each of these six lines coincides with the junction. Moreover, these six lines need to be independent so that the CAD-modeling-package solids processor can associate each line with a different face of the object.

When checking entity junctions, special attention should be given to arced faces. For example, Figure 8.13 (b) shows the wireframe of a fastener. The two junction locations in each cylinder show the endpoints of three entities. Even when only two entities define that curved face, each junction still has three endpoints. This case may be seen as an exception. If the designer tries to include additional entities to better define this cylinder, the processor will find errors.

A designer must remember that 3-D modeling packages following the boundary strategy will try to break down the model into regular faces (flat, arced, or meshed), and then will see that all the faces define a bounded volume or solid. Figure 8.13 (b) also includes junctions of four entities coming out of a single junction. In these cases, the designer has added a line to better define the object. Without that line, the program would have created a composite

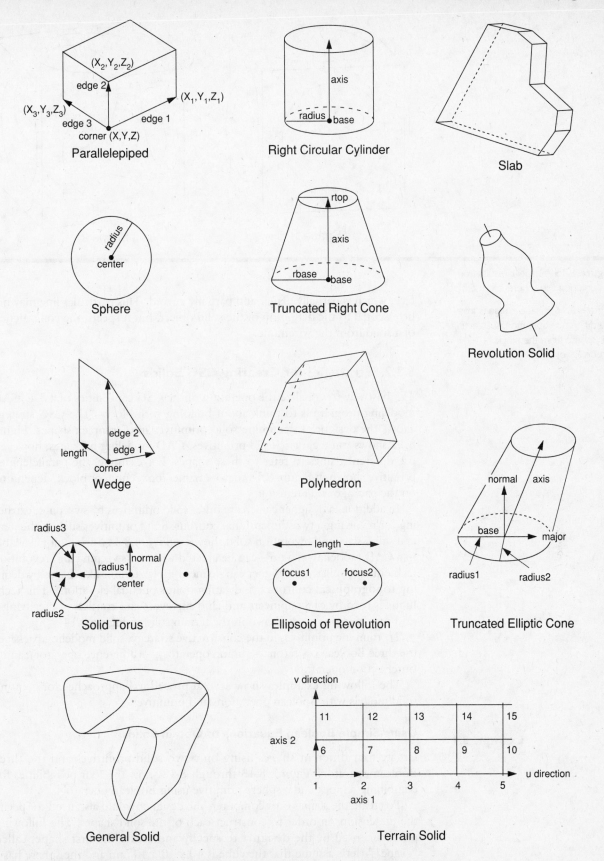

Figure 8.14 Generic primitives used in the constructive modeling strategy. (Courtesy of CDC)

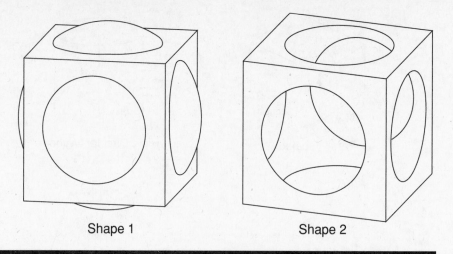

Shape 1   Shape 2

Figure 8.15 Shape 1 results from the union of the sphere and the block.

Figure 8.16 Shape 2 results from the difference operation, subtracting the sphere from the block. (Courtesy of CDC)

face, which is partially planar and partially curved. This particular line may not be essential to the definition of the solid object, but it speeds the construction of a solid from the wireframe.

8.3.2. Strategies for Creating CSG Solids

The best way to visualize the operation of the CSG capabilities of a 3-D CAD modeling program is to think about building with blocks. The CSG strategy allows the designer to combine solid primitives into complex shapes. Figure 8.14 shows some generic solid primitives. CAD modeling packages, however, use different names to refer to these shapes. For example, the parallelepiped primitive shown in Figure 8.14 may be named box, cube, or block, depending on the package you are using.

In addition, a designer can create other solid primitives by sweeping, extruding, or revolving a two-dimensional contour. Solid primitives such as the general solid, slab, and revolution solid shown in Figure 8.14—when not available in a CAD modeling system—can be created with the sweeping and revolution techniques. Similarly, a designer can define complex terrain-like shapes by defining **topographical contours** (indicating points of equal elevation). This technique is used by civil engineers and land surveyors and consists of specifying a grid matrix of points, as shown in the terrain solid in Figure 8.14.

To combine primitives in the constructive strategy, solid modeling packages use three Boolean operators: + (union operator), – (difference operator), and * (intersection operator).

The following examples show several procedural approaches for creating solid models with Boolean operations and primitives.

Example 8.1

Using Simple Boolean Equations to Obtain Solids

Create four different shapes using only two solid primitives and the three Boolean operators. Figures 8.15 through 8.18 show the four possibilities for combining a block and a sphere primitive using Boolean operators.

To create the shapes on a computer, the designer would also need to specify the dimensions in order to construct each of the solid shapes. The following process is used by the designer to specify and create the first shape, called "shape1" (let's assume that the cube is 40 x 40 x 40 mm and the sphere has a radius of 25 mm and is located at the center of the cube).

The designer indicates that he or she wants to create a block called "cube" and enters the parameters that define the cube as he or she is prompted for them by the computer.

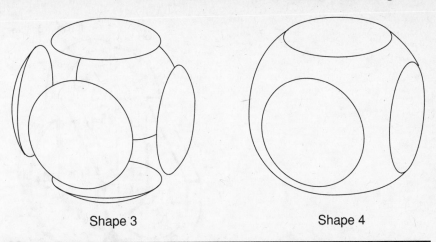

Shape 3   Shape 4

Figure 8.17 Shape 3 results from another difference operation, this time subtracting the block from the sphere.

Figure 8.18 Shape 4 results from the intersection operation, giving the mass held in common by the block and the sphere.
(Courtesy of CDC)

a. Corner of the cube (parallelepiped), i.e., coordinates at the origin or any vertex of the cube: (0,0,0).

b. Three edges relative to the corner, i.e., coordinates of the edges relative to the origin: {40,40,40}. Although this set looks like the coordinates of a point, the system recognizes the data as the edge lengths.

The designer then indicates that he or she wants to create a sphere called "sphere" and enters the parameters that define the sphere, as follows:

a. Center of the sphere relative to the corner of the cube: (20,20,20).

b. Radius of the sphere: 25.

Note that so far we have used the names "sphere" and "cube" to designate a sphere primitive and a block primitive, respectively; however, this is not absolutely necessary. In fact, many designers prefer to use other names to distinguish between the solids they are specifying and the primitive names used by the system.

Figure 8.15 shows the results of combining the cube and sphere primitives by using the Boolean operator+. The designer calls this shape "shape1." It can be expressed in an equation, as follows:

$$shape1 = sphere + cube$$

The + operator has the effect of adding these two shapes together to create shape1. Similarly, the − operator subtracts two shapes. For example,

$$shape2 = sphere − block, \text{ and}$$

$$shape3 = block − sphere$$

The results of these operations are shown in Figures 8.16 and 8.17, respectively. Note the effect that the ordering of the names has on the final result.

The * operator does not multiply two shapes together. Rather it gives the intersection, that is, those portions of the two primitives that coincide. The result of the equation

$$shape4 = sphere * block$$

is shown in Figure 8.18. In this case, as with the + operator, the order of the variable names has no effect on the final result.

The most difficult part of the equation procedural approach we have just reviewed is to divide the object we are trying to model into its component parts

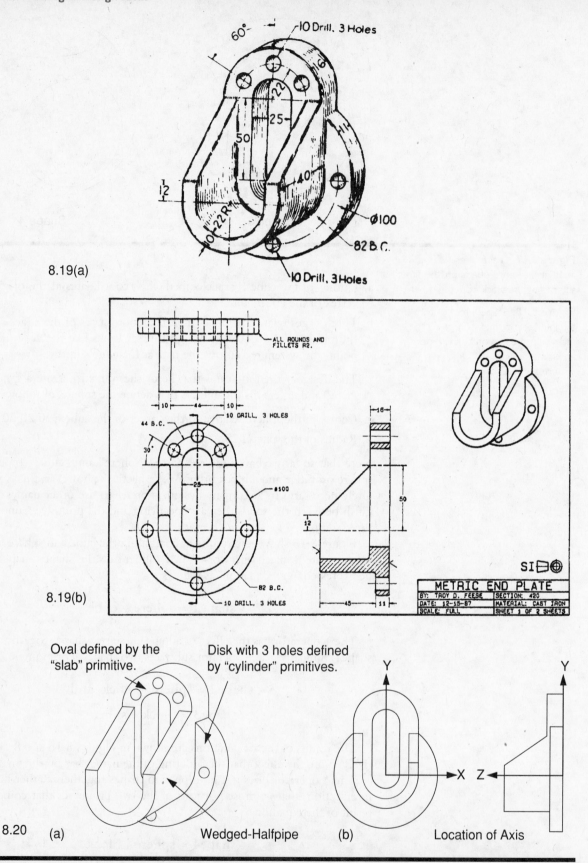

8.19(a)

8.19(b)

8.20 (a)   Oval defined by the "slab" primitive.   Disk with 3 holes defined by "cylinder" primitives.   Wedged-Halfpipe   (b)   Location of Axis

Figure 8.19 (a) Oblique sketch of an end plate. (Courtesy of McGraw-Hill; Source: Foster, *Graphic Science and Design*) (b) End plate's detailed drawings. (Courtesy of T. Feese and R. Barr)

Figure 8.20 Strategy for modeling an end plate: (a) divide the object in three parts, (b) choose coordinate origin at the center of the large disk.

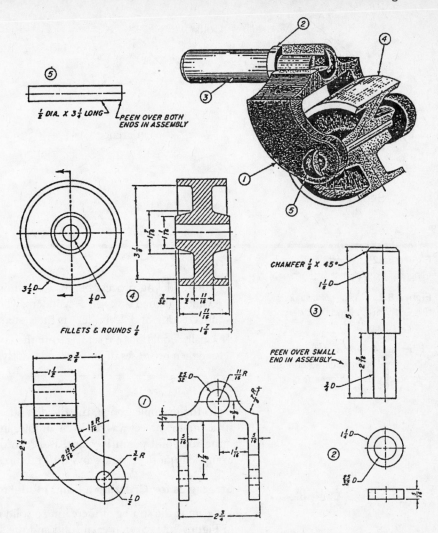

Figure 8.21 Caster assembly detail drawings. (Barr, et al.)

and primitives; that is, to develop a divide-and-conquer strategy. It is also important to select a strategic location for the *axes origin*; that is, in a way that would facilitate the modeling process. The next example illustrates these two important points.

Example 8.2

Creating a Solid Model for an End Plate

Propose the general strategy for creating a solid model for the given oblique sketch and detail-drawings given in Figure 8.19 (a) and (b).

1. Divide-and-conquer: The process of modeling this object may be considered to consist of creating three parts and combining them into the final object (see Figure 8.20 (a)). These parts are:

    *   The large disk with the three holes drilled in it.
    *   The large oval with the small oval slot.
    *   The wedged-halfpipe that protudes from the oval.

2. Define the axes-origin location: For the end plate, the designer chooses the part's coordinate origin to be at the center of the large disk (which is also the center of the bottom of the large oval) on the back surface of the part. This gives a good axis of symmetry about the Y-axis and ensures that all values in the Z direction will be positive, as shown in Figure 8.20 (b).

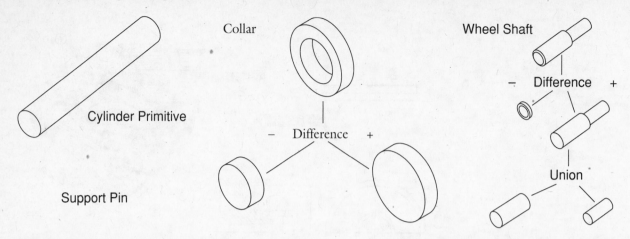

Figure 8.22 Support pin created using a cylinder primitive. (Barr, et al.)

Figure 8.23 Collar created using cylinder primitives and the difference Boolean operator.

Figure 8.24 Wheel shaft created using the cylinder primitives and the difference and union operators.

3. The modeling process begins by defining each of the parts; for example, a cylinder named disk (disk=cylinder), where "disk" is the name of the part we are creating and "cylinder" is the system's function for creating a cylinder.

4. Finally, equations are set to create the final model. The CAD modeling package then processes the model and displays the resulting rendered solid model.

In the example above, the divide-and-conquer strategy necessary for constructing the object was relatively simple, and no CSG tree was needed to determine the solid primitives and Boolean operators required. The following example is more complex and thus requires more planning by the designer.

Example 8.3

Strategies for Creating a Solid Model for a Caster Assembly*

Determine the strategy for creating a solid model of the caster assembly shown in Figure 8.21. Sketch each solid and the sequential Boolean and unary operations needed to construct the final solid model for the caster.

The strategy for constructing the assembly consists of dividing the caster assembly into five different parts, numbered in Figure 8.21: wheel frame (1), collar (2), wheel shaft (3), wheel (4), and support pin (5). Due to their simplicity, the support pin, collar, and wheel shaft can be created using similar procedures. For instance, the support-pin solid can be created by beginning with a cylinder primitive of the specified size and using unary operations (rotation and translation) to position it within the assembly (Figure 8.22). The collar solid can be created using a Boolean difference of two cylinder primitives, as shown in Figure 8.23. The wheel-shaft solid can be created using either the Boolean approach shown in Figure 8.24, or by performing a sweep contour operation; that is, creating a profile and revolving it 360 degrees around a reference axis, as shown in Figure 8.25.

The wheel solid can be created by drawing a profile of the wheel and revolving it 360 degrees around a reference axis (see Figure 8.26). The profile is created with the geometric-entity construction capabilities of the CAD modeling package, then revolved using the sweeping operation.

---

*This example has been reproduced with permission of Mrs. Laneda Barr, Dr. Davor Juricic, and Dr. Ronald Barr. The example has been paraphrased from the paper titled "A Study of Procedural Approaches to Creating a Solid Model in a Freshman Engineering Design Graphics Course," *Engineering Design Graphics Journal*, Vol. 55, No. 1, pp. 24–36.)

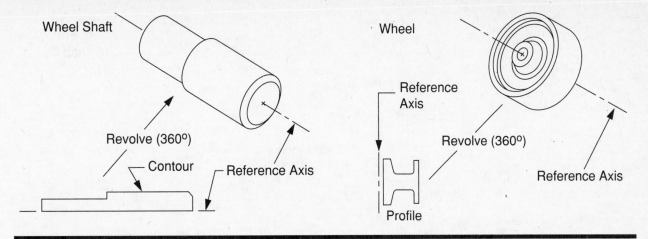

Figure 8.25 Wheel shaft created using the sweep-contour capability.

Figure 8.26 Wheel created using the sweep-contour capability or drawing a profile and revolving it 360°. (Barr, et al.)

The wheel-frame solid can be created according to at least five different procedures, designated here as Methods A through E. The CSG tree for Method A is shown in Figure 8.27. The contour of the top of the wheel-base frame and a circle for the hole in it can be generated with the geometric-entity construction capabilities, then extruded to give depth to each. The difference operation leaves the hole in the top part of the frame (Figure 8.27, right). The outside contour of the legs can be generated and extruded, in a similar fashion, and then duplicated. A difference operation again leaves holes in the legs of the wheel shaft (Figure 8.27, left). Note that the holes were not included in the creation of the contour, and were extruded separately. The three resulting solids can be joined together with the union Boolean (Figure 8.27, top). The rounding of the edges can be executed using the blending and filleting capabilities of the package. Note that these operations have been omitted from the figures to reduce the complexity of the drawings.

The CSG tree for Method B is shown in Figure 8.28. This method is similar to Method A, but eliminates the need to duplicate the legs; treating them as a single component. In this method, the leg contour is extruded the entire width of the wheel frame, and then a block primitive is used with a difference operation to remove the material between the sides. As in Method A, the difference operation is used with a cylinder primitive to produce the holes.

Figures 8.27 & 8.28 Wheel frame–Methods A & B. (Barr, et al.)

Wheel Frame (Method A)

Union

Duplicate and Union

+ Difference −

Extrude Extrude

+ Difference −

Extrude Extrude

Wheel Frame (Method B)

− Difference −

+

Union

Extrude

+ Difference −

Extrude

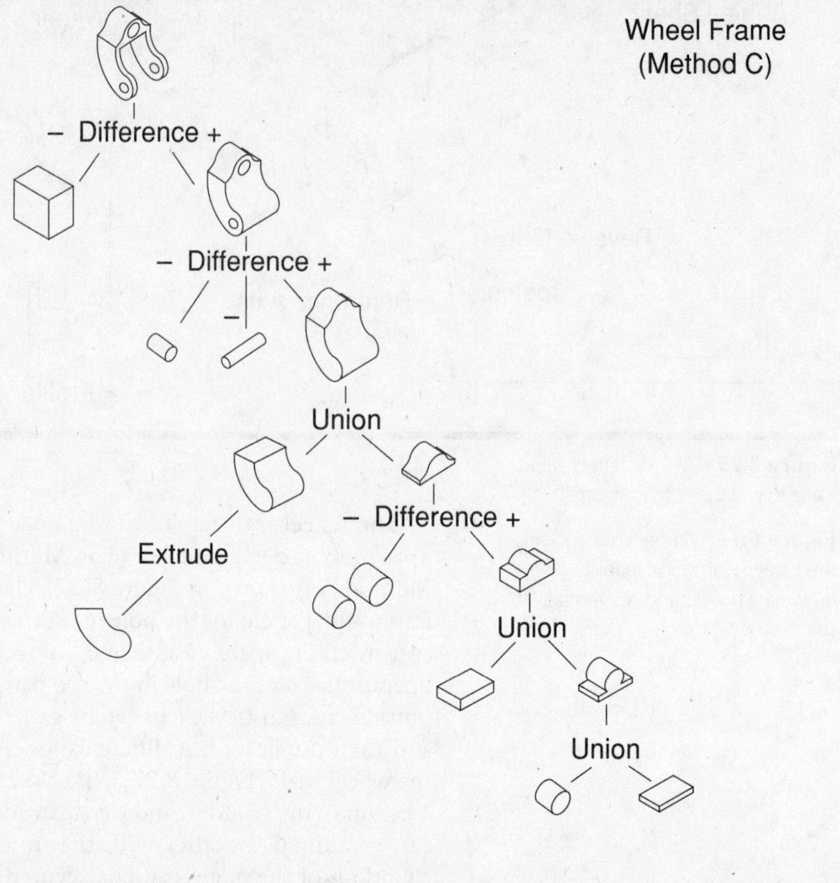

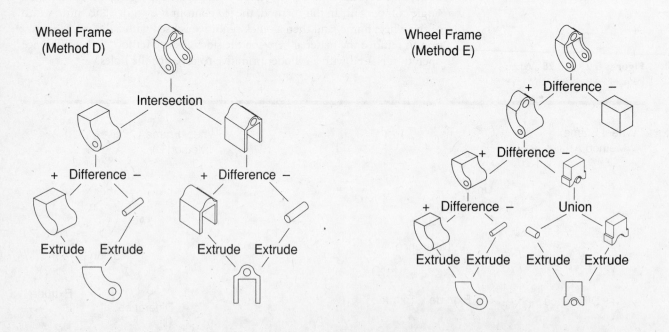

Wheel Frame
(Method C)

Figure 8.29 Wheel frame–Method C. (Barr, et al.)

Wheel Frame
(Method D)

Wheel Frame
(Method E)

Figure 8.30 Wheel Frame–Method D.

Figure 8.31 Wheel Frame–Method E. (Barr, et al.)

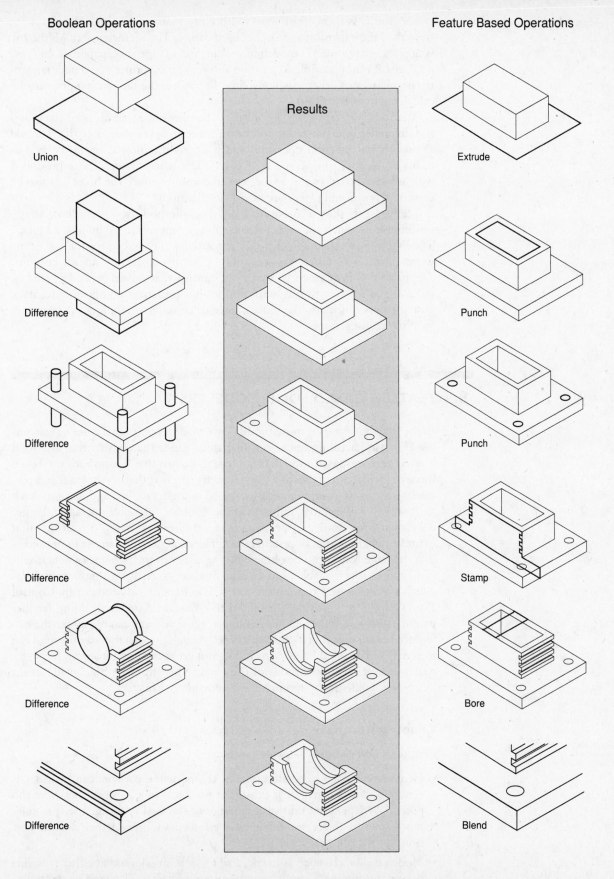

Boolean Operations

Union

Difference

Difference

Difference

Difference

Difference

Results

Feature Based Operations

Extrude

Punch

Punch

Stamp

Bore

Blend

Figure 8.32 Comparing Boolean and feature-based operations. (Courtesy of Professor William Ross and Michael Gabel)

Method C is shown in Figure 8.29. Note that this method requires more steps than the extrusion approaches used earlier. The inefficiency of Method C is aggravated if our CAD modeling package lacks tangency capabilities. In these packages, it is not possible to position automatically a primitive cylinder tangent to the surfaces of other existing solids. Therefore, the tangent points must be calculated mathematically.

Method D is shown in Figure 8.30. The previous methods used the union and difference operations but not the intersection operation. Note that Method D uses the intersection operation and is clearly the most efficient method in terms of number of operations involved. The wheel frame can be produced with an intersection of just two extruded contours. Since the holes can also be extruded, positioning steps are kept to a minimum.

Method E is shown in Figure 8.31. This method uses a "machine shop" procedure, in which the wheel-frame solid is conceived by "milling a block." The figure shows that a pattern was generated and extruded for the top of the wheel frame. The difference operation is used to create the surface contour. The pattern is positioned by matching cutouts that served as tool guides, or index marks. Although this method does not present a significant advantage over the previous methods, it does make us consider machining operations in solid modeling systems.

8.4 FEATURE-BASED SOLID MODELERS

In the previous paragraph (method D), we made a point for the use of machining and manufacturing operations that could guide the construction of a solid model. **Feature-based modelers** attempt to do just that. Using a feature-based modeler, a designer can identify the geometry of a part that corresponds to a particular machining operation. Feature-based modelers use machining terms such as "bore" to make a hole, rather than the Boolean difference operation. Figure 8.32 compares Boolean operations with the feature-based operations that extrude, punch, stamp, bore, and blend. The center column in the figure shows that the same results can be obtained using either of the two sets of operations.

Commercially available feature-based modelers such as ProEngineer by Parametric Technology Corporation and ICEM Parametric Modeler by Control Data Corporation provide capabilities to create solid geometry using familiar manufacturing terminology. For example, these systems can recognize the difference between boring a "through hole" (which goes all the way through the material) and a "blind hole" (which does not go all the way through). If the designer changes the dimensions of the object, the "through hole" will remain "through" while the "blind hole" will remain unchanged.

Chapter Summary

Chapter 8 detailed the following points:

- Geometric models generated on a CAD modeling package can provide an economical and convenient substitute for a real object, since they have the potential (depending on the capabilities of the CAD package used) to fully represent the object, including all the information needed to analyze and simulate the object's operation.

- Models can be classified as iconic, analog, or symbolic, and as either prescriptive or descriptive. Geometric models are generally classified as symbolic-descriptive, since they are abstract representations that characterize a device. Some designers, however, prefer to classify geometric models as iconic-descriptive, since a rendered model closely resembles the actual object.

- Three-dimensional (3-D) geometric models can be classified as wireframe, surface, or solid models.

- Wireframe models represent objects by the edge lines, curves, and points on the surface of the object. Since surfaces are not visible, wireframes can be difficult to interpret and are tedious to create. They are, however, the fastest to display and do not require sophisticated hardware.

- Like wireframes, surface models provide an accurate mathematical description of an object, but surface models appear more realistic. Surface models are relatively easy to construct by creating plane surfaces and by sweeping, revolving, or extruding entities. The usefulness of surface models is limited, however, because they do not represent the interior of the model and because they approximate curved surfaces with polyhedrons.

- A solid model is an unambiguous and informationally complete description of the object being represented.

- One method for creating solid models, called constructive solid geometry, or CSG, is to combine solid primitives, such as blocks, spheres, and cylinders, using Boolean and unary operations. Creating a solid using CSG techniques often involves creating a CSG-tree to diagram the construction process.

- Another method for creating solid models, called boundary representation, or B-Rep, is to first describe the faces, edges, and vertices that bound the object, thus creating a 3-D wireframe. The wireframe undergoes a geometrical analysis process to ensure that the model is completely bounded before it can be turned into a rendered solid model.

- Feature-based modelers provide the capabilities needed to create solid models using familiar manufacturing terms, such as extrude, punch, stamp, bore, and blend.

REFERENCES AND SUGGESTED READINGS

Barr, L., Juricic, D., and Barr, R., "A Study of Procedural Approaches to Creating a Solid Model in a Freshman Engineering Design Graphics Course," *Engineering Design Graphics Journal*, 55(1), 24-36.

Chiyokura, H. *Solid Modelling with DESIGNBASE*. Reading, Mass.: Addison-Wesley, 1988.

Dieter, G. *Engineering Design: A Materials and Processing Approach*. New York: McGraw-Hill, 1983.

Francis, R., et al. *Facility Layout and Location: An Analytical Approach*. Englewood Cliffs, N.J.: Prentice-Hall, 1974.

Santelle, T. "3-D CAD Modeling." *The Autodesk Guide for Teachers Trainers*, 1989.

Turner, W. et al. *Introduction to Industrial and Systems Engineering*. Englewood Cliffs, N.J.: Prentice-Hall, 1978.

Weiler, K. "Two Taxonomies for Geometric Modeling Representations." ACM SIGGRAPH 1989 COURSE NOTES.

EXERCISES

8.1. Figure 8.33 (a) shows two Boolean operations. In Figure 8.33 (b), darken in all the visible edges for the solid model that would result from the operations (courtesy of Prof. William Ross).

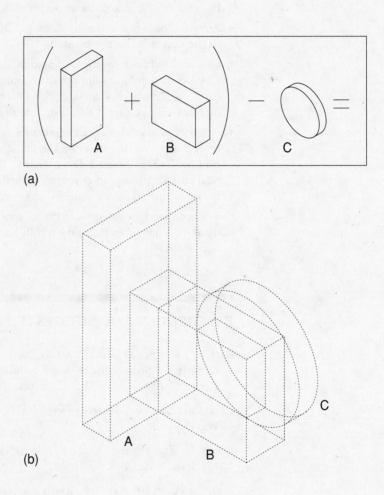

(a)

(b)

Figure 8.33 (Courtesy of Prof. William Ross)

8.2. Develop a strategy for constructing a solid model for the objects shown in Figures 8.34, 8.35, and 8.36. Sketch the object's primitives using a CSG tree. Label the point coordinates for each vertex or edge of the object.

Figures 8.34, 8.35 & 8.36

8.3. Generate a solid model using any 3-D CAD modeling package for the shapes shown in Figures 8.37, 8.38, and 8.39. (Scale 1:1, mm)

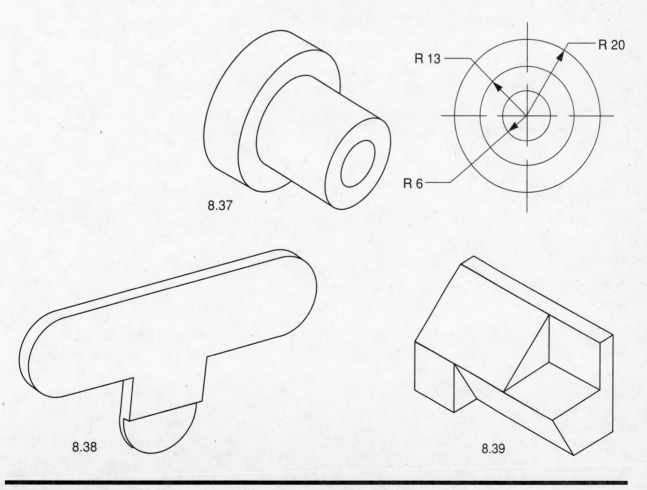

8.37

R 13

R 20

R 6

8.38

8.39

Figures 8.37, 8.38 & 8.39

8.4. Draw an image and/or write a short statement that describes or defines each of the key terms, listed below, used in this chapter.

Ambiguous representation	Model
Analysis (processing)	Nodes
Analog models	Nonsense object
Boolean algebra	Patch
Boolean operations	Planarity of a face
Boundary representation (B-Rep)	Prescriptive models
Constructive solid geometry (CSG)	Rotation
CSG trees	Segmentation value
Descriptive models	Solid models
Divide-and-conquer strategy	Solid primitives
Extrusion	Surface model
Feature-based modeler (mathematical models)	Sweeping
Geometric modeling	Symbolic models
Geometric models	Topographical contours
Iconic model	Unary operations
Junction locations	Wireframe models

CHAPTER 9 Design Documentation

Although a geometric model—particularly a solid model—can provide us with the complete 3-D database needed to build our designs, we must still document our design for legal and record-keeping reasons. **Design documents** consist of detail drawings that use acceptable industry standards to specify the material, size, proportion, and quality of a product.

Most structures and devices in use today have been built or manufactured from the information contained in detail drawings and written specifications. Contractors and manufacturing engineers still use detail drawings (such as construction plans and working drawings) to visualize the device or system that they are going to build.

At the core of detail drawings are the orthographic multiview, pictorial, and 3-D CAD modeling techniques, the essence of which have been covered in previous chapters. There are, however, other design documentation techniques that must be used to prepare detail drawings. In this chapter, we discuss the following design documentation techniques: generating cross sections to describe the interior of a product; providing dimensions to specify size and proportions; and indicating tolerance, or allowable margin of error, for a specified shape. The material is based on publications from the American National Standard Institute (ANSI) and International Standards Organization (ISO).

9.1 CROSS SECTIONS: INTERNAL REPRESENTATION

In preparing design documents we normally use 2-D representations. In many cases, multiviews with hidden (dashed) lines are enough to describe the interior as well as the exterior of the object we are documenting. However, in the case of complex devices, multiviews often do not provide a clear and unobstructed view of the object's interior features. For this reason we use **cross sections** to show portions of the internal geometry of the object.

To obtain a cross section of an object, we need to imagine that it has been sliced by a **cutting plane**. The cutting plane acts like an imaginary knife, cutting the object in half across an axis of symmetry. The internal features of the resulting "half-object" are projected onto the cutting plane in a similar fashion as when we are sketching orthographic multiviews. Figure 9.1 shows the process for creating a cross-section right-side view by using a cutting plane. Since we are not actually (physically) cutting the object, the resulting front, top, and sectional right-side multiviews are that of the original (uncut) object. Note that hidden lines are still drawn in all multiviews except in the sectional

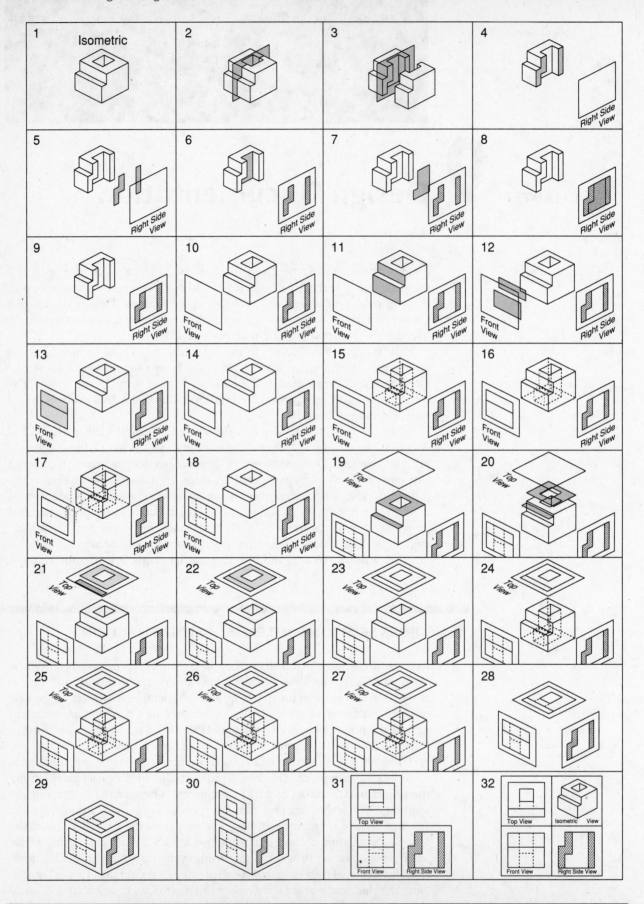

Figure 9.1 Sequence showing a cutting plane slicing an object and the process for visualizing a cross-sectional view.

view. It is recommended that hidden lines be excluded from a sectional view because they defeat the cross section's intended purpose.

Note that the solid features (those coming in contact with the cutting plane) are shaded with a pattern of diagonal lines called **section lining** or **crosshatching**. In cross sectioning, we use different symbols or patterns of lines to indicate the type of material touching the cutting plane. The crosshatching patterns used to represent some of the most commonly used materials are shown in Figure 9.2. However, if the entire product is made of a single material, we use the cast-iron-crosshatching symbol shown in Figure 9.2 (a) as the general symbol, regardless of the actual material.

We can pretend to cut an object in many ways—longitudinally, transversely, all-the-way-through, or partially—depending on the internal features that we are trying to convey or visualize. The simplest type of cross section is a **full section**, in which the cutting plane goes all the way through the object along the object's axis of symmetry.

Figure 9.3 shows the frontal multiview (left) and the right-side full section of a mechanical part. Although the cutting plane slices the object in half, the view is called a "full section" because the cutting plane passes *fully* through the part along its center line or axis of symmetry. Note in the full section that only the portions of the object that touch the cutting plane are cross-hatched, and only the visible lines of the exposed background features are depicted (no hidden lines are drawn). In this case, since the position of the cutting plane is obvious, there is no need to mark it on the front view. However, as we shall see, there are many cases where it is convenient to mark and label the cutting plane in an adjacent view.

Figure 9.2 Crosshatching symbols. (Courtesy of ASME & ANSI)

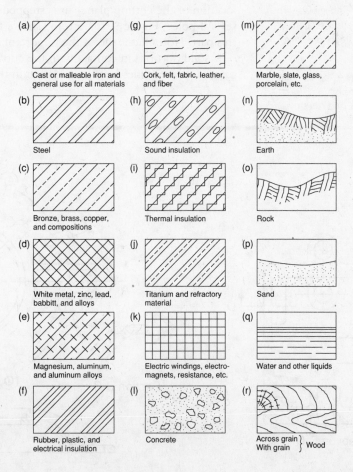

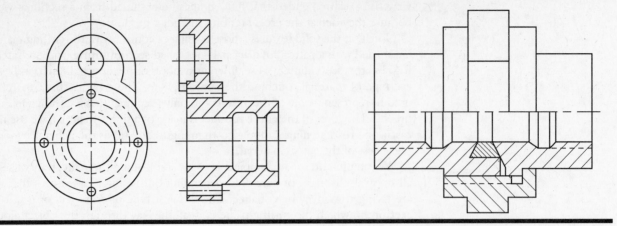

Figure 9.3 (left) A frontal multiview and a full section created by treating the vertical axis of symmetry as a cutting plane.

Figure 9.4 (right) Half section. (Courtesy of ASME and ANSI)

Figure 9.5 (left) The multiview of the top of this object shows the position of the vertical cutting plane. The frontal view is the offset section resulting from the stepped cutting plane.

Figure 9.6 (right) A top view and two aligned sections. (Courtesy of ASME and ANSI)

Figure 9.4 shows a **half section** view of another mechanical part. This drawing exposes only half of the part's inside features (the other half shows the orthographic projection multiview without hidden lines). Note that although one quarter of the part has been "removed," the view is called a "half section" because the part shows *half* of its interior features and the cutting plane passes half-way through the part. Again, the cutting plane line has been omitted since it coincides with the center line, and its location is obvious. However, in this case, some hidden lines have been drawn in the cross-hatched portion because they help the viewer to visualize the part.

Figure 9.5 (top view) shows a cutting plane as a heavy dark line (D-D) drawn on the top view of a mechanical part. In fact, line D-D represents the edge view of the cutting plane. Since some important features of the object (i.e., holes) are not positioned in a straight line, we have had to indicate the location of the cutting plane—it is stepped at right angles and passes through several holes. Figure 9.5 (bottom) shows the frontal **offset section** view for this part. Note that it shows the important internal features of the object, and only solid portions in contact with the cutting plane are cross hatched. In this case, no hidden lines have been drawn in the cross-hatched surface, but some

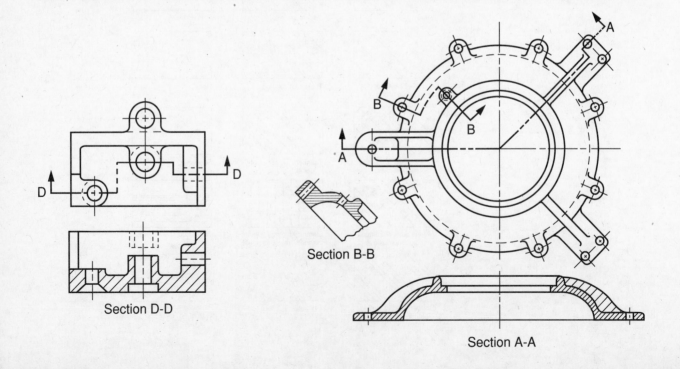

Section D-D

Section B-B

Section A-A

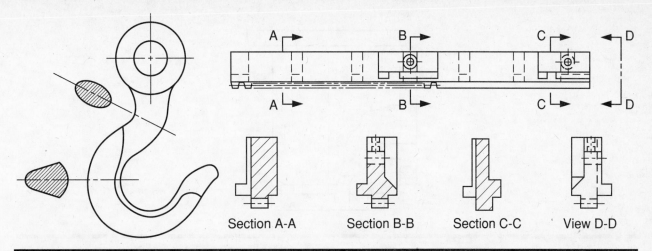

Section A-A   Section B-B   Section C-C   View D-D

Figure 9.7 (left) A front view and two removed sections.

Figure 9.8 (right) The top figure shows the front view of the object. Sections A-A, B-B, and C-C are magnified removed sections, and View D-D is a magnified right-side view. (Courtesy of ASME and ANSI)

hidden lines appear in the background to assist in the interpretation of the upper portion of this detail drawing.

In cases where an object contains angular features, we can use variations of offset sections. Figure 9.6 shows an **aligned section**. Note that this section (A-A) is obtained by rearranging the cutting plane so that it passes through an important feature of the object. Figure 9.6 shows another aligned section. Note that section B-B has been broken-out and is oriented parallel to cutting plane B-B.

Two **removed sections** are shown in Figure 9.7. ANSI defines a removed section as a section displaced from its common projection position. Some designers draw removed sections at a different scale from the scale of the reference view (that is, the view that contains the cutting plane arrow-lines). Figure 9.8 shows examples of magnified removed sections. Note that sections A-A, B-B, and C-C have been removed and are twice as large as the top reference view. View D-D provides a magnified right-side multiview of the detail drawing (Note that although D-D is not a section, we are using a cutting-plane symbol to indicate the direction from which we are viewing the object.)

An alternative to a removed section is to pass a cutting plane perpendicular to the part and revolve it 90 degrees. This results in a **revolved section**, an example of which is shown in Figure 9.9. When there is no space to place a revolved section in the drawing, a removed section is used rather than a revolved section. Both removed and revolved sections are particularly useful in depicting shafts, rods, columns, and wide-flange beams (I-beams).

Figure 9.9 Revolved section. (Courtesy of ASME and ANSI)

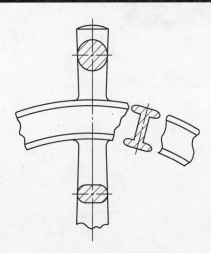

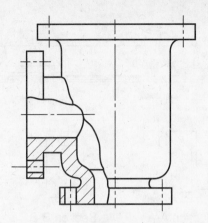

Figure 9.10 Broken-out section.
(Courtesy of ASME and ANSI)

Finally, Figure 9.10 shows a portion of a device that has been broken-out to expose part of the device's interior. These **broken-out sections** improve the representation of the device or object without having to draw a complete section.

Although the creation of cross sections is usually a 2-D representation technique, there is no reason why we could not use the technique on solid models to show the interior details of products. Figure 9.11 shows a full section of a geometric solid model. The designer, in this case, obtained a cross section of the model by executing a solid slice or cut command on a 3-D CAD modeling package. Similar results could be obtained with a difference – Boolean operation by subtracting a primitive (Block or Cylinder) from the frontal portion of the object.

Figure 9.11 A full section of a solid model.

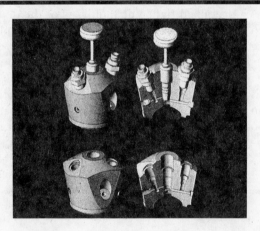

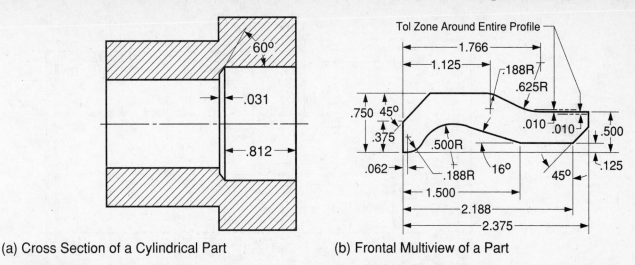

(a) Cross Section of a Cylindrical Part   (b) Frontal Multiview of a Part

Figure 9.12 Using arrowheads to show dimensions. (Courtesy of ASME/ANSI)

Solid-section models are very useful for visualization and presentation purposes; however, they need to be supplemented with 2-D cross sections specifying the size of each internal feature.

9.2 DIMENSIONING: SPECIFYING THE SIZE

Dimensioning is another important design documentation technique. It is used in conjunction with sectioning, orthographic multiviews, and CAD modeling to specify the desired size and proportions of the product. This section reviews the rules used for specifying dimensions, while the next section discusses how to specify the allowable margin of error for each specified dimension.

To appreciate the value of dimensioning in design, we should mention that prior to the 1800s designed products were typically defined by iconic (physical) models that were then reproduced. For example, to manufacture a rifle barrel, a laborer had to measure each barrel component on the designer's prototype by using a pair of calipers and transfer the measurements from the original prototype to the product. Since each laborer needed a model barrel to work from, the greater the number of workers a shop had, the greater the number of prototypes it had to supply. Also chances of error increased, because it was impossible to make all models identical, given the rudimentary tools of the time. Therefore, all rifle barrels were different, and it was nearly impossible to interchange parts.

Since the industrial revolution, designers have used dimensions to communicate the designer's intent. A **dimension** specifies the desired size of a product feature. It is a magnitude measured in a specified direction, or along a diameter or principal axis of an object. Dimensions are normally indicated using arrowheads, as shown in the cross section drawings shown in Figure 9.12. However, this is not always true; Figure 9.13 shows the foundation plan of building for which dimensions are given without using arrowheads.

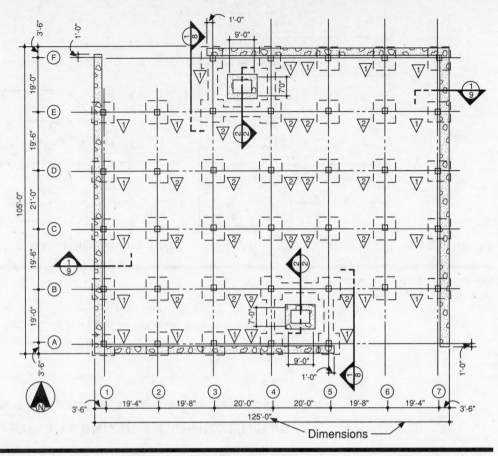

Figure 9.13 Foundation plan of a building showing dimensions in feet and inches. (Note: This is a sectional top view drawn by passing a cutting plane parallel to the basement floor of the building.)

9.2.1 ANSI Dimensioning Rules*

ANSI standards state that detail drawings shall clearly define the design's intent and shall conform with the following rules:

1. Each dimension shall indicate the allowable variation from that size, except for those dimensions specifically identified (see Section 9.3).

2. Dimensions for indicating the size, form, and location of the object's features shall be complete to the extent that there is full understanding of the characteristics of each feature.

3. All dimensions needed to completely document the design are necessary. However, no more dimensions than those necessary for a complete definition shall be given. The use of generalized or overall dimensions that apply to all the details on a drawing should be minimized. It is better to indicate each dimension directly in the particular feature of the part.

4. Dimensions shall be selected and arranged to suit the function and mating relationship of a part (i.e., where one part interfaces with another) and shall not be subject to more than one interpretation.

5. The drawing should define a part without specifying the manufacturing method that is to be used to produce the part. Thus, only the diameter of a hole is given without indicating whether it is to be drilled, reamed, punched, or made by any other operation. However, in those instances where manufacturing, processing, quality assurance, or environmental information is

---

*The material in this subsection has been reproduced with permission of ASME and ANSI. It is based on ANSIY 14.5M-1982. Some segments have been modified for clarity.

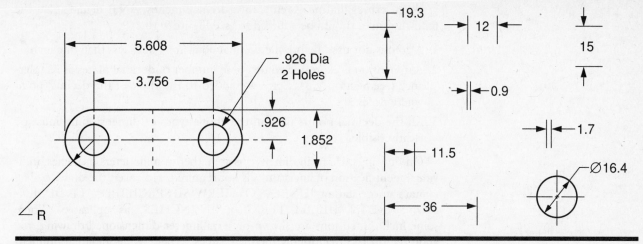

Figure 9.14 Dimensions should be indicated to the visible outlines or center lines. Do not give dimensions for hidden lines. (Courtesy of ASME/ANSI)

Figure 9.15 Proper format for expressing millimeter dimensions. (Courtesy of ANSI/ASME)

essential to the definition of design's functional requirements, it shall be specified on the drawing or in a document referenced on the drawing.

6. Dimensions should be easy to read. Dimensions should be shown in true size using orthographic multiviews and/or auxiliary views. Also dimensions should be indicated for the object's visible outlines or center lines as shown in Figure 9.14; do not give dimensions for hidden lines.

7. Wires, cables, sheets, rods, and other similar objects shall be specified by linear dimensions indicating the object's diameter or thickness.

8. A 90° angle is implied where center lines and lines depicting features are shown on a drawing at right angles and no angle is specified.

9. Unless otherwise specified, all dimensions are applicable at 20° C (68° F). Compensation may be made for measurements made at other temperatures.

9.2.2 Units of Measurement and Standard Decimal Formats

For uniformity, all dimensions in the ANSI Y14.5M-1982 standards are given in SI (international system) units. The most common SI linear unit used on working drawings is the millimeter. There are, however, a few industries that still use other measurement systems; for example, the U.S. construction industry uses the U.S customary system, although this is being phased out. The most common U.S. customary linear unit used on working drawings is the decimal inch.

Decimal dimensions are used on drawings except in certain industries, such as the construction industry, where dimensions are identified by standardized nominal designations such as pipe and lumber sizes.

ANSI dictates that the following standard rules should be adhered to when expressing measurements in millimeters (Figure 9.15).

1. Where the dimension is less than one millimeter, a zero precedes the decimal point.

2. Where the dimension is a whole number, neither the decimal point nor a zero is shown.

3. Where the dimension exceeds a whole number by a decimal fraction of one millimeter, the last digit to the right of the decimal point is not followed by a zero.

4. Neither commas nor spaces shall be used to separate digits into groups in specifying millimeter dimensions on drawings.

When expressing measurements in decimal inches, ANSI dictates that the following rules should be adhered to (see Figure 9.16):

1. A zero is not used before the decimal point for values less than one inch.

2. A dimension is expressed to the same number of decimal places as its tolerance (see Section 9.3). Zeros are added to the right of the decimal point where necessary.

3. All the decimal points used in the above types of dimensioning must be clearly visible.

On drawings where all dimensions are either in millimeters or inches, individual identification of linear units is not required. However, the drawing shall contain a note stating "UNLESS OTHERWISE SPECIFIED, ALL DIMENSIONS ARE IN MILLIMETERS" (or "IN INCHES," as applicable). Where some inch dimensions are shown on a millimeter-dimensioned drawing, the abbreviation IN. shall follow the inch values. Where some millimeter dimensions are shown on an inch-dimensioned drawing, the symbol mm shall follow the millimeter values.

9.2.3 Linear and Angular Dimensions

Linear dimensions specify features that can be measured in a straight line, while **angular dimensions** are used for circular features. Linear dimensions can be specified in either the millimeter or decimal inch format. On the other hand, **angular dimensions** are expressed in either degrees and decimal parts of a degree or in degrees, minutes, and seconds (see Figure 9.17). These dimensions are expressed by symbols: for degrees °, for minutes ', and for seconds ". Where degrees are indicated alone, the numerical value is followed by the symbol °. Where only minutes or seconds are specified, the number of minutes or seconds shall be preceded by 0° or 0° 0', as applicable.

9.2.4 Stylistic Elements for Specifying Dimensions

Dimensions are specified by means of dimension lines, extension lines, chain lines, and leader lines from the dimension to the appropriate feature (refer to Figure 2.7). Written notes are used to convey additional information. The following subsections describe the stylistic elements used to specify dimensions.

Leader Lines. A **leader line** is a slim angular line with an arrow at one end and a horizontal shoulder at the other end. They are used to point to a dimension or note and are usually inclined at a 30- or 60-degree angle. Leader lines are

Figure 9.16 Proper format for expressing decimal inch dimensions. (ASME/ANSI)

Figure 9.17 Proper format for expressing angular units. (ASME/ANSI)

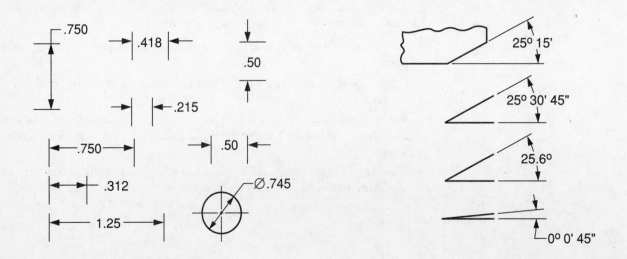

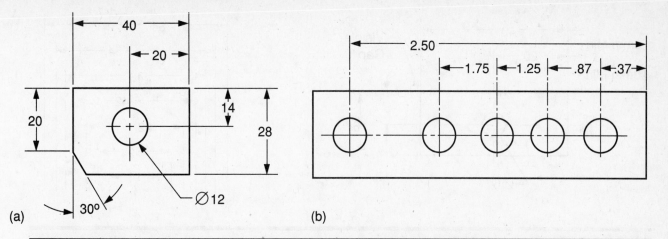

(a)   (b)

Figure 9.18 (a) Application of leader lines and dimension lines. (b) If several circles are to be dimensioned, they should be dimensioned from center to center of each circle. (Courtesy of ASME/ANSI)

used mainly to specify the dimensions of arcs and circles, but they are also used to specify notes or symbols concerning a surface.

There are several basic ways to dimension a circular feature using leader lines. Figure 9.18 (a) shows a leader line pointing to a circle and specifying a 12-mm diameter. Note that the Ø symbol is used to indicate that this magnitude refers to the circle's diameter, not its radius. In this case, the leader line touches the circumference and points to the centerpoint of the circle. Figure 9.16 shows another method of specifying a diameter. In this case, the leader line's arrowhead has been omitted and a dimension line was placed inside its circumference. Alternatively, the dimension also could have been placed directly within the circle—without a leader line—but only if it served to clarify the dimension.

Dimension Lines. A **dimension line**, with arrowheads at each end, shows the direction and extent of a dimension (see the linear dimensions given in Figure 9.18 (a)). Dimension lines can also be a pair of lines with each arrowhead pointing toward the other line, as shown in the angular dimension given in Figure 9.18 (a). Preferably, dimension lines should be broken for insertion of numerals, as shown in the figure. Where horizontal dimension lines are not broken, numerals are placed above and parallel to the dimension lines (refer to Figure 9.13) or outside the extent of the dimension (as shown in Figure 9.16).

As indicated in Figure 9.18 (a), the center of a circular feature should be positioned in relation to a corner. In the same way, if several circles are to be dimensioned, they should be dimensioned from center to center of each circle (see Figure 9.18 (b)).

Dimension lines shall be aligned if practicable and grouped for uniform appearance, as shown in Figure 9.19. This alignment gives the detail drawing a neat and organized appearance and helps in readability.

Figure 9.19 Grouping and alignment of dimensions. (ASME/ANSI)

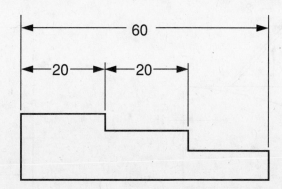

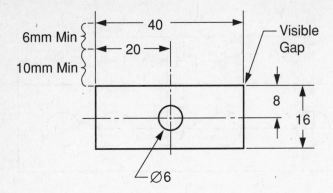

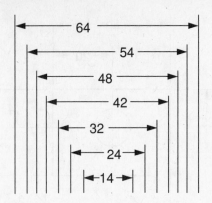

Figure 9.20 Proper spacing of dimension and extension lines. (ASME/ANSI)

Figure 9.21 Staggered dimensions. (ASME/ANSI)

Dimension lines should be drawn parallel to the direction of measurement to facilitate reading. The space between the first dimension line and the part outline should not be less than 10 mm; the space between succeeding parallel dimension lines should not be less than 6 mm (see Figure 9.20). However, these spacings are intended as guides only. If the drawing meets the accepted design documentation requirements in a particular industry, nonconformance to these spacing requirements is not a basis for rejecting a working drawing or a construction plan.

Where there are several parallel dimension lines, the numerals should be staggered for easier reading, as shown in Figure 9.21.

The dimension line of an angle is an arc drawn with its center at the apex of the angle. The arrowheads terminate at the extensions of the two sides (refer to Figures 9.17 and 9.18 (a)).

Whenever possible, dimension lines should not cross. Where this situation is unavoidable, the dimension lines should not be broken.

Extension Lines. Extension lines are used to indicate the projection (extension) of a surface or point to a location outside the part outline. Normally, a short visible gap is left between the extension line and the outline of the part, and the line extends beyond the outermost related dimension line (refer to Figure 9.20). Extension lines are usually drawn perpendicular to dimension lines. Where space is limited, extension lines may be drawn at an oblique angle to clearly illustrate where they apply. Where oblique lines are used, the dimension lines are still shown in the direction in which they apply (see Figure 9.22).

Wherever practicable, extension lines should neither cross one another nor cross dimension lines. To minimize such crossings, dimensions are staggered,

Figure 9.22 Oblique extension lines. (ASME/ANSI)

Figure 9.23 Breaks in extension lines. (ASME/ANSI)

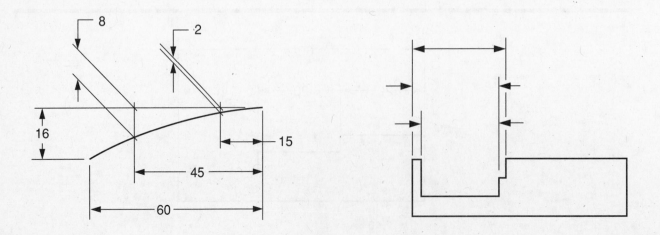

12.70 ± 0.25

Figure 9.24 A proper format for indicating the tolerance of a length.

with the shortest dimension line shown nearest the outline of the object (refer to Figure 9.21). Where extension lines must cross other extension lines, dimension lines, or lines depicting features, they are not broken. Where extension lines cross arrowheads (or dimension lines are close to arrowheads), a break in the extension line is advisable, as shown in Figure 9.23.

9.3 TOLERANCING: VARIATION OF ALLOWABLE SIZE*

Since it is difficult and very costly to manufacture a device or build a structure to the exact desired dimensions, designers use **tolerances** to specify the permissible variation in size and shape. Tolerances are an integral part of the design documents. In fact, tolerances are intimately linked to each specified dimension in the detail drawings. By specifying a tolerance, the designer makes it possible for the manufacturing (or building) inspector to verify that the particular components of the designed product fall within the allowed limits.

A manufacturer (or builder) should never scale a drawing to obtain dimensions and geometric tolerances—the data must be explicitly provided on the drawing. Dimension and tolerance specifications have significant legal and contractual implications. For example, when a designer indicates that a hole is to be drilled to a given dimension of .708 R (radius), it becomes part of the contractual design documents. When a designer specifies that the finished size of a part has to fall between 3.883" and 3.875", the quality inspector will reject parts that do not fall within those limits.

Designers use notes and standardized symbols to specify the geometrical quality and the degree of precision for each of the important features of their design. When the shape (geometry) is also specified—which is usually the case—we use the term **geometric tolerancing** instead of "tolerancing."

When specifying allowable tolerances, designers should check with an experienced manufacturing engineer or machinist. The designer should also be familiar with the definitions and symbols used to specify geometrical quality.

9.3.1 Basic Tolerance Definitions

A **tolerance** is the total permissible variation allowed in a dimension. In Figure 9.24, for example, the tolerance is $\pm$ 0.25, or a total variation of 0.50. This specification means that the width of the object can be as much as 0.25 greater than 12.70 or 0.25 less than 12.70. The **tolerance limits** of a dimension are the largest and the smallest that a part can be. Thus, in Figure 9.24, the tolerance limits are 12.70 + 0.25 = 12.95, and 12.70 − 0.25 = 12.45. The **specified**

---

*The material in this section has been reproduced with permission of ASME and ANSI. It is based on ANSI Y14.5M-1982. Some segments have been modified for clarity.

dimension, also know as the **nominal size**, is the basic size from which we calculate the tolerance limits. The specified dimension in Figure 9.24 is 12.70. In detail drawings, the tolerance dimension can be specified in either of the following ways: 12.70 ± 0.25 or $^{12.95}_{12.45}$.

A **bilateral tolerance** designates a dimension that can be either greater or smaller than the specified dimension, as the case in Figure 9.24. A **unilateral tolerance** can only be greater (or can only be smaller) than the specified dimension. For example, a unilateral tolerance given by $12.70 \, ^{+0.25}_{-0}$ would mean that the part can be no bigger than 12.95 and no smaller than the specified dimension, 12.70.

Maximum material condition (MMC) is the size of a part feature that results when the part has the most material. An object is at MMC when the feature is at its upper tolerance limit, unless the feature is a hole, in which case the object is at MMC when the feature is at its lower tolerance limit. The **least material condition (LMC)** is the opposite of MMC. In Figure 9.24, MMC is at 12.95 and LMC is at 12.45.

9.3.2 Fit of Mating Parts

Tolerancing is particularly important when a designer needs to specify two parts that have to fit together, for example, a shaft and a hole (Figure 9.25). Two parts that fit together are called **mating parts**. When providing dimensions for two mating parts, a designer needs to consider the possibility of both clearance fit and interference fit.

A **clearance fit** occurs when an external feature (for example, a shaft) will fit into an internal feature (for example, a hole or collar) as long as the mating parts remain within the given tolerance limits. Figure 9.25 (a) shows a part with a drilled hole and a diameter tolerance of $^{8.83}_{8.78}$. Figure 9.25 (b) shows the specified diameter tolerance for the shaft as $^{8.75}_{8.70}$. Note, in this case, that for any tolerance limits the shaft and hole will always have a clearance fit. For example, if we combine the smallest possible hole (8.78) with the largest possible shaft (8.75), there will still be a clearance of 0.03.

Fit is the range of tightness that may result from the specific tolerances of two mating parts. The **tightest fit** results at the minimum clearance or allowance. The **allowance** in the figure is given by the maximum material conditions of the hole minus the maximum material conditions of the shaft ($\text{MMC}_{\text{hole}} - \text{MMC}_{\text{shaft}}$). In Figure 9.25, the allowance is 0.03. The **loosest fit** will be obtained at the maximum clearance and is given by ($\text{LMC}_{\text{hole}} - \text{LMC}_{\text{shaft}}$).

Figure 9.25 Mating parts. (a) Part with a drilled hole indicating the tolerance of the hole's diameter. (b) Shaft (solid cylindrical part) and tolerance of its diameter.

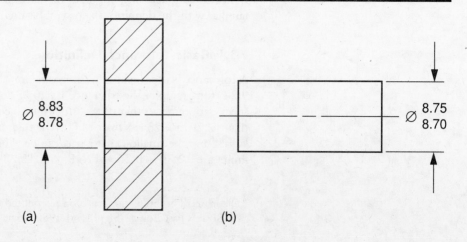

$\varnothing \begin{array}{c} 8.83 \\ 8.78 \end{array}$

$\varnothing \begin{array}{c} 8.75 \\ 8.70 \end{array}$

(a)   (b)

An **interference fit** occurs when two mating parts will be in contact (pressed together) because the shaft is actually larger than the hole. The smallest possible amount of interference will result from (LMC_{shaft}–LMC_{hole}), and the tightest amount of interference from (MMC_{shaft}–MMC_{hole}).

9.3.3 General Tolerancing Symbols (Extracted from ANSIY 14.5M 1982)

Along with the specifications of tolerance and type of fit, a designer needs to be able to convey information about the shape of each part of a design. This subsection discusses the standard symbols used for specifying geometric characteristics and tolerance requirements on working drawings. Situations may arise where the desired geometric requirement cannot be completely conveyed by symbols. In such cases, a note, supplementing a geometric tolerance symbol, may be used to describe the requirement. In other occasions, a note suffices to specify the desired design requirement.

Let's now discuss the types of symbols used to specify the product's shape quality with geometric tolerances.

Geometric characteristic symbols serve to specify the shape quality of the product being designed. Figure 9.26 shows the main geometric characteristics used in describing a product. Note that these symbols describe more than just the tolerance limits of each part: they specify shape attributes, such as required straightness, flatness, and so on.

Figure 9.26 Geometric characteristic symbols. (Courtesy of ASME/ANSI)

	Type of Tolerance	Characteristic	Symbol
For Individual Features	Form	Straightness	—
		Flatness	▱
		Circularity (Roundness)	○
		Cylindricity	⌕
For Individual or Related Features	Profile	Profile of a Line	⌒
		Profile of a Surface	⌓
For Related Features	Orientation	Angularity	∠
		Perpendicularity	⊥
		Parallelism	//
	Location	Position	⊕
		Concentricity	◎
	Runout	Circular Runout	↗ *
		Total Runout	↗↗ *
* Arrowhead(s) may be filled in.			

Datum Identifying
Letter

Figure 9.27 Datum feature symbol. (ASME/ANSI)

Figure 9.28 Basic dimension symbol. (ASME/ANSI)

The **datum feature symbol** is used as a reference to identify certain features on a product. In this way, other dimensions and tolerances can be referenced to a particular datum feature symbol. The datum feature symbol consists of a frame containing the datum identifying letter preceded and followed by a dash (Figure 9.27). All letters of the alphabet, except I, O, and Q, can be used as datum identifying letters. Each feature of an object requiring identification is assigned a different **datum identifying letter**. When data requiring identification on a drawing are so numerous as to exhaust the single alpha series, the double alpha series is used—AA through AZ, BA through BZ, etc.

The **basic dimension symbol** is used to identify the **specified dimension** (refer to Section 9.3.1). The specified dimension is drawn inside a rectangular box, as shown in Figure 9.28.

Material condition, or **modifying**, **symbols** are used to indicate conditions, such as "at maximum material condition (MMC)," "regardless of feature size," and "at least material condition (LMC)" (see Figure 9.29). The projected tolerance zone symbol, for instance, is used to indicate an intended tolerance zone (refer to Figure 9.12). The symbols used to indicate **diameter**, **spherical diameter**, **radius**, and **spherical radius** are also shown in Figure 9.29. These symbols precede the value of a dimension or tolerance. Occasionally, a designer may need to use a reference symbol to specify a dimension that will be alluded to frequently (Figure 9.29). The **arc-length** symbol is used to indicate that a linear dimension is an arc length measured on a curved outline. The symbol is placed above the dimension.

Figure 9.29 Modifying symbols. (ASME/ANSI)

Term	Symbol
At Maximum Material Condition	Ⓜ
Regardless of Feature Size	Ⓢ
At Least Material Condition	Ⓛ
Projected Tolerance Zone	Ⓟ
Diameter	$\varnothing$
Spherical Diameter	S$\varnothing$
Radius	R
Spherical Radius	SR
Reference	( )
Arc Length	⌒

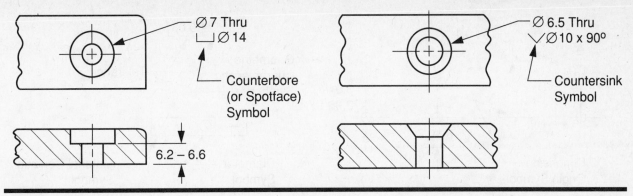

Figure 9.30 Counterbore or spotface symbol. (ASME/ANSI)

Figure 9.31 Countersink symbol. (ASME/ANSI)

The **counterbore**, or **spotface**, **symbol** is used to specify the shape of drilled holes. An enlarged cylindrical portion of a drilled hole is called **counterbore**. This hole is used to provide a recessed area in which to seat the head of a bolt below the surface of the part. This situation is called **spotface** when the hole is just a finished round depression on the surface, used to provide a true and accurate bearing surface on which to seat the head of a bolt. The symbolic means of indicating a counterbore or spotface is shown in Figure 9.30. The symbol precedes the dimension of the counterbore or spotface.

The **countersink symbol** is used to specify an enlarged conical portion of a hole that provides a place to seat a beveled head of a flathead screw. The symbolic means of indicating a countersink is shown in Figure 9.31. The symbol precedes the dimensions of the countersink.

The **depth symbol** indicates the desired depth of a hole. This symbol should always precede the desired depth dimension, as shown in Figure 9.32.

The **square symbol** is used to indicate that a single dimension applies to a square shape. The symbol should precede the desired dimension, as shown in Figure 9.33.

The **dimension origin symbol** is used to indicate that a toleranced dimension between two features originates from one of these features. This is used when a designer wants a dimension to be referenced to only one side, as shown in Figure 9.34.

9.3.4 Using Feature Control Frames to Specify Tolerances

Geometric characteristic symbols, the tolerance value, and datum reference letters are combined in a **feature control frame** to express a geometric toler-

Figure 9.32 Depth symbol. (ASME/ANSI)

Figure 9.33 Square symbol. (ASME/ANSI)

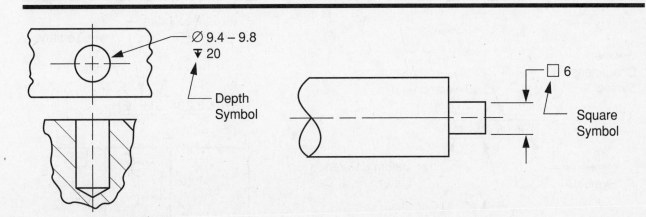

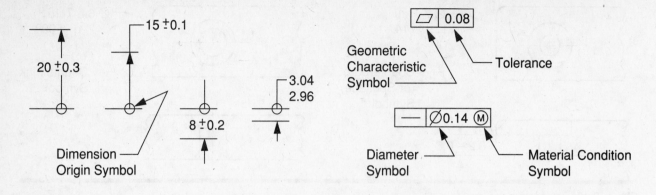

Figure 9.34 Dimension origin symbol. (ASME/ANSI)

Figure 9.35 Feature control frame. (ASME/ANSI)

ance (see Figure 9.35). The feature control frame is divided into two compartments, the first containing the geometric characteristic symbol, and the second containing the tolerance. When specifying a circular feature, the tolerance is preceded by the diameter (or radius) symbol and followed by a material condition symbol.

Where a geometric tolerance is related to a datum, this relationship is indicated by entering the **datum reference letter**—which is the same as the datum identifying letter, used in the datum feature symbol (refer to Figure 9.27). The datum reference letter is placed in a compartment following the tolerance, as shown in Figure 9.36. When the specified geometric tolerance needs to be referenced to more than one datum, we use different datum reference letters. To avoid confusion each letter is ordered according to its precedence as primary, secondary, or tertiary (Figure 9.37).

The feature control frame is placed in relation to the feature by one of the following methods, as shown in Figure 9.38:

1. locating the feature control frame using a leader directed note pertaining to the feature;

2. running a leader from the frame to the feature;

3. attaching a side or an end of the frame to an extension line from the feature.

Figure 9.36 Feature control frame incorporating a datum reference. (ASME/ANSI)

Figure 9.37 Order of precedence of datum references. (ASME/ANSI)

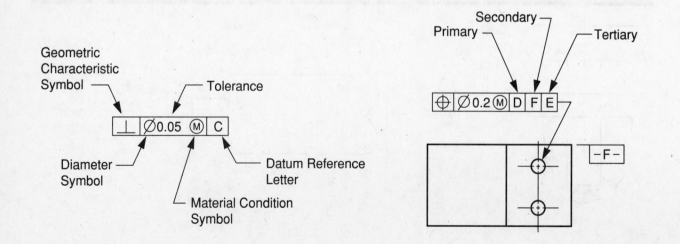

9.4 PATENTING: PROTECTING THE DESIGN

Design documentation techniques are used by designers, not only to communicate their design ideas, but also to protect them. A **patent** allows a designer to exclude others from manufacturing, building, using, or selling similar designs or inventions for a period of time (17 years in the U.S.). Any person who invents or discovers a new and useful device, process, or system may obtain a patent. The term "useful" is very important and refers, for example, to a machine that performs a specified purpose. Generally, if the invention has been described in any publication previous to submitting it for patent, or has been in public use, or has been on sale in the country where it is to be patented, a patent cannot be obtained (of course, the rules vary from country to country). One way to check if the invention is new is to perform a patent search in a large scientific or university library. There are also computerized databases available for this purpose.

Several government booklets describe the process for preparing patent documents. For example, the booklet *Guide for Patent Draftsmen*, from the U.S. Printing Office, describes the procedures for preparing patent drawings in the U.S. Application forms may be obtained from U.S. Department of Commerce, Patent and Trademark Office, Washington, D.C. 20231. In addition, the booklet *General Information Concerning Patents*, available also from the Patent Office, answers many of the questions commonly asked related to patents. Of course, a detailed explanation of the application procedure to submit a patent is beyond the scope of this book. Let's then concentrate on the drawings and verbal explanations that must accompany a patent application.

Figure 9.38 A working drawing showing examples of feature control frame placement. (ASME/ANSI)

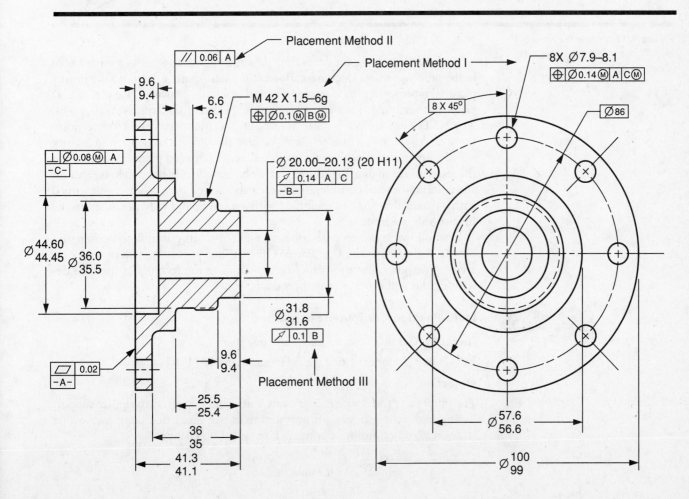

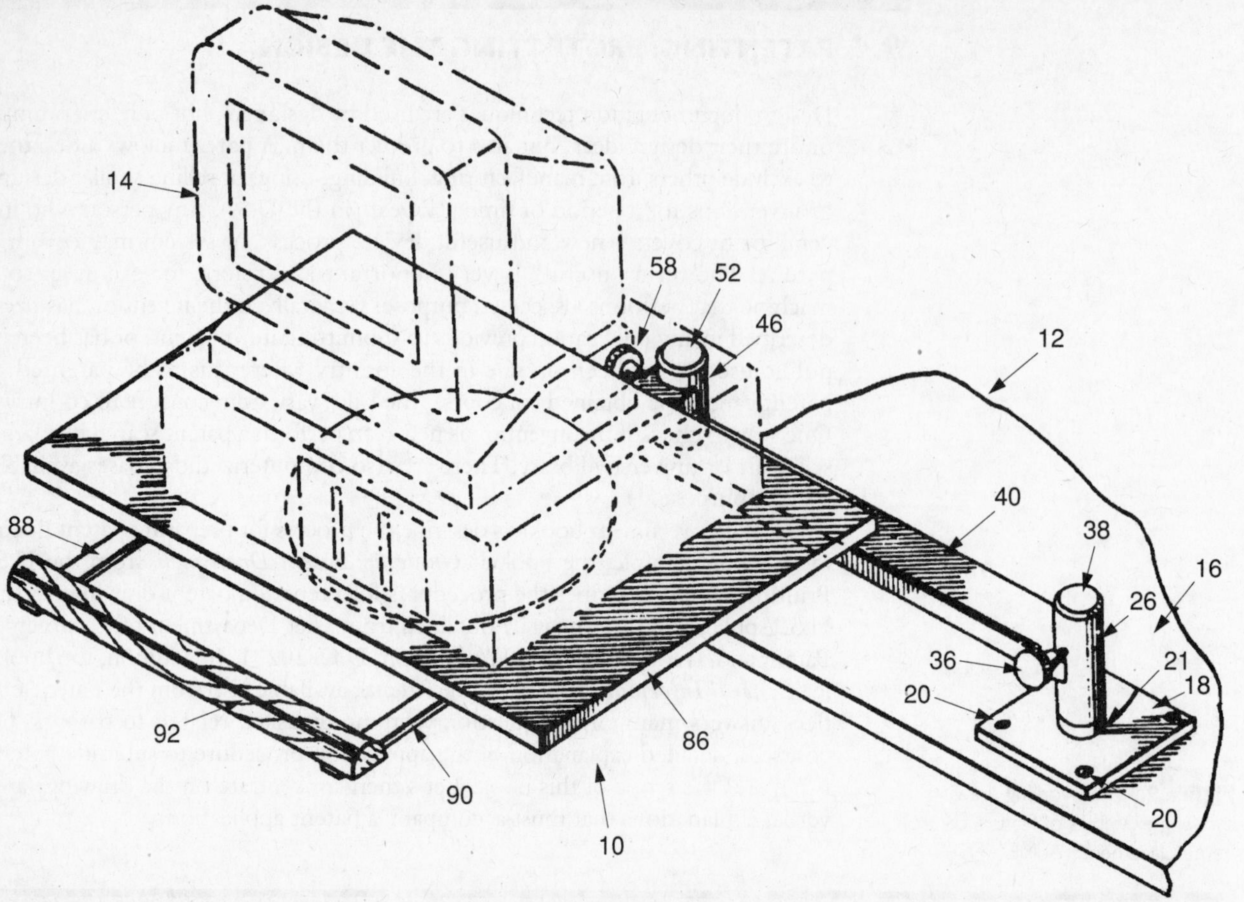

Figure 9.39 Perspective view of the Multi-Position Computer Support. (Courtesy of Mr. Skalka)

Rather than relying on detail drawings and specifications—as we have seen in the previous design documentation techniques—patent drawings use mostly pictorial representations, such as rendered isometric drawings. Rendered 2-D views and sectional views are also occasionally used for clarification purposes. These 2-D views are very similar to orthographic multiviews and cross sections; however, the drawings are rendered to give the illusion of depth and are not usually dimensioned. This is the main difference between patent drawings and the standard detail drawing techniques we have studied in the previous sections. In addition, for legal considerations, each component of a product—described with a patent drawing—is identified with a number and fully described in the **invention's abstract**.

The following example describes a patented multi-position computer support, as registered in the U.S. Patent Office. When presenting patent drawings, a young designer/inventor should *closely* emulate the techniques used for describing this and other patented products.

Example 9.1

Multi-Position Computer Support*

Inventors: Gerald P. Skalka and Stanley Skalka

U.S. Patent Number: 4,687,167; Date: August 18, 1987

Objective

The purpose of the device is to provide a new and improved computer support having high strength, ease of positioning of the supported computer over a large area, and economy of construction and maintenance.

---

*Reprinted by permission of the inventors.

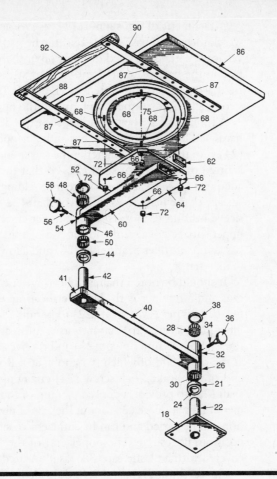

Figure 9.40 Exploded perspective view of the device as viewed from a position below and forward thereof. (Courtesy of Mr. Skalka)

Background

It is desirable to position a computer and its monitor in a variety of positions to permit multiple users to use the computer or to provide adequate space for other materials. A number of devices and systems have been proposed for this purpose (i.e., including desk-mounted attachments). Such systems have suffered from a number of shortcomings, including lack of adequate strength, high-friction pivot couplings between the pivot arms and between the inner pivot arm and its supporting structure, high expense, and an inability to easily and accurately position the computer or other items supported on the outer end of the outer pivot arm. Other devices have employed parallelogram type linkages and/or complicated arrangements for supporting a workstation platform.

Invention's Abstract

A computer support includes a base member to which an inner swing arm is pivotally mounted with an outer swing arm being pivotally mounted on the outer end of the inner swing arm and supporting a platform support by a lazy-susan bearing on its outer end (Figure 9.39). The pivotal connections are provided by pivot shafts over which pivot sleeves are positioned with upper and lower spaced roller bearings sets and a low-friction load bearing sleeve of substantial hardness engaging the lower end of each pivot sleeve. Brake/locks at each pivot permit retention of the arms in any desired rotational position in separate horizontal planes of movement.

Description: Figure 9.39 shows the preferred embodiment of the device, designated (10), mounted on a table (12) and providing support for a computer and monitor designated (14), and illustrated in phantom lines.

Attachment of the support (12) is enabled by a fixed positioned base (16) which includes a base plate (18) attached to the table (12) by bolts (20) and a vertically extending fixed or inner pivot shaft (22), mounted in a central aperture in the base plate (18) and welded at the upper (18) and lower surface of the base plate, as illustrated in Figures 9.39 and 9.40. The weld provides a strong and rigid connection between the pivot shaft and the base plate.

A tubular sleeve bearing (21) (see exploded view in Figure 9.40), formed of hardened low-friction steel, has an inner opening defined by a conical surface (24) with the larger diameter at the lower end of the sleeve bearing (21), which is fitted over the pivot shaft (22) so that the larger diameter portion provides adequate space to accommodate the welding bead at the juncture of the upper surface of the plate (18) and pivot shaft (22). The lower surface of the tubular sleeve bearing (21) rests on the upper surface of the base plate (18), and its upper surface engages the lower end of a first or inner pivot sleeve (26), which has an upper roller bearing set (28) and a lower roller bearing set (30) provided in its interior.

It should be noted that each bearing set consists of a plurality of roller bearings and a retainer with the roller bearings engaging the outer surface of the fixed and inner pivot shaft (22) to permit a low-friction rotation of the first or inner pivot sleeve (26) about its axis. A threaded aperture (32) extends through the wall of the inner pivot (26) and receives a threaded brake/lock screw (34) at the outer end of which is a knob (36). Rotation of knob (36) results in the end of the brake/lock screw (34) engaging the outer surface of inner pivot shaft (22) to provide a desired amount of friction in resistance to pivotal movement of pivot sleeve (26) about the axis of pivot (22), where the amount of friction can be varied and can be sufficient to simply lock the pivot sleeve (26) in position, if desired. The upper end of the first or inner pivot sleeve (26) is covered with a plastic cap (38), as illustrated in Figures 9.40 and 9.41.

Figures 9.40, 9.41, and 9.42 describe the first or inner swing arm (40) of the hollow rectangular transverse cross section that has its inner end welded to the first or inner pivot sleeve (26) and extends outwardly in perpendicular manner therefrom at a location approximately midway between the upper end and lower end of the pivot sleeve (26). An outer or second pivot shaft (42) extends vertically upward from the outer end of swing arm (40) through which it extends and to which it is welded, in a manner analogous to the connection of inner pivot shaft (22) to the base plate (18).

A tubular sleeve bearing (44) identical to tubular sleeve (21) is fitted over the outer or second pivot shaft (42) to cover a weld bead (45), as shown in Figure 9.43, and a second or outer pivot sleeve (46) identical to the first or inner pivot

Figure 9.41 Side elevation. (Courtesy of Mr. Skalka)

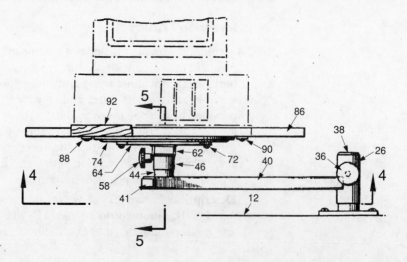

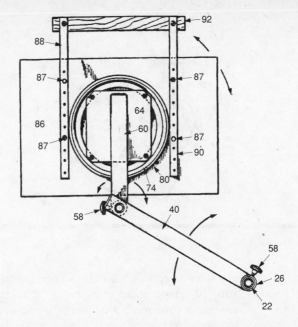

Figure 9.42 View along reference line 4-4 in Figure 9.41. (Courtesy of Mr. Skalka)

sleeve (26) is fitted over the second pivot shaft (42). Upper roller bearing set (48) and lower roller bearing set (50) are provided on the interior of the outer pivot sleeve (46) to engage the outer surface of pivot shaft (42) in exactly the same manner that bearings (28) and (30) engage the outer surface of the pivot shaft (22). A plastic cap or plug (52) is received in the upper end of the second pivot sleeve (46). Also, sleeve (46) is provided with a threaded aperture (54) receiving a brake/lock screw (56) having a knob (58), as shown in Figure 9.44, on its outer end and being identical in construction, purpose, and operation to elements (34) and (36) associated with the inner pivot sleeve (26). It should be observed that the inner end of the brake/lock members (34) and (56) can be provided with a friction-enhancing pad or the like, or that either engaging the outer surface of the associated pivot shafts or metal-to-metal contact can be employed, if desired.

A second or outer swing arm (60) is welded to the second or outer pivot sleeve (46) and extends outwardly therefrom in a perpendicular manner. Swing arm (60) is identical in cross section to the inner swing arm (40) but is of reduced length as compared thereto. Additionally, a plastic end cap or plug (62) is provided in the outer end of the outer swing arm (60) and a single similar

Figure 9.43 Sectional view along line 5-5 in Figure 9.41. (Courtesy of Mr. Skalka)

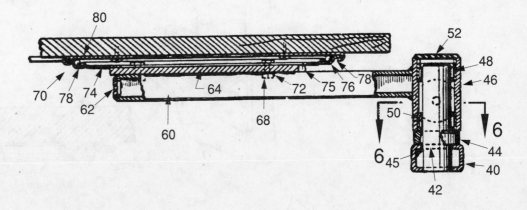

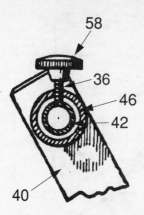

Figure 9.44 Sectional view along line 6-6 of Figure 9.43. (Courtesy of Mr. Skalka)

Figure 9.45 Views of alternative embodiments. (Courtesy of Mr. Skalka)

plastic end cap or plug (41) is provided in the outer end of the inner swing arm (40). A metal carrier plate (64) is welded to the upper surface of the outer swing arm (60) and is provided with four openings (66) through which mounting bolts (68) extend.

A lazy-susan bearing assembly, generally designated (70), is attached to the metal carrier plate (64) by bolts (68) that are held in position by nuts (72). The lazy-susan bearing assembly comprises a fixed annular bottom tray (74) having an inner edge (75) and a coaxial annular bearing groove (76) in which spherical roller bearings (78) are positioned to support an upper or top tray (80) for rotation in a well-known manner. Additionally, upwardly extending

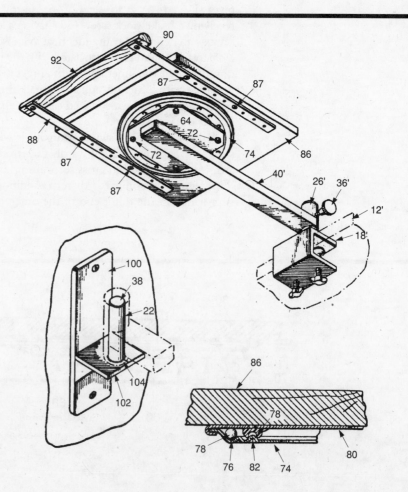

dimples (82) are provided at equal angular spacings about the axis of the fixed circular bottom tray (74) to engage a plastic detent (84) having a recess engageable with dimples (82) to permit angular rotational positioning of the upper tray (80) in an obvious manner.

A wooden support platform (86) is attached to the upper or top tray (80) by screws or the like (87). First and second handle support plates (88) and (90) are connected to the lower surface of the wooden support platform (86) by screw means (87) and extend forwardly thereof. It should be observed that the handle support plates (88) and (90) are provided with a plurality of apertures to permit their positioning forwardly and rearly with respect to the wooden support platform in a desired position. A wooden handle (92) is connected to the outer ends of the support plates (88) and (90).

In operation, manual movement of wooden handle (92) allows the positioning of the computer (14) in any desired position. Brake/lock means that (34) and (56) can be adjusted to lock the computer in such a position if desired and can also be adjusted to hold the computer in position with sufficient frictional force while still permitting subsequent manual adjustment of the computer position with minimal effort.

Figure 9.45 illustrates a second embodiment in which the second swing arm (60) is not employed, and the carrier plate (64) is directly affixed to the outer end of a modified swing arm (40'). The inner end of swing arm (40') is welded to a sleeve (26') fitted over a pivot shaft identical to pivot shaft (22) but attached to a base plate (18') that is unitarily part of a clamp assembly mounted on the edge (12') of a table.

Chapter Summary

Chapter 9 detailed the following points:

- To view the interior of complex objects, designers often generate cross sections that supplement the standard multiviews.

- Cross sections are obtained by passing an imaginary cutting plane through an object. Differences in the position of the cutting plane required and the placement of the resulting section determine the type of cross section to be used: cross sections can be classified as full, half, offset, aligned, removed, revolved, or broken-out sections.

- Working drawings are annotated with dimensions that specify the size and proportions of the object.

- The format for dimensions on working drawings is governed in the U.S. by ANSI dimensioning rules. The ISO standards are used in most other countries. The stylistic elements governed by these rules include the use of leader lines, dimension lines, and extension lines.

- Many industries use SI units (the millimeter is the most common) to measure linear dimensions, though several continue to use the U.S. customary units. Angular dimensions are measured in degrees and decimal parts of degrees or in degrees, minutes, and seconds. Decimal formats for both sets of linear units and formats for both types of angular measurement are governed by ANSI or ISO standards.

- The dimensions that are included on working drawings are generally accompanied by tolerances, which specify the allowable variation in the dimension.

- Tolerances are particularly important when a designer must specify the dimensions of two parts that must fit together.

- The symbols and format used for specifying tolerances are governed by ANSI or ISO standards. The symbols commonly used include the geometric characteristic symbols; the datum feature symbol; the basic dimension symbol; the material condition or modifying symbols; counterbore or spotface symbols; countersink, depth, and square symbols; the dimension origin symbol; and the feature control frame. In addition, tolerances are often referenced to each other with a datum reference letter, contained in the feature control frame.

- A patent is a piece of design documentation that legally protects the rights of the designer or inventor. In the U.S., the process for creating patent drawings is determined by the Department of Commerce's patent and Trademark Office. Patent drawings use mostly pictorial representations, such as rendered isometric drawings, to communicate the design.

REFERENCES AND SUGGESTED READINGS

Basic Facts About Trademarks. U.S. Department of Commerce, Patent and Trademark Office, Washington, D.C., Revised 1989.

Dimensioning and Tolerancing. ANSI Y14.5 – 1982. New York: American Society of Mechanical Engineers, 1982.

General Information Concerning Patents. U.S. Department of Commerce, Patent and Trademark Office, Washington, D.C., Revised 1989.

Henschel, M. *Metric Supplement to Technical Drawing*. Stratford, Conn.: Charles Quinlan Publisher, 1976.

Madsen, D. *Geometric Dimensioning and Tolerancing*. South Holland, Ill.: Goodheart-Willcox, 1984.

French, T., C. Vierck and R. Foster. *Engineering Drawing and Graphic Technology*. New York: McGraw-Hill, 1986.

EXERCISES

9.1. Sketch a full section for the multiviews shown below.

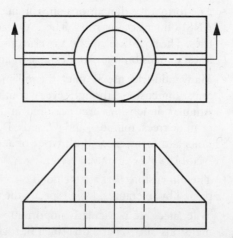

9.2. Sketch an offset section for the multiviews shown below.

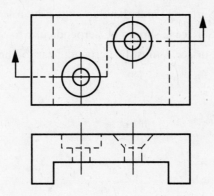

9.3. Specify the dimensions for the multiviews shown below.

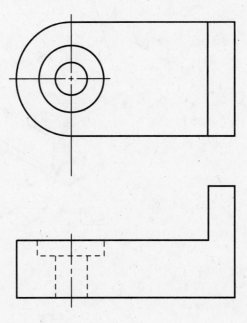

Scale 1:1 metric (mm)

9.4. Sketch the missing right-side multiview for the dovetail shown below. Specify the dimensions and tolerances for each view, based on the following information:

a. Surface D must have an angularity tolerance of 0.05 mm with Surface A.

b. Surface C should be perpendicular to Surface A within 0.03 mm.

c. Surface E must be perpendicular to Surfaces A and D within 0.02 mm.

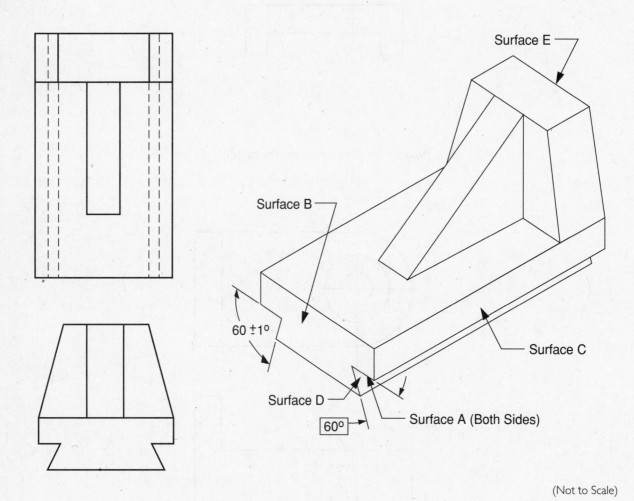

(Not to Scale)

Courtesy of McGraw-Hill and Profs. C. Jensen and J. Helsel

9.5. Draw an image or write a statement that describes or defines each of the key terms, listed below, used in this chapter:

Allowance

Aligned section

Angular dimensions

Basic dimension symbol

Bilateral tolerance

Broken-out section

Clearance fit

Counterbore

Counterbore (or spotface) symbol

Countersink symbol

Cross section

Cutting plane

Datum feature symbol

Datum identifying letter (datum reference)

Depth symbol

Design document

Dimension

Dimension line

Dimension origin symbol

Extension lines

Feature control frame

Fit

Full section

Geometric characteristic symbols

Geometric tolerancing

Half section

Interference fit

Invention's abstract

Leader line

Least material condition (LMC)

Linear dimensions

Loosest fit

Material condition (or modifying symbol)

Mating parts

Maximum material condition (MMC)

Offset section

Patent

Removed section

Revolved section

Section lining (crosshatching)

Specified dimension (nominal size)

Spotface

Square symbol

Tightest fit

CHAPTER 10 Design Presentation

"**A** picture is worth a thousand words." Actually, a picture—whether a simple graph showing market research data, a realistic rendering of a design, or an animated sequence showing a proposed product in action—may be worth quite a bit more, since most people would rather look at an interesting picture than read a long and tedious design report. Pictorials, rendered models, physical prototypes, and animated sequences are closer approximations of an actual product than are text descriptions; therefore, they can convey design information in less time and hold the attention longer. These techniques are particularly useful when making a presentation to an employer or selling a design idea to a client.

This chapter covers the most common methods used to present design results and data: creating effective graphs and charts, displaying eye-catching 3-D renderings and animations, and presenting simple cardboard prototypes.

10.1 PRESENTING DESIGN DATA

Graphs and charts are used in the fields of mathematics, science, business, and engineering to present quantitative information. Engineers and designers depend on graphs to explain physical behavior. If data have been gathered about a particular physical behavior, a similar or related behavior may be predicted without the aid of a rigorous mathematical solution by analyzing a graph. For example, if an engineer is designing a machine for driving piles underground, he or she may analyze a graph, such as the one shown in Figure 10.1, to see the relationship between time of fall and drop-hammer distance.

Figure 10.1 A rectilinear graph used to predict the physical behavior of a pile driver. (Courtesy of McGraw-Hill)

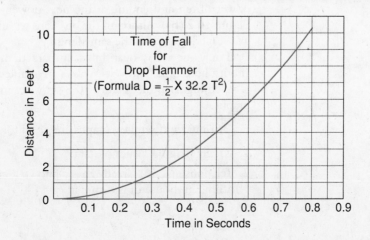

Time of Fall
for
Drop Hammer
$$\left(\text{Formula } D = \frac{1}{2} \times 32.2 \, T^2\right)$$

Distance in Feet

Time in Seconds

Design feasibility studies and reports should, therefore, be enhanced with graphs and charts showing, for example, product performance, marketing data, and so on. Good design presentations, without exception, include graphs to explain the specific characteristics or properties of the design.

There are as many types of graphs as there are ideas to visually represent them. Over the years, five basic types of graphs have gained popularity. The five main categories of numerical graphs are: rectilinear, logarithmic, polar, bar graph, and pie chart.

10.1.1 Rectilinear Graphs

A **rectilinear graph** presents a relationship on a coordinate plane. One coordinate of the data point (e.g., time or distance) is positioned along the horizontal axis. The distance along the axis at which the point is marked is proportional to the value of the number. The other coordinate of the data point is positioned along the vertical axis. The unit spacing distance is dependent on the size of the paper and the highest and lowest values of the data to be graphed, and the unit spacing must be constant along an entire axis. The units used on the horizontal axis, however, need not be the same size as those used on the vertical axis. Notice, for example, in the rectilinear graph shown in Figure 10.1, that each increment on the vertical axis equals one foot but on the horizontal axis only one twentieth of a second.

Rectilinear graphs are good for

1. Displaying a large amount of data.
2. Comparing more than one relationship or more than one curve on the same graph.
3. Filling in missing values.
4. Displaying a series of values, instead of a change in them.

Rectilinear graphs are *not* recommended for

1. Displaying only a few data points.
2. Displaying changes or differences.
3. Showing drastically fluctuating data or data that span a wide range of values.

10.1.2 Logarithmic Graphs

A **logarithmic graph** differs from a rectilinear graph in that it does not have equal spacing of unit markings along a given axis. Instead, equal spacing is related to powers of 10 as shown in Figure 10.2 (a). The distance between lines 1 and 10 (i.e., 10^0 and 10^1) is the same as between lines 10 and 100 (i.e., 10^1 and 10^2). A group of ten divisions along a logarithmic axis beginning at some power of ten and ending at the next power of ten, is called a **log cycle** (see Figure 10.2 (b)). Although the divisions within a cycle vary in length along the axis, each log cycle is the same length.

If only one axis is logarithmically marked, the graph is called a **semilog chart**. If both horizontal and vertical axes are marked logarithmically, then the graph is called **logarithmic**. Figure 10.3 shows examples of semilog and logarithmic graphs.

Logarithmic and semilog graphs are good for

1. Widely ranging values of data.
2. Relationships that already have a known logarithmic behavior (e.g., the logarithmic response of the human ear).

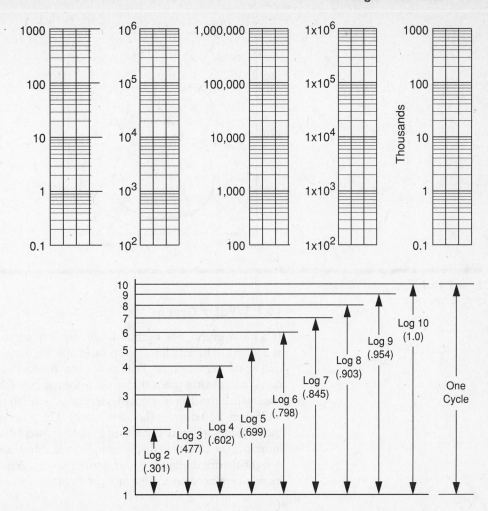

Figure 10.2 (a) Logarithmic spacings. (b) Log spacings and a log cycle.

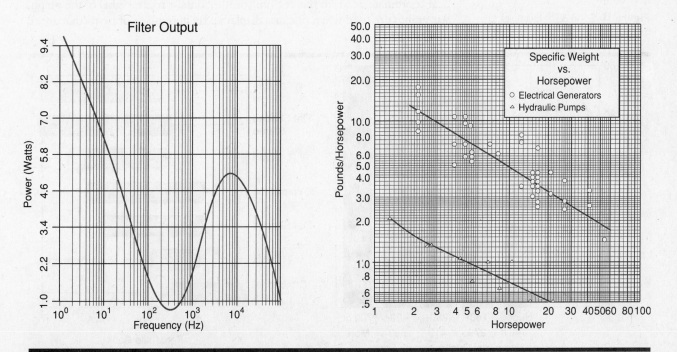

Figure 10.3 (a) Semilog chart. (b) Logarithmic graph.

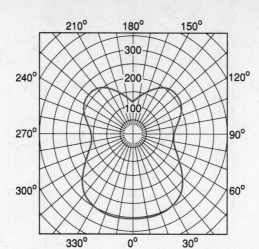

Figure 10.4 Polar graph. (Courtesy of GTE Sylvania, Inc.)

10.1.3 Polar Graphs

In a **polar graph**, one of the coordinates is an angle while the other is graphed as a length. The grid lines of a polar graph form concentric circles, with the origin at the center point. Data points are marked in the same manner as positional coordinates given in the polar format (see Chapter 7). Polar graphs are used where the data is angularly dependant, and in most cases, the data repeats itself every 360 degrees (i.e., it is cyclic). The polar graph in Figure 10.4 shows the luminous intensity (measured in candlepower) distribution curve for a diffuse luminaire (i.e., a source that gives light in all directions, though not uniformly). A light-fixture designer may construct such a graph by measuring the illumination produced on a plane at right angles to the source, at a known distance.

10.1.4 Bar Graphs

A **bar graph is** similar to a rectilinear graph, but bars are shaded under the vertical coordinate down to the bottom (or horizontally to the right) of the graph. Bar graphs are used when one axis displays a small number of items that are to

Figure 10.5 (a) & (b) Examples of bar graphs.

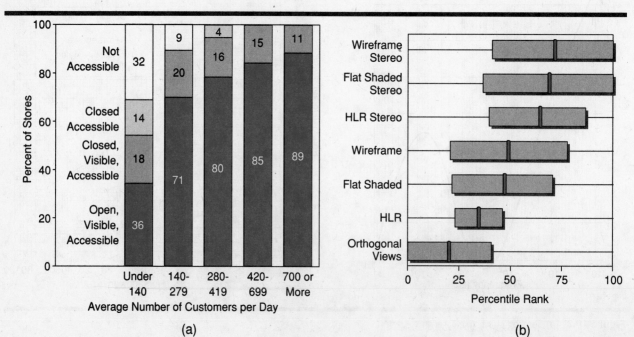

(a)

(b)

be compared, or the values along one axis can be broken down into a few ranges. Bar charts are easily understood, since the size of the bar is indicative of the value of the data represented. Bar graphs are used to display a few data points, such as quantities, with emphasis on changes in the data, and are used extensively in engineering design and management. Figure 10.5 (a) shows data useful for designing a store. The figure shows the relationship between the visibility and accessibility of a store and the number of customers that visit it each day. Figure 10.5 (b) ranks the effectiveness of different computer display technologies used in design presentation.

10.1.5 Pie Charts

A **pie chart** is a polar bar graph. Different "pieces of pie" are shaded around the circular graph, and all the pieces add up to a whole circle. The greater the value of the data, the greater is the "piece of pie." Pie graphs are used when data values can be expressed as a percentage of the whole. For example, the pie chart in Figure 10.6 shows how much of the time taken to prepare a design presentation went to the various parts of that presentation. Since "art work" took 25% of the time, a quarter piece of the pie is designated "art work."

Pie charts are very effective for comparing small "chunks" of quantitative information quickly. Note that the pie chart in Figure 10.6 uses texture for emphasis. Shading and other rendering techniques can also be used to add depth to the chart.

Charts and graphs are often created on computers using spreadsheet packages, such as Lotus, which contain specific functions for creating graphs and charts. If a designer feels so inclined, the same types of figures can be created and greatly embellished with 3-D CAD modeling and rendering software.

10.2 METHODS FOR RENDERING 3-D MODELS

Although graphs are extremely useful for conveying data related to a product, the design itself, to be fully understood, should be modeled. Of the rendering methods available to the designer, multiviews are helpful for working drawings, but they are not as effective when trying to convey ideas to a prospective client. For this activity, the designer needs to use 3-D CAD modeling software capable of displaying realistic rendered models.

In Chapter 8, we studied several geometric modeling techniques; however, at that time we were not focusing on the degree of realism obtained—all we

Figure 10.6 Pie chart.

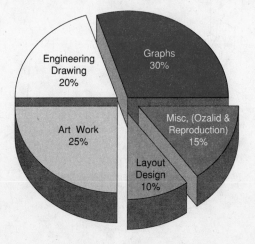

wanted was to produce an accurate 3-D model. In this section, we study the rendering and display techniques used for presenting realistic geometric models to a client. The three basic techniques for displaying three-dimensional objects are wireframe models with hidden line removal (HLR), shaded solids, and stereoscopic representations. This section discusses the first two techniques; section 10.3 will present an introduction to stereoscopic computer graphics.

10.2.1 Wireframe Models with HLR

Most modeling packages offer wireframe **hidden line removal (HLR)** to make wireframe models easier to understand. HLR is a program within most 3-D CAD modeling packages that calculates and only displays the edges and surfaces directly visible to the observer. Figure 10.7 shows an object before and after executing the HLR program. In addition to HLR, some systems also vary the intensity of the lines on the screen according to how close they are to the front of the object. This technique is known as **depth cueing**.

10.2.2 Effect of Light Sources on Solid Models

Despite the advantages of HLR and depth cueing, however, they do not provide an adequate degree of realism to create competitive design presentations. Modern rendering or shading methods must be used in conjunction with modeled solids to generate realistic presentations.

When rendering a solid object, the designer needs to consider first the light sources desired. For instance, designers must often decide whether the effect of light on the object should resemble that of the sun or a light bulb. For this reason, many 3-D CAD modeling and rendering systems offer two types of light source options: a **directional light** source, such as the sun, and a **positional light** source such as a light bulb.

For a directional light source, all of the light rays are assumed to be parallel; therefore, only the direction of the light has to be specified. The effect of a directional light source is analogous to the lines-of-sight in parallel projections: assuming light rays are parallel is equivalent to assuming that the light source is located an infinite distance away.

Figure 10.7 Wireframe displays: (a) before, (b) after hidden line removal (HLR)

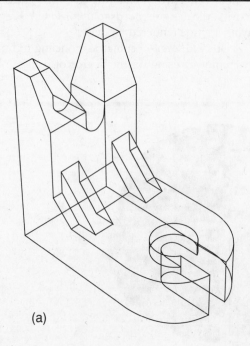

(a)

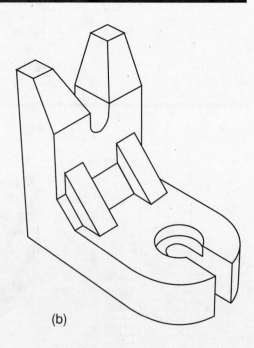

(b)

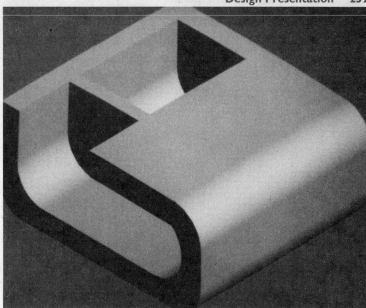

Figure 10.8 Flat shaded display of an object. Note that the intensity of the light is the same in all parallel surfaces.

For a positional light source, the user specifies the point location of the source. When a point light source is specified, the light rays all emanate from the point, and the rays reaching the object are not parallel (this situation is analogous to perspective projection). Some systems allow the user to define multiple-point light sources and even to assign different colors to each of the sources.

Just modeling where light strikes can leave ambiguous relationships between objects or parts of objects. Additional information about the geometric relationship between objects can be displayed by showing shadows. Any part of an object that does not have a direct view of the light source can be assigned a relatively low intensity because it is in shadow.

10.2.3 Reflectance of Solids

In addition to the source of light, another property that affects the appearance of an object is its **reflectance**, a term that refers to the fraction of incident visible light which the object reflects. Bright objects have a high reflectance, dark objects a low reflectance. Gray objects reflect the same fraction of light for all wavelengths of light. Colored objects reflect a different fraction of light at different wavelengths.

The first step in generating a shaded display is often to specify a percentage value for the reflectances. The user may choose an arbitrary color for each object, or, if color is important to the design, the user might specify the actual color that the object will have when it is manufactured. If some numerical analysis has been performed on the object, the surfaces of the object might also be assigned colors based on the results of that analysis; e.g., if temperatures were calculated, areas of low temperature might be colored blue, and areas of high temperature might be colored red (refer to Figure 1.12, Chapter 1).

Once the light source has been specified, the different surfaces on the object can be shaded with different intensities automatically. One way is to find the angle between the surface normal at the center of the surface and the direction of the incoming light. If this angle is near zero, a high intensity is assigned to the surface. If the angle is ninety degrees, a low intensity is assigned to the surface; if greater than ninety degrees, the surface is completely turned away from the light source. However, to avoid having some surfaces be completely black (and invisible), a constant, relatively low, ambient intensity is assigned to surfaces that are turned away from the light source.

If the intensity of a surface is the same for all points on the surface, the surface is said to be **flat shaded**. When directional light sources are used, surfaces are flat shaded (Figure 10.8). When positional light sources are used, surfaces can be **Gouraud shaded**. With a positional light, the angle between the direction to the light source and the surface is different at each vertex point of a surface. A surface is Gouraud shaded when a different intensity is computed for each vertex, and the intensity on other points on the surface are found by interpolation.

10.2.4 Surface Finishes of Solids

Besides assigning different reflectances for different objects, the differences between objects can be emphasized by assigning different surface finishes to objects. A **diffuse surface** is a matte-like, or dull, surface. You cannot see your reflection in a diffuse surface. A **specular surface** is shiny. If a system allows the user to specify surface finish, it usually asks for what percentage of the reflectance is diffuse, and what percentage is specular. The most popular method for making images with combined diffuse and specular reflectances is known as **Phong shading**.

Additionally, the user may be able to specify the level of glossiness for the specular portion of reflectance. A mirror, in which clear, sharp reflections can be seen, is an example of an extremely glossy surface. Reflections are less clear in less glossy surfaces. Specifying a high, glossy, specular component of reflectance for an object highlights changes in its shape. The combination of diffuse and specular shading methods provides a degree of realism acceptable for most design presentations.

Figure 10.9 Image produced using the ray tracing technique.

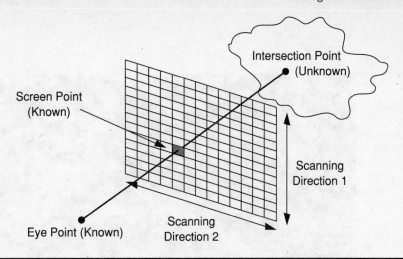

Figure 10.10 Ray Tracing Principle: Tracing a visual ray from the observer's location through the screen to the object to be displayed.

10.2.5 Advanced Shading Methods

The basic shading methods studied above do not produce truly realistic images of objects. The images are not realistic because they contain only point or directional light sources, but do not show the interreflection of light between objects. Moreover, point and directional light sources produce sharp shadows, whereas real light sources are area light sources, and may produce soft shadows. Several more advanced methods for shading objects have been developed to overcome these limitations and make objects look more realistic. Three of these newest methods are ray tracing, reverse ray tracing, and radiosity.

Ray tracing is a very popular and powerful technique used to produce realistic images (see Figure 10.9). This technique produces images which include different surface finishes, shadows, specular reflections between objects, and the refraction of light through transparent objects. Although it is believed to have been first suggested by Appel as early as 1967, this method became better known following the publication in 1980 of Whitted's now classic paper (Fujimoto et al., 1985). One of the numerous advantages of this technique is the simplicity of its principle, which consists of tracing a visual ray from the observer's location to the object being displayed (Figure 10.10). Unfortunately, finding the intersection of the ray vector and the object surface is not always an easy task to accomplish. For this reason, most of the computing time required to render an object with ray tracing is spent on finding the intersections.

Reverse ray tracing (RRT) was first conceived as a simple way of dealing with the problem of finding the intersection between the visual ray and complex

Figure 10.11 RRT Principle: A ray can be traced back from the known point through the screen to the observer's location.

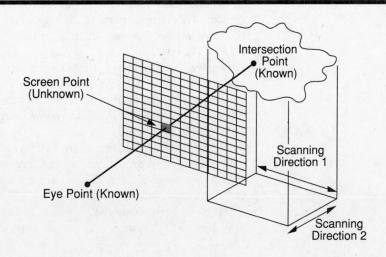

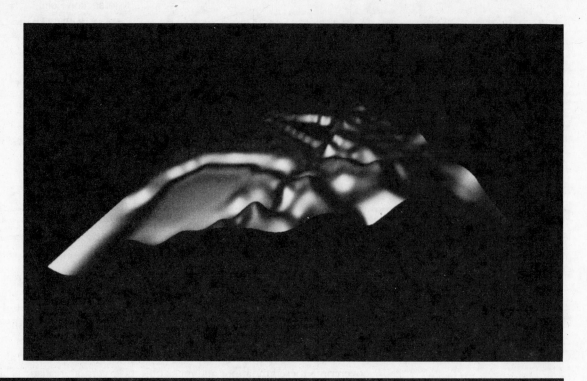

Figure 10.12 Image of a complex surface produced using the reverse ray tracing (RRT) technique.

surfaces (Opdenbosch and Rodriguez, 1991). If the surface can be defined by a given equation or by scanning or digitizing data points (see Chapter 7), we can trace these known points back from the surface model to the observer's location, as shown in Figure 10.11. Figure 10.12 shows a complex surface (a topographical map) rendered using RRT. This technique has the advantage of allowing the mapping of images on the object's surface; for example, we can map **contours** (points of equal elevation) on a complex surface to aid visualization. Figure 10.13 shows a complex surface with contour lines mapped on it.

Finally, another relatively new method is radiosity. **Radiosity** produces images that include soft shadows and diffuse reflections between objects (Rushmeir, 1989).

10.2.6 Selecting a Shading Method

In general, the major trade-off in selecting a shading method is speed versus realism. This issue is particularly important when a designer is presenting a rendered model, on the screen monitor, to a client or boss. For wireframe HLR, most systems can redisplay an object in **real-time**; that is, objects can be redisplayed as quickly as it takes the user to specify a new position. Many systems now do flat, Gouraud, or Phong shading using special hardware, so that objects shaded with these techniques can be redisplayed in near real-time. As objects or groups of objects become more complex, it may be necessary to add shadows or other realistic effects such as transparency or specular reflections in order to make sense out of the display. More complex methods, however, take more time to display, and complex raytraced or radiosity images can take several minutes to display. This of course affects the effectiveness of design presentations using those techniques.

Today only the basic shading methods are available on most commercially available graphics systems. As computer processing speeds increase, and more efficient computational techniques are developed, however, even the most advanced shading methods discussed here will become available.

10.3   STEREOSCOPIC GRAPHIC DISPLAY

Three-dimensional computer graphics usually refers to images that are computed based on a three-dimensional coordinate system and then displayed as a parallel or perspective projection onto a flat CRT screen. An observer's perception of depth in an image can be conveyed by cues such as the angular perspective effect (see Chapter 3), object structure, motion, and the size of objects, as well as by shading and shadowing.

To these techniques, **stereoscopic computer graphics** adds the additional depth cue of **stereopsis** (Hodges, Johnson, and Dehoff, 1988). When an observer looks at a three-dimensional scene, because the eyes are horizontally separated, the images formed at the back of each eye for any particular point in the scene differ in their horizontal position. This effect is referred to as **binocular disparity** or **binocular parallax**. Stereopsis involves the merging of these two slightly different two-dimensional images by the brain into a single three-dimensional image. Stereo graphics achieves this effect by generating two views of a scene and displaying them so that only the left eye sees the left-eye view and only the right eyes sees the right-eye view (see Figure 10.14). The result is that the observer sees an image that appears to be truly three-dimensional (Hodges, Johnson, and Dehoff, 1988; McWhorter, Rodriguez, and Hodges, 1991).

Figure 10.13 RRT is used here to map contours on a surface and thus help the observer visualize points of equal elevation.

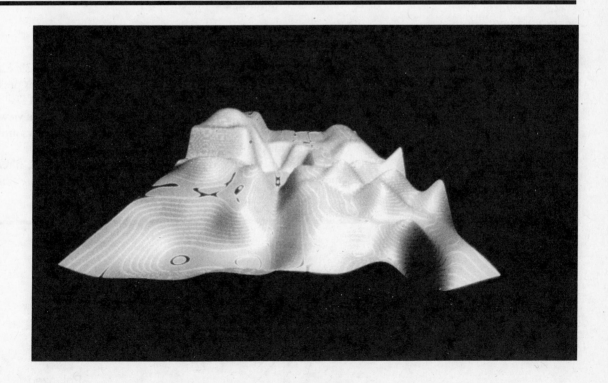

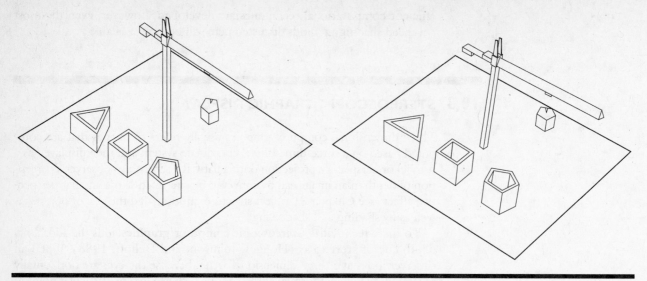

Figure 10.14 Two views of a scene are needed to obtain a stereoscopic image since a slightly different scene is observed by the left and right eye. (Note: If possible, cross your eyes to see the image in the middle.)

During the past five years there has been significant advancement in the technology for stereoscopic computer graphics. The introduction of liquid crystal shutters, circular polarization, and 120 Hz CRT refresh rates have made possible bright, flickerless, three-dimensional display stations that can be viewed by multiple observers wearing passively polarized glasses. Numerous application areas have recognized that the depth perception provided by stereoscopic display systems is an important part of understanding relationships between objects in a scene. Such areas include medical imaging, crystallography, cartography, remote positioning, and meteorology.

10.3.1 Stereoscopic CRT Displays

Stereoscopic CRT display systems are usually divided into two basic categories: time-parallel and time-multiplexed displays. Time-parallel systems present left- and right-eye views simultaneously on a separate or single CRT screen and require special optical apparatus to deliver the correct perspective view to each eye. Examples of time-parallel systems include anaglyph displays and certain types of polarized displays.

In **anaglyph displays**, the right- and left-eye perspectives are filtered with complementary or near-complementary colors and are superimposed on a CRT

Figure 10.15 Dual-CRT time-parallel display.

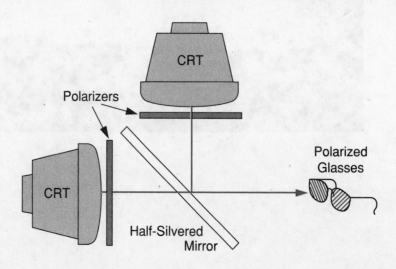

screen. If you have seen a 3-D movie, you are familiar with this type of display. The spectator wears glasses with filters that match the projection filters. For black and white images, red and green filters are usually used. For color images, red and cyan or green and magenta filters are used. A problem with this technique is that it distorts the colors of an image.

Polarized time-parallel displays have been created using two CRTs arranged at right angles to each other and a partially silvered mirror, as shown in Figure 10.15. Polarizers are placed on each monitor with the filters arranged at right angles to each other. The half-silvered mirror is placed between the monitors so that it reflects one perspective view and transmits the other. The observer wears corresponding polarized glasses so that each eye sees the correct perspective view.

Time-multiplexed stereo pair systems require a viewing shutter that presents the paired stereo images by alternating right- and left-eye perspective views of an object on a CRT. Early implementations of this technique used an alternation rate of 60 Hz (thirty left-eye views and thirty right-eye views per second), but this approach suffers from an observable flicker. To eliminate the flickering effect, commercial systems based on 120 Hz non-time-interlaced monitors have been developed by Stereographics Corporation and Tektronix.

10.3.2 Recent Developments in CRT-Based Displays

A different approach to a stereo display system that does not require special glasses or other viewing apparatus has been constructed using a slit that moves across the screen of a CRT at approximately 20 hertz. This type of display is known as a **parallactiscope**. With this technique, images can be produced on the screen that can be seen from wide angles, up to forty degrees on each side of the slit. Thus, different views can be seen from different angles. This technique allows for several viewers at the same time.

Multiplanar displays create a three-dimensional image by partitioning a scene into multiple two-dimensional cross sections. The cross sections are positioned in space so that a 3-D image is perceived by the observer. Current multiplanar displays are usually based on the concept of the varifocal mirror invented by Traub while at Mitre. Varifocal-mirror displays combine a vibrating circular mirror, held stationary at its circumference, with a CRT (see Figure 10.16). Traub discovered that if he used a circular, flexible material fastened at the edges, the mirror can be made to approximate a spherical mirror with a focal length that varies as the mirror vibrates, hence the name **varifocal**. The vibrations are synchronized with the display of an object on a CRT so that each point on an object is reflected from the mirror at a position corresponding to the depth of that point.

Figure 10.16 Varifocal mirror display.

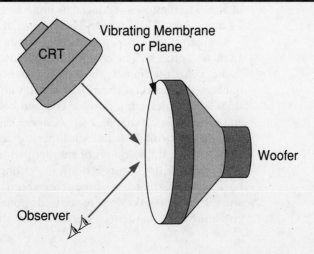

The mirror is vibrated by air pressure generated from an acoustical woofer that can be driven at low frequencies. A simple sine wave is passed through a high-quality amplifier and drives the woofer. Physical limitations limit the size of the mirror to a maximum of 18 to 19 inches. A larger mirror may cause sympathetic vibration in surrounding structures. Acoustical considerations place the frequency of the vibration of the mirror at approximately 30 hertz. A very fast phosphor is required to preclude image smear. Currently, the only phosphor available with sufficiently fast decay is a green phosphor so that only monochrome displays are viable. Efforts to add color using color wheels or liquid crystal π cells have been only marginally successful.

Varifocal mirror displays have several characteristics that set them apart from stereo pair and perspective displays. Hidden line and surface removal have no meaning since the observer can change his position and see a different perspective. Since the mirror is constantly moving in space, the resolution is limited both by the CRT resolution and the speed of point plotting by the CRT. Current CRT technology limits the number of image points to less than forty thousand. Hence only wireframe images are possible. In addition, images are translucent, which can cause confusion in viewing complex scenes.

10.3.3 Competing Display Technologies

There are many competing technologies that provide true three-dimensional display of synthetic images. Those technologies that are cost effective and permit real-time interactive manipulation of high-resolution computer generated scenes will survive. The recent development of large, circularly polarized liquid crystal shutters combined with 120 Hz monitors and fast graphics frame buffers has made time-interlaced stereo pair systems the most competitive. Regardless of which technologies survive, true 3-D display is no longer a curious innovation but a useful design presentation tool. By combining stereographics with the rendering techniques we studied in Section 10.2 a client, for instance, can be brought to a design workstation to see a truly realistic presentation.

10.4 ANIMATION

Rendered and stereo models are fascinating and provide an ever-greater approximation of real images, but they are static. However, we can add another dimension, time, to this virtual space and therefore display the movement of an object by creating animated sequences and visual simulation. Conventional **animation** can be defined as "a technique in which the illusion of movement is created by photographing a series of individual drawings on successive frames of film. The illusion is produced by projecting the film at a certain rate (typically 24 frames/sec)" (Magnenat-Thalmann et al., 1985).

Computer animation focuses on a number of different aspects of the entire animation process. The computer can be used to create the drawings for each frame, color the frames, shoot the sequences, edit, and synchronize the sequences. Animation software has proved valuable for analyzing spatial relationships and for detecting possible collision between the components of devices and systems. For example, a site designer can see if two cranes on a construction site may collide with each other, or can check if a mechanical part will interfere with the workings of another part in a device. Animation can also be used for predicting future actions. For example, when ice built up dangerously on a nonvisible portion of the space shuttle, the camera on the manipulator arm did not allow the crew to see well enough to remove the ice buildup. Precise animation sequences were used by the NASA Mission Planning and

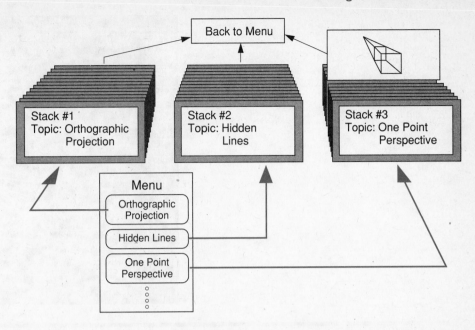

Figure 10.17 Sample menu created with hypertalk software for viewing stacks of cards as animated sequences.

Analysis Division to examine the removal operation before it was attempted (Robertson, 1987).

Animation software can be categorized by four different animation levels (Magnenat-Thalmann and Thalmann, 1985):

Level 1: The system simply acts as a graphics editor for the creation of drawings.

Level 2: The system computes in-between scenes and object trajectory.

Level 3: The system provides object operations such as translation and rotation.

Level 4: The system provides facilities for defining objects that possess their own animation.

Existing key frame animation systems are currently at Levels 1 and 2. Current Level 3 and Level 4 systems are primitive and will require extensive development in order to attain adequate modeling capabilities. Current animation systems are descriptive (of an object's surface geometry) rather than prescriptive (of an optimal course of action). The more sophisticated programs require very powerful workstations; however, it is possible to create very simple animations on less powerful desktop computers.

One popular way to animate sequences is using **hypermedia** software available in computers such as Macintosh and IBM-clones. In the Mac, Hypercard pictures and text are stored in "cards" that are subsequently stored in "stacks." The animation is created by displaying quickly and in sequence the cards contained in a specific stack. Generating an animation sequence in hypercard implies the creation of the pictures of each frame on single cards. A simple object animation requires a stack of about 50 cards. The stack contains a master code written in a very user-friendly language called hypertalk. In this case, the code is a simple loop that instructs the computer to display sequentially the cards in the stack. The program stipulates how much time each card has to be displayed and the visual effects to be used, such as "dissolve." Figure 10.17 shows a diagram of how animation card stacks can be organized in a menu structure. The various animation stacks can be selected from a menu designed by the programmer. In this case, the user makes a selection of a particular topic, for example, "orthographic projection" to see the orthographics projection animation sequence (refer to Figures 2.5 and 2.6). Animated sequences produced by Hypercard have been used in this book to show engineering visualization techniques.

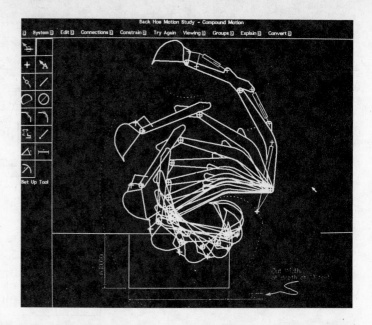

Figure 10.18 Animation of a new backhoe design. (Courtesy of Cognition, Inc.)

There are several commercial animation packages currently available to the designer. Wavefront and Alias make two of the animation packages able to animate objects for conceptual engineering design and manufacturing. Given the right workstation, these animation packages can generate computer images in real-time. That is, they can generate "lifelike" animation of mechanical parts. The most important feature of animation is that it can be used as a "Will-the-design-work?" tool. For example, with packages such as the Mechanical Advantage by Cognition a designer can simulate the performance of a design product, such as a backhoe, by displaying an animation sequence, as shown in Figure 10.18, of a new excavator design. In this case, the software package helps to present not only what the product looks like, but also how it will work.

10.5 DESIGN PROTOTYPES

All the techniques studied so far provide the designer with a high degree of virtual realism and movement. However, what can be better than the object itself to present a design idea? Cardboard prototypes are not the "real-thing," but they add the sense of touch.

The best way to learn how to present design prototypes is to see real-life examples or case studies. In Chapter 4, we saw a design prototype made out of wood. Ordinarily, however, designers prefer to use soft materials such as cardboard, poster board, and balsa wood to build their prototypes. These prototypes are used for conducting simple tests. For example, a designer can use a prototype to feel if a product is bulky, if it fits inside another product, or how it feels to the user.

Nevertheless, there is always a need to manufacture a real design prototype because there are tests that cannot be performed using a cardboard prototype. These tests consist, among others, of stress tests, such as trying to crush the product and checking its ability to perform as expected.

The following example explains the use of a cardboard prototype to present a design solution.

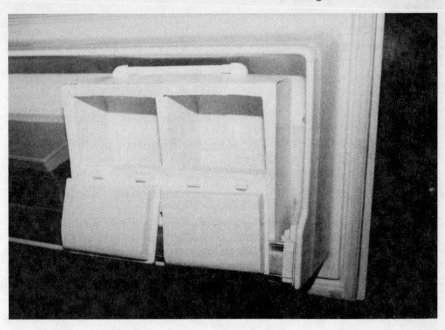

Figure 10.19(a) The Chill 'N' Fill design prototype made of cardboard and balsa wood. Place Chill 'N' Fill in the freezer, allow to cool overnight..

<table>
<tr><td>Example 10.1</td></tr>
</table>

Self-Contained Can Cooler

Conventional coolers do what they were designed to do—keep things cold. However, these coolers are sometimes messy, do not always keep drinks as cool as they should, and often fail to make the drinks easily accessible. For these reasons, a new-style cooler will be presented here to replace conventional coolers and to correct the problems associated with them.

Within the design process, a cooler solution eventually evolved into what was named the *Chill 'N' Fill* cooler. A geometric model of the final solution was developed, but a physical prototype was needed to assure that it had the "feel" and "appeal" needed for marketing the product.

Figures 10.19 (a-b) show the use of this new cooler. Note that the *Chill 'N' Fill* cooler prototype is totally self-contained. The design prototype was built of poster board and balsa wood. It has two openings and cavities to hold the canned drinks. A cardboard division was placed in the cooler between the

Figure 10.19(b) The cooler is portable and the drinks are easy to remove.

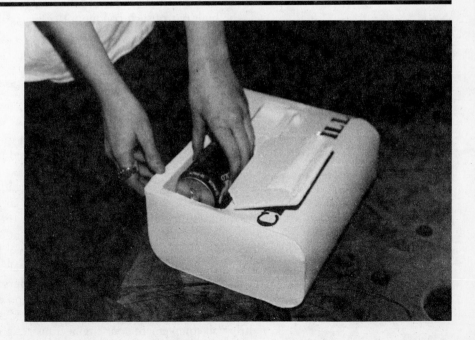

cavities and the outside of the case to separate the "insulation" from the "refrigerant." A foam-style insulation was installed in the outer portion of the inside of the case. A gel, similar to the commercial product blue ice, was pumped into the inner chamber of the case's interior to simulate the "refrigerant liquid" effect. The handle and lids were made of recycled cardboard.

Chapter Summary

Chapter 10 detailed the following points:

- Data related to a design are generally best presented using a graph or chart.
- The most common types of graphs are the rectilinear, logarithmic, polar, and bar graph, and the pie chart.
- The rendering of wireframe models can be enhanced with hidden line removal, a program within most 3-D CAD modeling packages that calculates and displays only the edges directly visible to the observer. With a program called depth cueing, thicknesses of lines in the model can be varied according to how close they are to the front of the object.
- The rendering of solid models can be enhanced with various methods of shading.
- To shade a model effectively, a designer must stipulate whether the light source is directional or positional and whether shadows should be displayed. He or she must also indicate the reflectance and surface finish of each object in the model.
- In addition to the light source, reflectance, and surface finish, advanced shading programs may take into account the reflection of light from one object to another and may allow the creation of contours in complicated surfaces.
- The realism of 3-D models can be increased with stereoscopic displays that simulate depth with binocular disparity. Binocular disparity can be created with time-parallel or time-multiplexed stereoscopic displays, with a parallactiscope, or with multiplanar displays.
- The illusion of movement can be added to geometric models with the use of animation software. Animation software can be especially useful for detecting possible collisions between parts or for predicting future actions.
- To add the sense of touch to the realism of a design, a design prototype can be built out of such commonplace materials as cardboard, posterboard, or balsa wood.

CONCLUSION

This book has presented traditional visual thinking and state-of-the-art geometric modeling techniques that are needed to conceptualize and implement design ideas.

The use of concurrent design principles and visual thinking/modeling techniques is just the beginning of a career as an engineer, designer, inventor, or technologist. Following an introduction to these skills, a professional in one of these fields must learn how to engineer solutions, a skill that will require courses ranging from mechanics and structural analysis to construction and manufacturing. If you are interested in learning more about computer graphics visualization, we suggest taking some elective courses in vector algebra, computer programming (particularly, C language), and computer graphics in your computer science department. The marketable skills you pick up in these classes will help you complement your engineering design and visualization background.

REFERENCES AND SUGGESTED READINGS

Alias Research. "ICEM Alias." *Control Data Literature Distribution Services.* St. Paul, Minn., 1987.

Hodges, L., P. Johnson, and R. Dehoff. "Stereoscopic Computer Graphics." *Journal of Theoretical Graphics and Computing,* 1(1), 1988, 1–11.

Julesz, B. *Foundations of Cyclopean Perception.* Chicago: University of Chicago Press, 1971.

Ladner, R. "Construction, Display, and Manipulation of Three-Dimensional Models of Biopolymers." *SPIE Proc.,* 1982.

Magnenat-Thalmann, N., and D. Thalmann. *Computer Animation Theory and Practice.* Tokyo: Springer-Verlag, 1985.

Magnenat-Thalmann, N., D. Thalmann, and M. Fortin. "Miranim: An Extensible Director-Oriented System for the Animation of Realistic Images." *IEEE Computer Graphics and Applications,* 5(3), 1985, 61–73.

Opdenbosch, A., W. Rodriguez, and L. Hodges. "Reverse Ray Tracing Technique for Complex Surface Visualization." *Journal of Theoretical Graphics and Computing,* 3(1), 1990, 31–36.

Opdenbosch, A. and W. Rodriguez. "Visualizing Parametric Surfaces with the Enhanced Reverse Ray Tracing Technique." *Proceedings,* Engineering Design Graphics Mid-Year Conference, ASEE, Norfolk, Virginia, Nov. 3–5, 1991.

Robertson, B. "Animation for Engineering." *Computer Graphics World,* 10(2), 1987, 46–50.

Rushmeier, H. "Application of the Radiosity Method to Computer Graphics: A Brief Review." *Journal of Theoretical Graphics and Computing,* 2(1), 1989, 18–22.

EXERCISES

10.1. Plot the data given below. The "Frequency" axis should be logarithmic, and the "Power" axis should be linear.

Filter Output

Frequency	Power
1 hertz	10.0 watts
10	6.0
200	1.5
5,000	2.0
30,000	3.5

10.2. Draw the graph of the data given below. The intensity of a test lamp, in candle-power, is given as a function of the angle (in degrees).

Angle	Candlepower
0	10
90	60
180	130
270	60

10.3. Using a 3-D CAD modeling package, draw a pie chart illustrating your use of time in a typical day.

10.4. Create a presentation (including a physical prototype) for a design problem assigned by your instructor.

10.5. Draw an image and/or write a statement that describes or defines each of the key terms, listed below, used in this chapter.

Anaglyph displays

Animation

Bar graph

Binocular disparity (binocular parallax)

Depth cueing

Diffuse surface

Directional light

Flat shaded

Gouraud shaded

Hidden line removal (HLR)

Hypermedia

Logarithmic graph

Log cycle

Multiplanar displays

Parallactiscope

Phong shading

Pie chart

Polar graph

Polarized time parallel displays

Positional light

Radiosity

Ray tracing

Real-time

Rectilinear graph

Reverse ray tracing

Reflectance

Semilog chart

Specular surface

Stereographics

Stereopsis

Time-multiplexed stereo pair

Varifocal

Glossary

This section contains terms used in computer, engineering, and graphics; many of them have been extensively discussed in this book. Additional terms have been included to serve as a reference source for other courses and future design work.

absolute coordinates Coordinates defined in relation to an origin location.

ACM SIGGRAPH The computer-graphics interest group within the Association for Computing Machinery.

adapter An interface card that allows a computer to use a peripheral device.

addresses The locations of stored electronic information on RAM chips.

adjacent views Two aligned adjoining multiviews.

adjoining views Two multiviews that share a common boundary.

algorithm A set of well-defined instructions for solving a problem in a finite number of operations. Contrast with *heuristic*.

aliasing When a computer image has jagged or stairstepped edges.

aligned section A cross-sectional view obtained by rearranging the cutting plane so that it passes through an important feature of an object.

aligned views Orthographic multi-views placed side by side, so that their corresponding points are placed on the same projection line.

alphanumeric A set of characters consisting of letters and numbers (digits).

alternating pair display A technique in which an image consists of two alternating views of a scene.

ambiguous representation A non-rendered model in which it is impossible for a viewer to determine which lines are in the foreground or background of a geometric model. Wireframe models often provide ambiguous representations.

anaglyph display A stereographic display in which the right- and left-eye perspectives are filtered with complementary or near-complementary colors and are superimposed on a CRT screen.

analog Relating to quantitative physical data that varies continuously. Contrast with *digital*.

analog computer A system that processes data in the form of voltage fluctuations, not in the form of digitally encoded data.

analog model A model that substitutes one property of the system being described for another.

analysis In solid modeling, lso called processing, refers to the computational process involved in rendering a model. Also referes to calculating stresses and deformations.

angular bearing The direction of a line with respect to the north/south axis.

angular dimension The dimension of a circular feature, measured in degrees.

angular perspective Another name for two-point perspective; when two of an object's axes are inclined and one axis is parallel to the projection plane.

animation Creating the illusion of movement on a video display.

ANSI American National Standards Institute. The organization in the U.S. that works, in coordination with ISO, to establish acceptable standards.

application Software designed for a specific type of work, such as word processing, spreadsheets, or CAD modeling.

architect's scale A scale in which the major divisions represent feet and the subdivisions represent inches.

arithmetic logic unit (ALU) The part of the computer system containing the circuitry that processes arithmetic and logical (comparison) operations.

array In programming, a specified sequence of positions in computer memory. A regularly ordered set. An image can be represented as an array of numbers corresponding to the brightness of each point in the image.

artificial intelligence (AI) A branch of computer science that uses computers to solve problems that appear to require human imagination and/or intelligence.

ASCII American National Standard Code for Information Interchange. A standard code used to exchange information among data processing and communications systems.

assembly language A low-level means of communicating with a computer. This language lies between high-level languages and machine language.

assignment To give values for color, opacity, and refractive index to each volume element that is to be rendered in a computer graphics image.

attributes Elements that control characteristics, such as the color of an entity.

autoexec.bat In DOS, a file that contains an automatic set of commands that are executed when the computer is turned on.

automatic hiding Also called hidden-line removal. Computer-generated hiding of lines and surfaces that would not be seen by a viewer observing a three-dimensional object in the real world.

auxiliary projection A type of orthographic multiview that is inclined to the principal planes of projection. It is used to display the true shape of a feature that is not parallel to any of the principal planes of projection.

axonometric drawing A drawing that resembles an axonometric projection. However, distances along axes are measured in true length.

axonometric projection A type of pictorial in which the lines of sight used to created the projection are parallel to each other.

A/UX A version of the Unix operating system used in Apple's Macintosh computers.

backup disk A disk containing duplicate data. Backups are made so that information is not lost when the original disk is damaged or destroyed.

backup information Up-to-date material that supports a design feasibility study.

bar graph A type of graph that uses shaded bars of different length to compare items.

BASIC Beginners All-Purpose Symbolic Instruction Code. A high-level interactive programming language frequently used on personal computers.

basic dimension symbol The symbol used to identify a specified dimension.

batch processing A technique in which a number of similar items or transactions are grouped and processed in a designated sequence during a machine run without user interaction.

baud rate A unit for measuring data transmission speed. Usually referred to as a measure of bits per second (bps); more precisely, however, the baud rate measures the number of signal changes that occur in one second.

bicubic bezier patches Two cubic functions that are used to represent a curved surface. A patch that blends well at boundaries with adjacent patches.

bilateral tolerance Designates a dimension's tolerance that can be either greater than or smaller than the specified dimension.

bill of materials A table containing part names, materials, specifications, quantities needed, and costs.

binary digit Abbreviated "bit." Either of the characters 0 or 1.

binary number system A number system with a base, or radix, of two.

binocular disparity Also called binocular parallax. The effect caused by the difference in the horizontal position of the human eyes.

biochip Integrated circuitry that is composed of protein molecules.

bit map A grid pattern of binary digits stored in memory. It is used to generate an image on a raster scan display. Each bit corresponds to a pixel on the display.

bit plane The hardware used to store a bit map.

blurring To model how the eyes see motion.

Boolean operations Math operations used to create geometric models by combining primitives.

brainstorm To identify or propose alternative solutions to a design problem, generally in a group setting. The objective is to generate a large number of ideas without negative criticism.

B-Rep Boundary representation. A modeling technique that describes the faces, edges, and vertices of an object.

broken section A type of cross section that exposes a portion of the inside of an object.

B-spline Beta spline. A mathematical model used to represent complex smooth curves. They are used to describe cross sections of complex three-dimensional surfaces.

buffer An electronic storage device used to compensate for the difference in rates of flow of data from one device to another.

bus Circuits that provide a communication path between two or more devices, such as between a CPU, storage, and peripherals.

byte A group of adjacent bits, usually eight, operated on as a unit.

cabinet oblique projection An oblique pictorial generated by lines of sight making an angle of approximately 63 degrees with the plane of projection. The receding axis measurements are half their actual size.

cache A high-speed storage device.

CAD/CAM Computer-Aided Design/Computer-Aided Manufacturing. A general term applied to the automation of design and manufacture operations.

CAE Computer-Aided Engineering. The use of software programs to perform engineering analysis of a design.

CAI Computer-Assisted Instruction. A general term that refers to a learning situation in which the student interacts with a computer through a course of study aimed at achieving certain instructional goals.

canned programs Programs prepared by an outside supplier and provided to a user in a machine-readable form.

case-sensitive The distinction made by an operating system or application between lowercase and uppercase characters.

Cartesian A coordinate format that defines points on a plane, or in space, based on their linear distances from mutually perpendicular axes.

cathode ray tube (CRT) A device, resembling a TV screen, on which images may be displayed.

cavalier oblique projection An oblique pictorial drawn by recessing an axis at an angle between 0 and 90 degrees (usually 45 degrees) with respect to the horizontal axis and using true-length depth measurements.

center lines Lines drawn in the center of circles and arcs to aid in the view's interpretation. Alternating long and short dashes that identify a circular feature of an object and locate its center.

central processing unit (CPU) The component of a computer system that controls the interpretation and execution of instructions. The CPU includes primary storage, arithmetic-logic, and control units.

central projection Also called perspective projection. A realistic projection in which the lines of sight emanate from a single point, and parallel features of depth converge toward a vanishing point.

character A letter, digit, punctuation mark, or other written symbol.

character string A string of alphanumeric characters.

chip A thin wafer of silicon on which integrated electronic components are deposited.

circle An arc with an included angle of 360 degrees.

clearance fit A situation in which the external feature (for example, a shaft) will fit into an internal feature (for example, a hole), as long as the mating parts are manufactured within the given tolerance limits.

clipping Removing those portions of an image that are outside the boundaries of the display.

clock speed Also called clock rate. The rate at which the electronic circuitry in a computer generates a steady stream of pulses. The rate is normally given in MHz.

color plane Each of the three areas of memory—red, green, and blue—in the display memory of a computer equipped with an RGB video monitor.

communication protocol A set of hardware and software standards used to allow computers to connect and exchange information with one another.

compiler A computer program that produces a machine language program from a program written in a high-level language such as C or FORTRAN.

computer A machine that is designed to accept input data, to process the data, and to produce output results under the direction of a software program.

computer graphics Images created on a computer.

concurrent Referring to a design process in which engineers design simultaneously both the product and the procedure by which it is to be built or manufactured; or referring to a coordinated effort of people working on several phases of a design project simultaneously.

construction lines Lines used to assist in guiding the drawing processes. These lines are drawn very lightly and are usually erased or deleted after they have served their purpose.

constructive solid geometry (CSG) The technique of combining solid primitives, using Boolean operations, to make complex solid objects.

constructive-tree Also called a CSG-tree. A strategy for planning the construction of a solid model by sketching the required primitives and Boolean operations.

control points Locations in three-dimensional space that influence the shape of a curve with equal force.

control unit A device that organizes the operations of the ALU and consequently the functions of the entire computer.

contour A line indicating points of equal elevation or height.

corpus callosum The nerve cable connecting the human brain's hemispheres.

counterbore An enlarged cylindrical portion of a drilled hole used to provide a recessed area in which to seat the head of a bolt below the surface of a part.

countersink An enlarged conical portion of a hole that provides a place to seat the beveled head of a flathead screw.

crosshatching Also called section lining. A pattern of lines or symbols used to represent the type of solid material exposed by the cutting plane.

cross section A view showing portions of the internal geometry of an object.

CSG *See* Constructive Solid Geometry.

cutting plane An imaginary plane used to establish the location of a cross section.

cylindrical coordinates A set of coordinates defining the location of a point in space using the distance from a reference location to the projection of the point on the X-Y plane, the included angle between the positive X-axis and the projection of the point onto the X-Y plane, and the distance of the point along the Z axis from the X-Y plane.

data Facts. The raw material of information.

database A stored collection of data needed by an organization or individual to meet information processing requirements.

database management system (DBMS) The comprehensive software system that builds, maintains, and provides access to a database.

data processing One or more operations performed on data to achieve a desired objective.

datum feature symbol A reference used to identify certain features of an object.

debug To detect, locate, and remove errors in programs and/or malfunctions in equipment.

decision matrix A table used to compare various design alternatives.

default The choice used by a piece of software when a user does not specify an alternative. In CAD, a user accepts a default by pressing the Enter key.

default drive The disk drive that will be searched if no specific disk is indicated in a path name.

delta The operation used to generate a point relative to the position of another point.

depth cueing A display technique that shows variation in the intensity of lines according to how close they are to the front of the object.

descriptive model A model that characterizes the behavior of a system, process, or product.

design annotation Techniques used for quickly recording design ideas.

design feasibility study A written report used for presenting the initial stages of the design process. It is used to determine if a product should be developed further.

design process A methodical approach used to reach the best solution to a design problem. The design process consists of three phases: ideation, simulation, and implementation.

design workstation Also called an engineering workstation. A system consisting of a set of integrated computer components assembled for an individual designer.

development The process involved in transforming resources into a useful product. In descriptive geometry, the process of unfolding the shape of a three-dimensional object onto a two-dimensional plane.

decision symbol The diamond shaped symbol used in flowcharts to indicate a choice or branch in a processing path.

descriptive geometry The construction of precise two-dimensional drawings to determine geometric information, such as the true size of oblique surfaces and the line of intersection between two planes.

device coordinates The coordinates used by the computer system to generate a display that fits on a screen monitor.

diagnostics Error messages printed by a computer to indicate system problems and improper program instructions.

diffuse surface A dull, matte-like surface.

digital computer A system that manipulates discrete data and performs arithmetic and logical operations on these data. Contrast with *analog computer*.

digitizer An input device used with a stylus to read in data from existing paper drawings. It is also used with a CAD menu overlay to execute operations by pointing at areas in the overlay.

dimensioning Specifying the size of a product feature in a drawing.

dimension line A thin line with arrowheads that shows the direction and extent of a dimension.

dimetric projection An axonometric projection in which two of the object's axes make equal angles with the plane of projection.

directional light A type of light source in which the light rays emitted are assumed to be parallel.

directory An organized list of files and subdirectories stored on a disk.

direct translator A single program designed to translate between two specific systems.

disk A revolving plate on which data and programs can be recorded in digital (binary) form. Made of flexible plastic or inflexible metal.

disk controller card A chip that assists in transmitting data to, or getting data from, a disk drive.

diskette Also called a floppy disk. A low-cost magnetic medium used for I/O and secondary storage purposes.

direct access Pertaining to storage devices where the time required to retrieve data is independent of the physical location of the data.

distributed data processing A general term describing the process of a logically related set of information processing functions and the use of multiple, geographically separated, computing and communication devices.

divide-and-conquer A technique used for solving a problem by splitting it into smaller, simpler problems.

DOS Disk Operating System. The most frequently used operating system used in 386- and 486-class machines.

dpi Dots per inch. A measure of printer resolution.

dual representation A technique used to maintain the desirable properties of both CSG and B-Rep modeling.

DXF Drawing Interchange File. A standard ASCII text file that describes an AutoCAD drawing file.

EBCDIC Extended Binary Coded Decimal Interchange Code. An 8-bit code used to represent data in modern computers. An alternate to the ASCii character set.

edge view of a plane A view with the direction of sight parallel to a plane so that the observer sees the plane as a straight line.

edit To correct, rearrange, and validate input data.

editor A program used interactively to review and alter text materials and other program data.

EDP Acronym for Electronic Data Processing.

electronic mail A general term to describe the transmission of messages through the use of computing systems and telecommunications facilities.

emulator A stored logic device or program that permits one computer to execute machine-language instructions to another computer different design.

engineering sketching Making scaled and proportional freehand drawings.

engineering visualization The use of geometric modeling, rendering, and animation techniques to help a client see a new design's shape and to study how it works before producing a real prototype.

engineer's scale A graduated rule in decimal parts of an inch; i.e., one inch is divided into 10, 20, 30, 40, 50, and 60 parts.

executive routine A master program in an operating system that controls the operation of other programs.

extends The portions of a center line that protrude beyond the circumference of a circle.

extension line A thin line used to indicate the projection of a surface or point to a location outside the part outline.

extrusion The creation of a three-dimensional object from two-dimensional entities displayed in the X-Y plane by pushing or pulling the displayed cross section along the Z-axis.

facsimile system (FAX) A system used to transmit pictures, text, maps, etc., between geographically separated points. An image is scanned at a transmitting point and duplicated at a receiving point.

feature-based models A modeling technique that uses manufacturing and construction terminology.

field A group of related characters or values treated as a unit.

file A collection of related records treated as a unit. An electronic container in which information such as text and programs is stored.

file processing The updating of master files to reflect the effects of current transactions.

file system A hierarchy of directories and files.

finite element mesh A set of simple elements that are connected together in a grid to represent a solid object. Used for engineering-stress and thermodynamic analysis.

first-angle projection standard A type of projection in which the object is positioned in the first coordinate quadrant; that is, between the observer and the plane of projection.

fixed coordinate system A stationary and permanent arrangement of the three principal axes (X, Y, and Z) in three-dimensional space.

flat shaded The rendering or shading obtained from directional light sources.

flowchart A diagram that uses symbols and interconnecting lines to show (1) a system of processing (a system flowchart) or (2) the logic and sequence of program operations (a program flowchart).

folding line The line of intersection between two projection planes. If an imaginary transparent box is unfolded, the folding line becomes an edge view of a projection plane.

formatting In general computing use, initializing a disk so that it can store drawing files. In word processing, to add style and presentation elements to a document.

FORTRAN FORmula TRANslator. A high-level language used to program and perform mathematical computations.

full section The simplest type of cross section in which a cutting plane passes fully though an object.

functional requirements (FRs) The essential design goals that must be met to solve a problem. The independence principle states that "functional requirements must be independently satisfied."

function keys Keys, usually located along the top of the keyboard, that access special commands. Commonly labeled F1, F2, and so on.

general-purpose language A programming language, such as C or FORTRAN, used to develop applications.

generator A computer program used to construct other programs that perform a particular type of operation, e.g., a report program generator.

genlock Synchronization of internally generated video to an external video source.

geometric characteristic symbols Symbols used to specify the shape quality of a product being designed.

geometric modeling A technique used to describe the physical shape of an object on a computer.

geometric primitive A polygon or patch used to describe the shape of a three-dimensional object.

geometric tolerancing A technique used to specify the size and shape of an object.

Gouraud shaded The rendering or shading obtained from a positional light source.

graphical-user-interface (GUI) A type of display format consisting of icons and pull-down menus used to choose options from the screen.

graphics The use of lines and figures to display data, as opposed to the use of printed characters.

graphic display A visual device that is used to project graphic images.

graphics editor An editor that revises and modifies a graphics design; the graphics equivalent of a text editor.

graphics tablet An input device consisting of a flat work surface and a stylus. Designs traced on the tablet are displayed on screen and stored in computer memory.

grid An equally-spaced pattern of dots displayed as a set of intersecting vertical and horizontal dotted lines on the screen's monitor.

half section A cross section that shows only one half of the inside features, created by passing the cutting plane halfway through the object.

hard copy Printed or filmed output, as opposed to electronically displayed output, as from a monitor.

hard disk A rigid aluminum plate coated with a substance that allows magnetic recording of data.

hardware Physical computer equipment such as electromagnetic and mechanical devices. Contrast with *software*.

hemisphere Half of a sphere. One side of the human brain.

heuristic A problem-solving method in which solutions are discovered by evaluating the progress made toward the end result. A directed trial-and-error approach. Contrast with *algorithm*.

hidden-line removal Elimination of lines that are obscured from the viewer's point of view by opaque foreground surfaces.

hidden lines Lines that are not visible in a multiview. They are represented with dashed lines.

high-level language A programming language oriented toward the problem to be solved or the procedures to be used. Instructions are given to a computer by using convenient letters, symbols, or English-like text, rather than by using the binary code that the computer understands.

host computer A main control computer in a network of distributed processors and terminals.

hybrid computer A data processing device using both analog and discrete data representation.

hypermedia Software for creating presentations, such as animation sequences.

hyperpatches A patch-bounded collection of points whose coordinates are given by a continuous, three-parameter, single-valued mathematical function.

iconic model A scaled prototype of a real object that looks similar to the object being represented.

icons A displayed graphic image used to represent an operation.

ideation The conceptualization phase of the design process, consisting of market research, problem definition, preliminary ideas, and preliminary decision on design choice. The ideation principle states that "early decisions greatly affect the final design outcome."

IGES Initial Graphics Exchange Specification. A standard file format used to exchange three-dimensional data between computer programs.

implementation The construction or manufacturing phase of the design process, consisting of prototyping and testing, generating a report, creating design documentation, producing the product, and marketing the product.

importing The action of bringing data from one computer program to another.

information Meaning assigned to data by humans.

information retrieval The methods used to recover specific information from stored data.

input/output *See* I/O.

input/output symbol A figure with the shape of a parallelogram, used to indicate both input and output operations in a flowchart.

interactive Describes a situation in which a person must provide input into a process and respond to the resulting effects or to direct prompts.

interactive system One that permits direct communication and dialogue between system users and the operating program.

interface A shared boundary, as between two systems or devices or between a system and a user.

interference fit A situation in which two mating parts will be in contact (pressed together) because the internal part is slightly larger than the external part.

internal storage The addressable storage in a digital computer directly under the control of the CPU.

I/O Input/Output. Basic functions of a computer system, consisting of gathering data and displaying and/or plotting the results.

ISO International Organization for Standardization. Usually referred to as the International Standards Organization. An association of member countries that works to establish acceptable standards around the world.

isometric drawing An axonometric drawing made by positioning the object axes at equal angles with respect to the plane of projection.

iterative Processes that do not follow a predetermined sequence of steps and can become repetitive.

job A collection of specific tasks constituting a unit of work for a computer.

junction locations The places where the end-points of a model's entities meet.

Kilobyte (K or KB) 2^{10}, or 1,024, bytes.

keyboard An input device that usually contains 128 alphanumeric characters.

label One or more characters used to identify a program statement or a data item.

LAN Local-Area Network. A connected, limited number of computers and output devices. A LAN can be connected by a bridge to a larger network.

laptop computer A small and lightweight portable computer.

laser An acronym for "light amplification by stimulated emission of radiation."

laser printer An electrophotographic device that uses a focused laser beam and rotating mirror to draw an image on paper.

layering In CAD modeling, the grouping of related geometric entities that allows a designer to display portions of a drawing rather than the entire drawing at once. For example, a designer may display electrical outlets (in one layer) independently from a floor plan (in another layer).

layout The arrangement of geometric entities, notes, dimensions, and other drawing elements on a screen display or paper.

LCD Liquid crystal display. A display that produces a dark image in a special liquid compound located between two transparent electrodes. It is frequently used in portable and laptop computers.

LCD printer Also called liquid crystal (display) shutter printer. It uses an electrostatically charged drum to transfer toner to the paper.

leader line A thin line used to point and specify a dimension or note. It is usually inclined at a 30- or 60-degree angle and has an arrow at one end and a horizontal shoulder at the other end.

least material condition (LMC) In tolerancing, the size of a part feature that results when the object has the least material.

library routine A tested routine maintained in a library of programs.

light pen A device that permits a designer to input data by pointing to the monitor screen.

line A geometric entity defined by two points or locations. Also a horizontal string of alphanumeric characters displayed on a screen.

linear dimension The combination of a symbol and value used to specify an object's features that can be measured in a straight line.

linear-sequence menu A menu structure used to guide a user through an orderly progression of commands.

line drawing A drawing of an object that is displayed using only visible (solid) lines; no shading is used to represent the object's surfaces.

line quality Describes the legibility of a drawing; judges the contrast between visible, hidden, dimension, and center lines.

link To connect two elements, programs, or files.

LISP List processing. A programming language used along with certain CAD packages (such as AutoCAD's AutoLISP) to manipulate drawing data. It uses a list of calls to functions for every expression needed to complete the program.

LSI Large Scale Integration. The procedure for integrating a large number of electronic circuits on a single small chip of silicon or other material.

lines of sight Visual rays used to project an object onto a standard projection plane.

linetypes The different types of lines that allow proper identification of an object's features in a drawing.

load The action of selecting and placing data to be processed from storage into memory.

local-area network *See* LAN.

logarithmic graph A graph that does not have equal spacing of unit markings along a given axis. Instead, equal spacings are related to powers of 10; i.e., the powers to which a base must be raised to equal a given number.

logging in Also called logging on. The action of connecting to a computer through a network. The system generally requests the user's name and password.

loosest fit The situation in which two mating parts are at their maximum clearance.

LPM Lines per minute. A measurement of printer speed.

M An abbreviation for mega, meaning million.

Mac Short for Macintosh, a computer manufactured by Apple Computer, Inc.

machine code Sequences of 1's and 0's that are understood by the computer; the end result of compiling a program written in a high-level language.

machine language A language used directly by a computer.

macros A set of functions and instructions abbreviated with a short key-sequence or code.

magnetic storage The use of the magnetic properties of materials to store data on disks.

mainframe computer A high-function computer, accessed by multiple users through terminals and workstations and used to perform computationally intensive tasks.

male connector A cable connector with pins exposed. Used for connecting output devices such as plotters and printers.

Mandelbrot set A mathematical set—ascribed to the inventor of fractals—used to generate natural-like images.

market research Investigation of consumer needs and wants.

math coprocessor Also called coprocessor or floating-point processor. A processor used in conjunction with the CPU that performs calculations using floating-point numbers, as opposed to whole numbers (integers). Used to speed up CAD modeling operations.

mating parts Two parts or objects that fit together; for example, a shaft and a hole.

matrix An arrangement of numbers (or dots) in rows and columns.

maximum material condition (MMC) In tolerancing, the size of a part feature that results when the part has the most material.

MCGA Multi-Color Graphics Array. A type of IBM video adapter that provides three graphics modes and is capable of displaying up to 262,144 colors.

media The material used to store data. Also the vehicle (audio, visual, etc.) used to convey information.

megabyte (M or MB) Means 2^{20}, or 1,048,576, bytes.

megahertz (MHz) A measure of frequency. One million cycles per second.

memory The capability of a computer to store and retrieve information.

menu A screen-displayed list of options from which users select an operation to be performed by typing certain characters, function keys, or by using a pointer such as a mouse.

menu-bar A thin rectangular block displayed at the top of a program, from which options can be selected.

merge To combine two or more elements, such as files.

mesh A surface defined by a collection of curves forming a grid pattern.

metafile A file used by an operating system to hold or define information about other files.

metric scale A scale used in the international system of measurements, or SI. According to the metric scale, 1:1 scale means 1 mm calibration equals 1 mm.

microcomputer The smallest category of computer, consisting of a microprocessor and associated storage and input/output elements.

microprocessor The basic arithmetic, logical, and storage elements required for processing (generally on one or a few integrated circuit chips).

microsecond One-millionth of a second.

millisecond One-thousandth of a second.

minicomputer A relatively fast but small and inexpensive computer with somewhat limited input/output capabilities. A minicomputer is more powerful than a microcomputer but less powerful than a mainframe.

MIPS One million instructions per second. A unit for measuring a computer's processor speed.

mnemonic Pertaining to a technique used to aid human memory.

model An accurate representation of an actual device, system, or process.

modem Acronym for modulator/demodulator. A communication device that allows the computer to send signals over telephone lines.

modular approach Dividing a project into segments or smaller units to simplify analysis, designing, and programming.

monitor The device used to display the images generated by the computer's video adapter.

monochrome A term used to describe a single color display.

motherboard The circuitry board on which the CPU is mounted.

mouse An input device used as a pointer for selecting entities or options.

mouse tracking An adjustment mechanism used to control the movement of a mouse on a pad in relation to screen cursor movement.

move A CAD modeling command to change the location of geometric entities or objects.

multimedia In computer graphics, also called hypermedia. The use of computer animation, graphics, simulation, sound, and video technology in a presentation.

multiplanar display A system that creates the illusion of a three-dimensional image by partitioning a scene into multiple two-dimensional cross sections.

multiplex To transmit messages simultaneously over a single channel or other communications facility.

multiprocessing The simultaneous execution of two or more sequences of instructions by a single computer network.

multiprocessor A computer network consisting of two or more central processors under a common control.

multitasking The capability of an operating system to run several applications and programs simultaneously. In many instances, only the foreground application is given processing time; to activate a background application the user needs to bring that application's window to the front of the screen.

multiuser environment A computer system that allows for more than one user at the same time.

multiview An orthographic projection view.

multiview projection The standard arrangement of orthographic projection views.

mylar A type of paper used to draw in ink.

nanosecond One-billionth of a second.

narrow bandwidth channels Communications channels that can only transmit data at slow speeds, e.g., telegraph channels.

network An interconnection of computer systems and/or peripheral devices at dispersed locations that exchange data as necessary to perform the functions of the network.

NLQ Near letter quality. A dot-matrix printer mode setting that allows a user to produce better looking printouts than in regular mode, though the printing speed is slower.

node A common junction of two or more geometric entities.

nonsense object A model that is a physical impossibility.

nonvolatile storage A storage medium that retains its contents in the absence of power.

normal Perpendicular to a tangent.

Novell A brand name for LAN operating systems used to share files and output devices among various types of computer systems, such as IBM-PCs and Macs.

NURBS Non-Uniform Rational B-Spline. A geometric primitive used to describe the shape of curved surfaces.

object In CAD modeling, a distinct entity.

object-oriented programming (OOP) A programming technique where the program is viewed as a collection of discrete objects.

oblique A pictorial produced by looking at an angle through the projection plane.

oblique line A line that is not in true length in any principal multiview.

OCR Optical Character Recognition. The recognition of printed characters through the use of light-sensitive optical machines.

offset section A type of cross section whose cutting plane zigzags to show the important internal features of an object.

one-point perspective Also called parallel perspective. Two principal axes of the object are parallel to the projection plane. Features parallel to the third axis converge toward a vanishing point.

operating system An organized collection of software that controls the overall operations of a computer.

optical disk Also called a compact disk (CD). A disk used to store multimedia presentations in digital form. In contrast with floppy and hard disks, CDs uses laser optics rather than magnetic media to store data.

optical mouse A mouse used on a small pad that reflects the light emitted by the mouse back into detectors in the mouse.

orthographic projection A projection using parallel lines of sight at right angles (90 degrees) to the plane of projection.

OS Abbreviation for operating system. (*See* DOS *and* Unix.)

painter's algorithm A graphics programming technique for deleting hidden surfaces and lines of an object.

palette The complete set of colors that a program can display.

parallactiscope A stereo display system that does not require special glasses or other viewing apparatus. It uses a slit that moves across the screen of a CRT at approximately 20 Hertz.

parallel perspective *See* one-point perspective.

parallel port An I/O connector for a parallel interface device.

parallel projection The type of projection that uses lines of sight parallel to one another.

parameter A variable whose value determines the location of an entity.

parent directory A relative term that refers to a directory that contains another directory (i.e., if directory A holds directory B, A is the parent directory of B).

parity check A method for checking the accuracy of binary data after those data have been transferred to or from storage. The number of 1 bits in a binary character is controlled by the addition or deletion of a parity bit.

Pascal A popular high-level programming language that facilitates the use of structured programming techniques.

patch A limited region on a larger surface.

path The route that leads the user from the root directory to a specific file on a disk.

patent A legal record that allows a designer or inventor to exclude others from manufacturing, building, using, or selling similar designs or inventions, without the inventor's permission, for a period of time.

patent search Looking up registered patents in a database.

pattern recognition A technique that allows a computer to recognize visual images from digital information.

password A unique group of characters that allows a particular user and/or a communication network to gain partial or total access to a computer system.

PC Personal computer.

peripherals The input/output devices and auxiliary storage units of a computer system.

perspective A representation of how humans perceive objects.

Phong shading A popular method of making images with combined diffuse and specular reflectance.

phantom line *See* reference line.

photorealism A term referring to computer output that is virtually indistinguishable from a photo.

picosecond One-thousandth of a nanosecond; one-trilllionth of a second.

pictorial A drawing or model showing three faces of an object in a given view or display.

pie chart A circular polar bar graph divided into shaded "pie pieces" representing spatially the breakdown of a data set.

piercing point The point of intersection between a line and a plane.

pitch The number of characters per inch in a line of print.

pixels Picture elements. The dots or picture elements on a computer screen, which make up the lines, shapes, drawings, numbers, and letters displayed on the screen.

pixel intensity The degree and variety of shadings in pixel color.

planarity of a face Term describing the flatness of a surface.

platform The hardware and software that supports a certain application.

PLATO Programmed Logic for Automatic Teaching Operations. The oldest CAI network, offering a variety of computerized educational programs for all levels.

plotter A device that converts computer output into a graphic hard-copy form, usually using pens and ink to draw the image on paper.

point A geometric entity defined by one location in space.

point view of a line A view with the direction of sight parallel to a straight line in space.

polar coordinates A subset of cylindrical coordinates. They represent a location on a plane defined by the radius and the angle from the positive X-axis to the point.

polar graph A type of graph where one of the coordinates is an angle while the other is graphed as a length.

polarized time parallel display A technique that uses two CRTs arranged at right angles to each other and a partially silvered mirror to create the illusion of three-dimensional viewing.

polylines A collection of connected line segments.

portability The ability of a program to run under more than one operating system or computer hardware.

portrait A printing mode in which the longer dimension of the paper is the length and the shorter dimension the width.

ports Places on the system unit used to connect other hardware components to it, such as a keyboard or a printer.

positional light A light source emanating from one point. In contrast to directional light, the light rays that emanate from the point are not parallel.

postprocessing Manipulation of data that has been manipulated previously.

PPM Pages per minute. A measurement of printer speed. (*See* LPM *and* CPS.)

preliminary decision An unbiased decision about which design solution has the most potential.

preliminary ideas Alternative solutions to a design problem.

preprocessor A device controlling the initial processing operations on the input.

prescriptive model A model that dictates a course of action.

primary auxiliary projection A projection constructed by drawing an imaginary auxiliary plane of projection parallel to a surface that is inclined in a principal view, and projecting its features onto that surface.

primitives Self-contained volumes or shapes that can be manipulated as discrete objects. A model can be constructed by combining various primitives.

principal planes of projection The frontal, horizontal, and profile planes of projection.

printer A device used to produce hard copy.

problem definition A clear and concise statement of a specific need a design is to meet; often identified through market research.

processing The numerical and character manipulation activities that transform data into information.

processing symbol A rectangular figure used in flowcharts to indicate a processing operation, e.g., a calculation.

program Software. A set of sequenced instructions to cause a computer to perform particular operations.

program manager Software that allows a user to work with several applications at the same time.

programming language A language used to define a set of instructions or algorithms.

projection An image produced by mapping a face of an object onto a plane.

projection plane An imaginary two-dimensional flat surface on which one draws or displays an object's multiviews.

projection theory The body of knowledge that comprises the rules and principles of analyzing, drawing, and displaying three-dimensional objects on two-dimensional planes.

prompt Alphanumeric characters appearing on a CRT screen, used to indicate that a computer program is awaiting input; for example, C> or /usr/people/guest>.

pseudocode A programming analysis tool. Counterfeit and abbreviated versions of actual computer instructions that are written in ordinary natural language.

puck A pointing device used with a digitizing tablet.

pull-down menu A type of menu that, when selected, descends from a menu bar.

quit The operation used to stop an activity.

RAM Random Access Memory. Also called read-and-write memory. The memory space within the computer that holds programs and data that are needed immediately for processing; a storage device structured so that the time required to retrieve data is not significantly affected by the physical location of the data. Data can be accessed in any order.

RAM capacity Available volatile memory; measured in kilobytes or megabytes.

RAM chip A semiconductor device used to store data.

raster A regular array of pixels.

raster image An image formed by a pattern of light and dark pixels.

raster-scan CRT A monitor that displays images by sweeping an electron beam across every row of pixels on the screen and varying the intensity of the beam as it sweeps.

ray tracing A popular technique used to produce realistic images on a computer. It consists of tracing a visual ray from the observer's location to the object to be displayed.

real-time Term describing the display of objects that can be re-displayed as quickly as it takes the user to specify a new position. The term is also used in the context of simulating in a computer the rate at which real-world objects move.

real-world coordinates The coordinates corresponding to the actual dimensions of the object being modeled.

record A collection of related data treated as a unit.

rectilinear graph A graph that presents the relationship of data on a coordinate plane.

reference line An edge view of a projection plane; the intersection line of adjacent projection planes.

reflectance A property that affects the appearance of an object. The term refers to the fraction of incident visible light that an object reflects. Bright objects have high reflectance.

refresh CRT A device consisting of electron guns, a focusing apparatus, horizontal and vertical deflection plates, and a screen coated with thousands of individual phosphors.

register A device capable of storing a specific amount of data.

related views Two multiviews bordering a common intermediate orthographic multiview between them.

relational symbols Symbols such as > (greater than), < (less than), or = (equal to) that are used to compare two values in a conditional branching situation.

relative coordinates Coordinates defined in relation to a previous point.

remote access Communication with a computer facility by a station that is distant from the computer.

removed section A type of cross section that is displaced from its common projection position.

rendering The use of shading and color to display a geometric model so that it looks real.

resolution The number of pixels per inch (or centimeter). The clarity obtained in a computer video display.

resources The people, money, materials, and machines used to design, build, and/or manufacture a product.

reverse engineering Analyzing the components of an existing product in order to develop a superior design for that product.

reverse ray tracing A way to render a surface by tracing known points back from the surface model to the observer's location.

reverse video Changing a video display so that what was originally dark is now light, and vice versa.

revolved section A type of cross section whose cutting plane passes perpendicular to the part and is revolved 90 degrees.

RGB video A graphics screen on which each pixel can receive red, green, and blue on/off signals.

ROM Read-Only Memory. Permanent memory that cannot be modified.

root directory The main directory.

rotate In CAD modeling, a command to turn a model so that it is viewed from a different angle.   .

saturation The amount (given as a percentage) of color in a certain hue.

scale To reduce or enlarge a display. To define a real size using a reduced or enlarged measurement gradation unit.

scanner An optical input device used to translate a pattern of light and dark images into a digital signal.

schematic diagram A drawing that uses lines and symbols to represent the interconnection of the components in a device. Usually used to draw electrical circuits.

scroll bar In GUIs, a vertical bar used with a mouse to move within a file.

SCSI Small computer system interface. An ANSI standard parallel interface used to connect peripheral devices to a computer.

secondary auxiliary projection A projection constructed when the surface of an object is inclined and does not appear as a line (an edge) in any of the principal planes of projection.

section lining *See* crosshatching.

segment A line of finite length.

segmentation The degree of smoothness used when modeling a curved object.

semiconductor storage A memory device whose storage elements are formed as solid-state electronic components on an integrated circuit chip.

semilog chart A type of graph where only one axis is logarithmically marked.

serial access Descriptive of a storage device or medium where there is a sequential relationship between access time and data location in storage; i.e., the access time is dependent on the location of the data. Contrast with *direct access* and *random access.*

simulation To represent and analyze properties or behavior of a physical or hypothetical system by the behavior of a system model, often manipulated by means of computer operations; the maturation phase in the design process.

single menu A one-menu structure used to accomplish a particular task, such as plotting.

snap A CAD function used to round-off the location of a digitized point to the closest designated position.

software A set of programs, documents, procedures, and routines associated with the operation of a computer system; programs that tell the computer what to do. Contrast with *hardware.*

solid model A rendered geometric model showing the surfaces of the object.

solid primitives A mathematically defined three-dimensional shape, used to construct solid models.

spatial analysis Determining specific geometric information about an object.

spatial geometry The use of descriptive geometry principles to analyze and solve problems involving spatial distances and relationships.

special-purpose language A programming language with a syntax designed for a particular field.

specular surface A surface with a shiny finish.

spherical coordinates A location defined by a radius and two angles.

spline A smooth curve defined by control points.

square symbol A symbol used to indicate that a square dimension applies to a square feature.

standalone A workstation that does not need to be connected to any other computers in order to work.

stereoscopic graphics A technique to create the illusion of depth by adding depth cues.

stereolithography apparatus (SLA) A device used to produce a plastic prototype from a computer-generated model.

stereoscopic vision Vision that infers depth from binocular disparity. The way the brain puts together the two slightly different signals obtained from each eye.

spatial functions The brain's creative and visual processing functions.

spotface A finished round depression on the surface of an object.

subdirectory A directory contained within another directory.

supercomputer Computer systems characterized by their very large size and high processing speeds.

surface model A shell-like model, used to define the boundaries of a geometric model.

sweeping In CAD modeling, an operation used for creating a three-dimensional model from two-dimensional contours that are extruded along a line or curve.

symbolic functions The brain's verbal, analytical, and logical information-processing functions.

symbolic model Also called a mathematical model. An abstract representation of a system, process, or product.

system clock A hardware device that coordinates computer circuit responses.

system unit The computer's housing.

tangent A line making contact with a curve at a single point.

telecommunications Transmission of data between computer systems and/or terminals in different locations.

terminal A device that performs I/O operations in a computer system.

third-angle projection standard A method of projection in which the plane of projection is positioned between the object and the observer; the object to be projected is positioned in the third coordinate quadrant.

timesharing The use of specific hardware by a number of other devices, programs, or users simultaneously in such a way to provide quick response to each of the users.

time multiplexed stereo pair A stereoscopic system that uses a viewing shutter that presents paired images by alternating right-eye and left-eye perspective views of an object on a CRT.

tightest fit The situation that occurs when two mating parts are at their minimum clearance.

tolerance The permissible variation in size and shape of an object.

tree A hierarchical data structure containing branches and nodes.

tree-structured menu A menu with the organizational characteristics of a tree.

trimetric projection An axonometric projection where no two axes make equal angles with the projection plane.

true-length view of a line (TL) A view in which distances on a line are not foreshortened. An orthographic view in which a line is parallel to the projection plane.

true view of a plane A view adjacent to an edge view of a plane, in which the plane is parallel to the projection plane.

two-point perspective Also called angular perspective. When two of the object's axes are inclined and one axis is parallel to the projection plane.

unary operations In CAD modeling, the operations used to manipulate and modify selected solid primitives.

UNIVAC I Universal Automatic Computer. The first fully electronic stored-program digital computer to be made commercially available (1954).

Unix A multiuser/multitasking operating system developed in the C language by A. T. & T. Bell Systems. It is less machine-specific than other operating systems.

unilateral tolerance A dimension that may only be greater (or may only be less) than a specified dimension.

user-defined coordinate system An alternative coordinate system that can be specified by a user. It is used, for instance, to facilitate the geometric construction of oblique (inclined) planes.

user-friendly A term describing a type of user-interface that is easy to use and operate.

user number Also called user name. The name (or number) by which a person is identified and addressed in a multiuser environment.

vanishing point (VP) In perspective projection, an imaginary point toward which parallel lines seem to converge.

varifocal In stereoscopic computer graphics, a mirror with variable focal length.

vector An operation used to describe a point location by its magnitude, direction, and point of application.

video display A screen monitor.

viewpoint In CAD, the designated point from which an observer is looking at an object.

virtual-reality models A computer display in which the user can manipulate a geometric model with greater freedom using devices such as electronic gloves and a helmet.

virtual storage Descriptive of the capability to use on-line secondary storage devices and specialized software to divide programs into smaller segments for transmission to and from internal storage in order to increase the effective size of the available internal storage.

visible lines Solid thick lines and curves delineating an object's edges; indicate the visible features of the object from the observer's point of view.

visual annotation To record design ideas using freehand sketching (also called design annotation).

visual display terminal A device capable of displaying keyed input and CPU output on a cathode ray tube.

visualization The creative ability to form mental images; includes perception, imagination, and communication.

visual perception The ability to see and understand the objects or environment we are observing.

visuals Images and models showing how a design works; usually used in a design presentation.

visual simulation A technique used for predicting and animating the response of a device, system, or process to operating conditions.

VLSI Very Large Scale Integration. The packing of hundreds of thousands of electronic components on a single semiconductor chip.

volatile storage A storage medium that loses its contents in the event of a power interruption.

voxel Volume element. The smallest unit volume of a three-dimensional object that has meaningful information. A three-dimensional pixel.

windowing Term describing an operating system environment in which the user is presented with delineated screen areas that resemble window openings. For example, the Microsoft Windows software allows a user of a DOS-based computer to work with multiple on-screen windows.

wireframe A computer model that appears to consist of wires or lines. It shows only the edges of the object being described.

word Also called word size or word length. The greatest number of bits a computer is capable of handling in any one operation. Depending on the microprocessor, it can be either 8-bits, 16-bits, or 32-bits.

word processor (WP) A computer software application package used to create, view, edit, store, retrieve, and print text material.

working directory The directory that is currently active.

working drawings The necessary multiviews, cross sections, dimensions, and tolerances needed to manufacture a product.

write-protect To make the information on a disk unalterable by covering a small opening or notch on the disk.

WYSIWYG An acronym for "what you see is what you get." WYSIWYG systems show graphics and text as they will appear in printed form.

zoom Reduction or enlargement of an image on the screen.

Index